FIELDS OF CONFLICT

FIELDS OF CONFLICT

Battlefield Archaeology from the Roman Empire to the Korean War

Volume 1
Searching for War in the Ancient and
Early Modern World

Edited by DOUGLAS SCOTT, LAWRENCE BABITS, AND CHARLES HAECKER

PRAEGER SECURITY INTERNATIONAL
Westport, Connecticut • London

Library of Congress Cataloging-in-Publication Data

Fields of conflict : battlefield archaeology from the Roman Empire to the Korean War /
edited by Douglas Scott, Lawrence Babits, and Charles Haecker.
  v. cm.
  Includes bibliographical references and index.
  Contents: v. 1. Searching for war in the ancient and early modern world — v. 2.
Nineteenth and twentieth century fields of conflict.
  ISBN 0-275-99315-9 (set : alk. paper) — ISBN 0-275-99316-7 (v. 1 : alk. paper) —
ISBN 0-275-99317-5 (v. 2 : alk. paper)
  1. Battlefields—History. 2. Excavations (Archaeology). 3. Military history. 4. Archaeology
and history. I. Scott, Douglas D. II. Babits, Lawrence Edward. III. Haecker, Charles M.
  D25.5.F53 2007
  930.1—dc22   2006029128

British Library Cataloguing in Publication Data is available.

Library of Congress Catalog Card Number: 2006029128
ISBN-10: 0-275-99315-9 (set)   ISBN-13: 978-0-275-99315-3 (set)
    0-275-99316-7 (vol. 1)   978-0-275-99316-0 (vol. 1)
    0-275-99317-5 (vol. 2)   978-0-275-99317-7 (vol. 2)

First published in 2007

Praeger Security International, 88 Post Road West, Westport, CT 06881
An imprint of Greenwood Publishing Group, Inc.
www.praeger.com

Printed in the United States of America

The paper used in this book complies with the
Permanent Paper Standard issued by the National
Information Standards Organization (Z39.48-1984).

10 9 8 7 6 5 4 3 2 1

Contents

Acknowledgments

THESE VOLUMES grew out of a series of papers presented at the third Fields of Conflict conference held in conjunction with the American Battlefield Protection Conference in April 2004 at Nashville, Tennessee. The ideas expressed in these volumes are an outgrowth of over 20 years of serious archaeological study of battlefield and conflict sites around the world. The Nashville conference brought many fresh ideas of how to view, study, and interpret archaeological evidence of conflict to the forefront. The editors, who also served as conference organizers, and the presenters all agreed that the works had a wider appeal than to just the researchers who were present. Thus the idea for these volumes was hatched.

We gratefully acknowledge Paul Hawke of the American Battlefield Protection Program, National Park Service, for allowing the Fields of Conflict conference to be held in conjunction with the ABPP conference. We owe a debt of gratitude to Paul, Kristen Stevens, and the ABPP staff for their very generous support, and for making the conference such a wonderful success and memorable event for all.

Elizabeth Demers of Praeger has been our friend and supporter from the inception of this project. We owe her a great deal. Elizabeth and the Praeger staff made this work happen, and to them a sincere thank you.

Introduction

> The history of technology is part and parcel of social history in general. The same is equally true of military history, far too long regarded as a simple matter of tactics and technical differentials. Military history too can only be understood against the wider social background. For as soon as one begins to discuss war and military organization without due regard to the whole social process one is in danger of coming to regard it as a constant, an inevitable feature of international behavior. In other words, if one is unable to regard war as a function of particular forms of social and political organization and particular stages of historical development, one will not be able to conceive of even the possibility of a world without war.[1]

MILITARY SITES HAVE long held the interest of archaeologists, and in the last two and a half decades there has been a growing interest in the archaeological investigation of battlefields or, as Freeman and Pollard[2] aptly named them, fields of conflict. Today there are a plethora of archaeological reports in the literature detailing the results of investigations at military forts, camps, prisons, and battlefields. These investigations have often been conducted as ancillary studies to the preservation, restoration, reconstruction, or interpretation of some military-related site. Many of the investigations have had little or no theoretical orientation or explanatory goal above that set by an architect or interpreter. This statement is not made as a negative criticism of the many fine reports that have resulted; it is a statement of fact made with the knowledge that, until recently, the archaeological study of military sites in general has had a limited research orientation.

That has begun to change, and dramatically so, over the last several years. The archaeology of conflict sites, battlefields, is still in its infancy, although growing at an exponential rate. The first Fields of Conflict conference that addressed international archaeological studies of battlefields was held in Glasgow, Scotland, in 2000, the second in Aland, Sweden, in 2002, and the third was held in association with the American Battlefield Protection

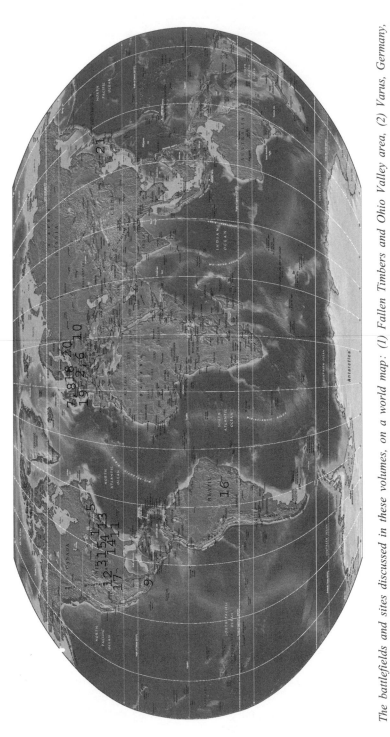

The battlefields and sites discussed in these volumes, on a world map: (1) Fallen Timbers and Ohio Valley area, (2) Varus, Germany, (3) Wilson's Creek, Missouri, (4) Lookout Mountain, Tennessee, (5) Monmouth, New Jersey, (6) Varus, Germany, (7) Edgehill, Nasbey, and English sites, (8) Towton, England, (9) Peñol de Nochistlán, Mexico, (10) Zboriv, Urkraine, (11) Camden, South Carolina, (12) Cieneguilla, New Mexico, (13) Evansport, Virginia, (14) Fort Davidson, Missouri, (15) Nashville, Tennessee, (16) Triple Alliance War, Paraguay, (17) Hembrillo Basin, New Mexico, (18) Iper, Belgium, (19) Pointe-du-Hoc, France, (20) Stalag Luft III, Poland, (21) Operation Manchu, South Korea.

conference in Nashville, Tennessee, in 2004. The continued interest in and growth of the archaeological study of battlefields are exemplified in this volume.

The works presented here build on endeavors of the two previous battlefield archaeological conferences as well as a variety of growing research interest in the area of conflict archaeology. We have chosen to organize these volumes in an essentially chronological fashion with literally 2,000 years of warfare from around the globe being covered in the various chapters. The initial chapters present the latest methods, techniques, and theoretical implications for the archaeological study of battlefields and other fields of conflict. These first chapters are rich in diversity of both time and space, ranging from Roman Germany in the first century AD to the late nineteenth century United States. They also range from presenting arguments of viewing battlefields as part of landscapes to using the powerful analytical capabilities of geographic information systems (GIS) to find new means to look at battlefields from a terrain analysis point of view, as well as the analytical potential of musket balls and firearms residue.

The succeeding chapters present contributions that range again from the first century, in Roman Germany, to the Korean conflict, and nearly everything in between in both time and space. While the chapters on the archaeological studies of battlefields in England, Europe, and the United States predominate, other chapters also present results of work in Mexico, South America, and the Ukraine. What we believe is impressive among the contributions in this volume is not the time depth nor even the global nature of archaeological studies of battlefields, but the fact that the studies are being done using variations of the same basic methods and theoretical models. What is also exciting in reading the various chapters is how each author has adapted, modified, and advanced both the basic methods and the theoretical underpinnings to meet the goals of a specific study. The methodological and theoretical advances presented in these chapters truly reflect the growth of battlefield archaeology in the last few years, and the wide-ranging interest in the definition of archaeological signatures of conflict and warfare.

NOTES

1. Ellis 1986.
2. Phil Freeman and Tony Pollard published the results of the first battlefield archaeology conference in 2001. They coined the term "fields of conflict" as part of the title for the conference and the resulting publication. The title has caught on and has been used as part of the title for each of the two succeeding conferences.

REFERENCES CITED

Ellis, John. 1986. *The Social History of the Machine Gun.* John Hopkins University Press, Baltimore (reprint of 1975 edition).

Freeman, P. W. M., and A. Pollard. 2001. *Fields of Conflict: Progress and Prospect in Battlefield Archaeology.* BAR International Series, 958.

How Do You Know It's a Battlefield?

G. Michael Pratt

BETWEEN 1995 AND 2002 the Center for Historic and Military Archaeology at Heidelberg College conducted multifaceted remote sensing, artifact recovery, and mapping projects at three eighteenth- and nineteenth-century battlefield sites in the Ohio Valley–Great Lakes region. The survey areas included portions of the sites of the Battle of Fallen Timbers (1794), a pivotal battle for control of the Old Northwest Territory; the Battle for Mackinac Island (1814), an unsuccessful U.S. attempt to recover the island after its loss to the British in 1812; and the Battle of Buffington Island (1863), the U.S. defeat of Confederate General John Hunt Morgan's attempt to escape across the Ohio River following his heretofore successful raid through Ohio and Indiana. All three battles were of short duration (less than one day), involved movement across the battlefield, and produced no significant earthworks or other modifications of the natural terrain. At the time of survey, all three sites were relatively undisturbed except for agricultural activities. Finally, all three were subjected to the same survey methods utilizing, for the most part, the same equipment and personnel. The survey method, presented here, provides an effective and efficient manner to assess the condition, content, and extent of a battlefield.

Archaeological surveys of all three sites produced lead shot as the most numerous battlefield artifact type. At the Buffington Island battlefield, recognizable carbine, pistol, and "Minié ball" shot could be identified by shape and size[1]; while spherical lead shot was recovered from all three sites. The recovery, identification, and mapping of shot types representing weaponry utilized by the combatants provided information that sometimes reinforced existing interpretations and sometimes forced a reinterpretation of the course of battle at each site. At each site the results of the survey provided previously unknown details, and at all sites the survey provided ground truth information for the location of battlefield events.

DETECTING THE BATTLEFIELD

Beginning in 1995, in conjunction with a developing battlefield survey program at Heidelberg College's Archaeological Survey (now Center for Historic and Military Archaeology), Richard Green of Historic Archaeological Research (HAR), West Lafayette, Indiana, developed metal detection methods for efficient and effective survey and mapping of battlefields. Under the direction of G. Michael Pratt, Heidelberg and HAR applied a combination of metal detection techniques and utilized Global Positioning System (GPS) mapping to identify the previously unrecognized site of the Battle of Fallen Timbers. The success of this project and national interest generated by efforts to preserve the battlefield provided CHMA and HAR access to several other eighteenth- and nineteenth-century battlefield sites. Over the next five years, Green refined his method and added techniques in an effort to perform a more balanced and intensive approach to remote and electronic investigations of historical battlefield sites. By 2000, CHMA and HAR had developed the specific approach described in this chapter. The sites discussed here were subjected to most or all of the following survey methods, usually in an ordered approach designed to recover an increasingly detailed dataset. All were subjected to metal detection and GPS mapping aspects.

ELECTROMAGNETIC CONDUCTIVITY SURVEY

Electromagnetic conductivity survey has long been utilized on both prehistorical and historical archaeological sites and has the capability to detect subsurface features as well as other types of conductive anomalies. On battlefield sites, an EM 38 ground conductivity meter and DL 600 Polycorder manufactured by Geonics, LTD, Mississauga, Ontario, Canada, are utilized to record conductivity measurements in the predetermined sample units where graves, trenches, or other features may occur. The EM 38 is configured to measure in the vertical dipole orientation and programmed to record data automatically in a 0.5-m resolution survey strategy. In this mode of operation, the technician scans the instrument over the surface along parallel survey lines at a 0.5-m/s pace. Survey lines are positioned at 0.5-m intervals. This technique results in an average of one data point per 0.5 m over the entire survey grid. The operator triggers fiduciary markers at 10-m intervals, permitting data coordinate adjustment between start and stop stations along each transect. The automatic mode is preferable for expeditious survey at the expense of coordinate resolution. Accuracy of the EM 38 thus configured is approximately +/− 0.5 m.

Variations in the measurements may be caused by differences in soil composition, buried features, disturbed areas, and by metal artifacts. These variations appear as anomalies in the data and may be graphically depicted following post-processing of the database. Recorded data is subsequently interpolated with contouring software and converted to color gradient image maps permitting investigators to filter, enhance, and analyze subsurface anomalies.

Following field survey, recorded data is downloaded from the DL 600 Polycorder and Geonics, LTD proprietary DAT38RT software is used to adjust survey line data and export the database to a contouring software package. Golden Software's Surfer 8 is utilized by HAR to create color image maps for analysis of the conductivity survey data.

Highly conductive metallic objects within the survey area tend to skew a dataset by introducing points well outside the normal range of ambient soil conditions. The signature of a metallic surface feature is observed to increase proportionally as it is approached. Buried metal anomalies may appear as both a large positive transition and a sharp negative spike. The buried metal object occurs as an increase in amplitude until the instrument passes directly over the object. At this point the EM 38 can reach a saturation level and a large negative transition takes place, followed by the high conductive reading tapering off as the operator moves out of the vicinity. In order to resolve smaller variations in the data during software manipulation, it is necessary to filter wide swings caused by metal features. The entities causing the sharp increase or decrease are not eliminated, but rather the data is filtered to permit upper and lower limits in a range essential for viewing anomalies of lesser magnitude. By significantly reducing the biasing factors, it may be possible to enhance minute variations inherent to disturbances with no associated metal artifacts.

METAL DETECTION SURVEY

Metal detection surveys have been performed successfully using a wide variety of instruments available on the open market.[2] Richard Green of Historic Archaeological Research (HAR) has refined detection methodology in an effort to develop a standardized, intensive approach which permits comparisons among diverse areas of a battlefield or between battlefields. The HAR approach, described below, was employed in the CHMA surveys of all three battlefield sites.

Three distinct types of metal detecting instruments exhibiting complementary performance characteristics are utilized both to optimize coverage and to reduce procedural variables. These instruments are generically specified as VLF motion, full range, discriminating detectors and are electronically designed with a critically fast response to accepted targets particularly when rejected items are in close proximity. The three kinds of metal detector will be referred to as Types I, II, and III for the purpose of this discussion.

The Type I instrument has an operating frequency at the low end of the VLF band typically in the 5–6 kHz range. The Type I detector has an affinity for ferrous items and is extremely sensitive to artifacts manufactured with materials found on the higher end of the conductivity spectrum (i.e., brass, copper, and silver.) The Type II detector operates at a somewhat higher frequency, generally 10–12 kHz. The high frequency detector is intrinsically sensitive to metal targets in the low to mid conductivity range such as lead, nickel, gold, and small irregularly shaped artifacts. The Type II detector is less sensitive to small iron items, making this instrument a better choice for working in concentrations of modern ferrous debris (i.e., fence wire, nails, etc.). The Type III detector operates on a frequency which overlaps that of both Type I and II.

By utilizing instruments that, when operated in tandem, offer high performance across the entire metal conductivity spectrum, a strategy for comprehensive metal artifact recovery is created. By virtue of the distinctly different operating frequency of each device, Type I and II detectors may be operated in relatively close proximity without cross-talk or spurious interference, while the Type III detector may be utilized in tandem with either of the other types. Thus, fieldwork is designed specifically to take advantage of metal detection attributes while minimizing inherent flaws of both the Type I and II instruments.

Sweep Metal Detection Survey

In the first stage of metal detection survey, the "sweep" method is conducted by alternating Type I and Type II or III metal detection technicians at 5-m intervals. Reconnaissance is carried out over transects established within the overall survey area. The sweep survey is carried out in the attempt to locate a battlefield and/or delineate areas of battlefield activity that merit further, intensive survey. After completion of this stage of the survey, decisions are made to determine the location and extent of additional, intensive metal detection operations.

2-2-90 Metal Detection Survey

Green designed this method of metal detection survey for recovery of a standardized sample of artifacts within a survey area. The method utilizes the propensities of both the detection instruments and the operators, and is referred to as the 2-2-90 method.[3] A grid of 15 × 15 m survey squares is established over the areas producing concentrations of artifacts in the sweep survey. Each grid unit is surveyed methodically in overlapping transects, resulting in 100 percent coverage. Following completion of a grid square, a second technician with an opposite Type I/II/III detector re-surveys the unit at a 90-degree axis with respect to the first operator's sweep. This methodology results in coverage by two operators using two different detectors and at a 90-degree angle of approach (2-2-90). Coverage is improved exponentially and typically either results in a drastic increase of collected artifacts or more thoroughly substantiates the lack of metal remains within a given survey unit.

In both types of survey, all metal artifacts detected are excavated and identified. Artifacts believed to be associated with the battlefield or other significant components are assigned a field specimen number and collected for cataloging and laboratory analysis. Fiberglass shaft flags bearing the field specimen number mark the artifact locations for subsequent GPS survey. All artifacts that are not to be identified in the field are treated the same as those slated for collection, permitting further analysis at a later date. Artifacts not attributed to the battlefield, but of potential significance to the other components are collected and recorded by the survey square. Metal objects deemed of no archaeological significance (such as aluminum foil, aluminum pull tabs, modern cartridges) are counted, recorded, and discarded off site.

GPS Survey and GIS Map Preparation

In all the CHMA battlefield surveys Historic Archaeological Research was retained for GPS/GIS work. HAR utilizes a state-of-the art Trimble Pathfinder Pro XRS GPS System with differential correction (DGPS) service provided by Omnistar, Inc. The Pro XRS is capable of real-time submeter horizontal coordinate accuracy in this configuration. In instances where Omnistar DGPS service is interrupted, raw pseudo-range data is collected for correction by means of post-processing following completion of field data collection. All field specimen locations are surveyed by GPS to meet or exceed +/− 1-m coordinate accuracy. Coordinate data is supplied to CHMA in the UTM system NAD 1927. Project delineation maps and maps indicating the distribution of artifact types are constructed using both CAD and ArcView GIS software. The post-analysis data from the CHMA laboratory and the GPS data files are exported to ArcView and plotted on the georeferenced USGS 7.5-minute quadrangle. HAR also prepares graphic presentation maps for illustrations and provides all geographic software materials for each project.

CASE STUDY 1: THE BATTLE OF FALLEN TIMBERS

On August 20, 1794, Major General Anthony Wayne led his Legion of the United States and two brigades of mounted Kentucky militia against a confederation of Native American tribes consisting of the Miami, Shawnee, Delaware, Ottawa, Wyandot, Mingo, Ojibwa, and Pottawatomie. The Legion approached the battlefield in five parallel columns, each spaced approximately 200 yards apart. Behind the Legion rode some 1,500 Kentucky militia. The battle area was characterized by a mature, open forest. To Wayne's right lay the steep valley of the Maumee River; to his left the forest became increasingly choked with underbrush.[4]

A screen of 150 mounted Kentucky volunteers rode some 400 yards ahead of two companies of regulars, who formed the front guard. These companies marched about 200 yards in front of the main columns. After advancing about five miles the mounted volunteers stumbled into the center of an ambuscade line containing as many as 1,100 Indian warriors and a company of Canadian Queen's Rangers. As gunfire erupted from the ambush, the militia screen collapsed and fled around the front guard of regulars. The front guard attempted to retreat while returning fire, but eventually was overwhelmed and fled the field. A large force of warriors, intent on assaulting the main columns, closely pursued the retreating soldiers of the front guard. A hastily formed skirmish line of light infantry and rifle companies forced the attacking warriors to seek shelter in an area of tornado-felled timber and stemmed the momentum of the initial Indian attack. A sustained firefight developed along this skirmish line and the Legionnaires were slowly forced back some 80 yards under the weight of superior fire.[5]

During this skirmish, the remainder of the Legion deployed from its columns into a battle line. The maneuver required each company to undouble its files, and advance obliquely to the left, forming on the right of the preceding company. On the right wing, the 1st and 3rd Sub Legions formed a single line, while on the left, the 4th Sub Legion formed on the battle line with the 2nd Sub Legion formed as a reserve. During the 30 minutes or so that it took the Legion to form, only the light infantry and artillery companies in the center column joined the battle.[6]

As the firefight spread along the length of the U.S. line, the Legion dragoons were ordered to ride to the river and flank the Indian line. Instead, Capt. Robert MisCampbell led his dragoons from behind the U.S. right wing and charged into the fallen timbers. MisCampbell was killed almost immediately and the cavalry charge quickly faltered when the troopers encountered heavy fire from concealed warriors. On the left side of the line the reserve (2nd Sub Legion) was ordered forward to extend the line and protect the left flank. Before this move was completed the entire Legion began a charge.[7]

The charge was little contested except on the left of the U.S. line where a party of Wyandot and Queen's Rangers attempted to fight a delaying action. The Wyandot and their allies suffered heavy losses before being driven from the field. As the charge developed the Kentucky militia was ordered forward to extend the U.S. flank further to the left; however, thick woods slowed their progress and prevented a major extension of the U.S. front. Nevertheless, hundreds of mounted men did move forward on the left flank of the Legion's line and participated in driving the warriors from the field.

Wayne's charge carried the army one to two miles downstream and was halted when the resistance dissipated and the charge became disorganized. The Legion was brought to a halt, then reformed its line, and remained in a defensive posture for several hours. No Indian counterattack developed. After selection of a campsite, the army moved to the high ground overlooking the foot of the rapids and within sight of Fort Miamis and its garrison, bringing the Battle of Fallen Timbers to an end.[8]

Two U.S. officers killed in the engagement were buried immediately after the battle. Wounded continued to straggle into Wayne's camp for two days and then a burial party found and interred 16 dead. The remainder of the approximately 50 battlefield dead were left unburied, a fact reported by both U.S. and British sources.[9]

A topographic feature mentioned in accounts of the battle and depicted on a contemporary map was a "steep ravine" behind the right wing of the Legion's position.[10] Only a single ravine system (some 600 m downstream from the Fallen Timbers National Historic Landmark property) matched the primary source descriptions. Contemporary accounts also place the battle in the forested and ravine dissected uplands, rather than in the prairies of the Maumee floodplain, where the battle was said to have occurred. Information from more than 20 contemporary accounts was developed into a detailed account of the battle which predicted a new location for the actual battlefield, based on the location of the ravine described above.[11]

Unfortunately, the proposed location was one of the most desirable parcels of undeveloped, agricultural land in the Toledo metropolitan area. After some discussion with the owner (City of Toledo) and the municipality in which the site lay (City of Maumee), an archaeological survey was conducted in 1995. The survey convincingly demonstrated the battle occurred in the predicted area and documented the location of several battlefield events as well as several battlefield casualties. Subsequent surveys were carried out on adjacent private lands in 1996 and 1997.[12] By 2000 the battlefield site had been designated as part of the new Fallen Timbers Battlefield and Fort Miamis National Historic Site, and in 2001 an additional survey was carried out in anticipation of an NPS General Management Plan for development of the NHS as an affiliated NPS unit.[13]

Fallen Timbers Archaeological Survey

The goal of the 1995 Fallen Timbers Archaeology Project was to assess the likelihood, based on contemporary accounts,[14] that the specific project area contained archaeological remains of the Battle of Fallen Timbers. Therefore, a metal detection reconnaissance survey designed to locate and map battlefield artifacts was carried out on a 20 percent sample that consisted of three 50-m-wide corridors spaced at intervals along the longest axis of the 160-acre project area. Corridors were oriented perpendicular to the suspected battle lines and divided into 25 × 25 m survey units.

The 1995 volunteer survey crew was assembled using a core of experienced metal detector operators, experienced members of the Toledo Area Aboriginal Research Society, an amateur archaeology group, and interested members of the general public. The project was directed by G. Michael Pratt, Heidelberg College, and volunteer detector operators were supervised by Richard Green and Larry Hamilton of HAR. Survey and mapping were carried out over

15 consecutive (12-hr) days and involved over 200 volunteers. Within transects, the 25 × 25 m units were surveyed by the 2-2-90 method. A sweep survey was developed to assess the area between high-density areas of two transects. The figure indicates artifact locations within the three transects and in the sweep area east of the forest. The figure also depicts the approximate locations of the original ambush line (right), the U.S. battle formation (left), and the skirmish that occurred in-between these positions.

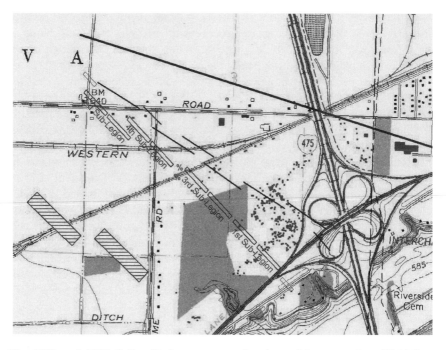

The 1995 and 1997 Fallen Timbers surveys: Results and interpretation. (Heidelberg College)

The 1995 Fallen Timbers Archaeological Project revealed the location of part of the battlefield site. Within the project limits, the area exhibiting the greatest artifact density appears as a 200-m by at least 350-m zone oriented parallel to and 300 m east of the ravine mentioned in a contemporary account. This area contained over 80 percent of the spent musket shot, nearly two-thirds of the spent rifle balls, and all of the buttons recovered from the site.[15] It appears to represent part of the skirmish in the fallen timbers, probably that in front of the 3rd Sub Legion's position. The buttons tend to occur in discrete clusters that often include both coat and vest size insignia buttons and plain buttons. These are interpreted as the remains of battlefield casualties who were left on the field unburied or interred in shallow graves subsequently disturbed by farming.

The 1995 survey successfully located the Fallen Timbers battlefield site, and provided information sufficient for designation of the property as a National Historic Site and an affiliate of the National Park System. As part of this effort, a 1998 ABPP grant to the Fallen Timbers Battlefield Preservation Commission supported the development of a locally produced videotape, *The Battle of Fallen Timbers—The Battle for Fallen Timbers.*

The 1995 survey was not adequate as a resource for the General Management Planning Process mandated by NPS for park planning purposes.[16] (1) The 1995 project addressed an area smaller than the present NHS property and therefore did not consider the northern area of the proposed park. (2) The survey focused on areas most likely to contain archaeological remains of the battlefield and did not attempt to assess the actual distribution of battlefield remains throughout the property. (3) No consideration was given to public use or interpretation of the site, so the potential impacts of such use were not considered. (4) Summer vegetation in the forest area precluded efficient survey, leaving this area under-represented in the sample. (5) Since no subsurface testing was carried out in the 1995 survey, the potential for disturbed or intact burials was not assessed, nor did the survey address the property's potential to contain earlier (e.g., prehistoric) or later (e.g., Canal-era) archaeological/historical components.[17]

The 2001 survey was a four-stage field survey designed to build baseline information necessary to the initial GMP process. The survey was designed to address many of the issues raised but not addressed by the initial survey of the Fallen Timbers Battlefield. By 2001 permanent survey data monuments had been placed to reference all future work at the site and a 15 × 15 m grid was developed over the NHS property. The project was carried out in separate stages in the spring, summer, and fall of 2001 by a crew of up to 14 and with the assistance of over 500 volunteers.

Stage I: Remote Sensing of Button Cluster Areas

The 1995 survey identified five clusters of five or more buttons representing Legion of the United States insignia and plain buttons. Two other button groups (of three and two buttons) and two isolated buttons were also recovered in the survey. The groups of buttons were interpreted as the remains of battle casualties.[18] Primary source accounts indicate the Legion's dead were treated in at least three different ways. The two dead officers (Capt. MisCampbell and Lt. Towles) were buried immediately after the battle, some 19 bodies were buried on the field two days later, and many were left unburied.[19]

Stage I of the 2001 survey gathered additional information on the distribution of buttons and their interpretation by an electromagnetic conductivity (EM) survey. Sample areas of 30 × 30 m were developed for each of seven multiple button locations and one single button find. The EM sample areas, designated EM 1–8, were established on the existing site grid. Heavy rains during March and April of 2001 left portions of the survey areas in standing water throughout the spring. As a result, three of the eight proposed 30 × 30 m areas (EM 3, 4, and 5) could not be explored with the EM 38.[20]

Anomalies in EM 1 (see figure), EM 2, and EM 6 that appeared to represent subsurface disturbances of greater than 1 m in length were selected for subsurface testing in Stage II. No such anomalies were identified in EM 7 or 8. The EM 38 survey also recorded the presence of two groundhog burrows, one each in EM 6 and 7. Openings for both were visible on the surface; however, the subsurface tunnels are identifiable in the image maps for these units.

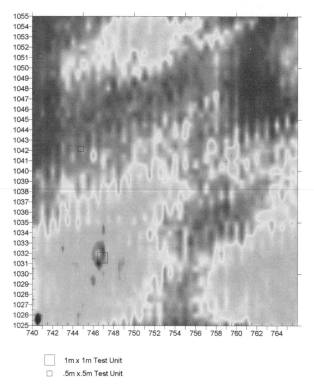

□   1m x 1m Test Unit
□   .5m x .5m Test Unit

EM 38 results: EM-1, Fallen Timbers. (Heidelberg College)

Stage II: Subsurface Investigation of the "Button Cluster" Areas

Three 1 × 1 m excavation units were placed to encounter the large conductive anomalies recorded in the EM survey. In each case, soil moisture or texture differences were noted within the excavations and these, rather than graves or other features, appear to be the source of the anomalies. All of the survey areas were subjected to 2-2-90 detection efforts that produced an additional 66 buttons and 105 shot, many of which were visible as small conductive spikes in the EM 38 data.[21] The following figure below depicts the distribution of buttons recovered in the 1995 and 2001 (Stage II) metal detection surveys.

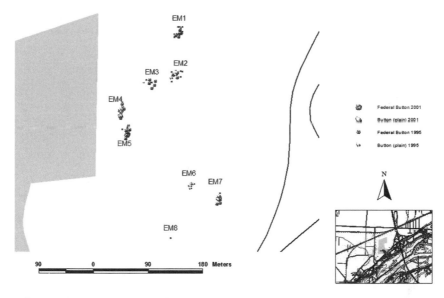

Fallen Timbers: Distribution of buttons 1995–2001. (Heidelberg College)

Stage III: Assessment of Potential NHS Access Area

Stage III activities involved 2-2-90 metal detection and artifact recovery within 15 × 15 m grid units, followed by hand excavation and screening of a 0.5 × 0.5 m test unit in the SW corner of each grid square. This stage of the survey was designed to sample portions of the NHS deemed most likely for selection for park access and facility development; 323 metal detection units were surveyed and 233 test units were excavated along the western edge of the battlefield portion of the NHS. A total of 183 battlefield artifacts, including 138 shot of various caliber, a federal button, a small axe head, and at least 14 pieces of a flintlock rifle were recovered by metal detection. Tool fragments, unidentified metal fragments, and lead waste fragments may also relate to the battlefield, but are equivocal. Two Civil War federal uniform buttons and two prehistoric flakes are clearly not associated with the Fallen Timbers Battlefield component. No battlefield-related artifacts and no significant prehistoric or other historic artifacts were recovered during excavation of the 233 test units. Nor was archaeological evidence of subsurface historic or prehistoric features encountered.[22]

Stage IV: Forested Area Survey

Intensive metal detection in the forest was designed to develop additional information on the location, artifact density, and condition of the archaeological remains of the "fallen timbers" area of the Battle of Fallen Timbers while testing the effectiveness of survey in this area under conditions of minimum vegetation cover. Due to the potential for encountering button clusters similar to those found just east of this section of the forest, EM 38 survey and sampling of subsurface anomalies were planned as contingent upon the recovery of buttons. These operations were not required; however, the stand-by excavation crew completed sixteen 0.5 × 0.5 m test units, arranged at 30-m intervals along four transects. These units documented the lack of a significant plow zone in this portion of the forest. Three musket balls, 19 rifle balls, five buckshot, an axe, and three fragments of unidentified ferrous metal were recovered from the forested area. No buttons or button clusters were encountered in this portion of the battlefield. No archaeological materials or features were encountered in these test units.[23]

CASE STUDY 2: THE BATTLE FOR MACKINAC ISLAND

In the summer of 1814 an invasion force of five companies of U.S. regulars drawn from the 17th, 19th, and 24th Infantry Regiments, Col. William Cotgreave's Ohio Volunteer Regiment, a detachment of the Corps of Artillery, and U.S. Marines were dispatched by ship to retake Mackinac Island, which had been lost in 1812 to a successful British invasion. On August 4, 1814, the ships of the invasion force sailed to the northern shore of the island and anchored in line of battle. Under the command of Lt. Col. George Croghan and Major Holmes, the invasion force was loaded in small boats; the ships opened fire and "cleared the shore"; and Croghan's force landed, uncontested.[24] Croghan's infantry and two artillery pieces set off upon a road which ran through Michael Dousman's farm and across the island to Fort Mackinac.[25]

Lt. Col. McDouall, the British commandant, responded to the invasion by rushing all available forces toward the center of the island to meet Croghan's forces as far from Fort Mackinac as possible.[26] McDouall's military force consisted of about 140 regulars; 50 militia under Lewis Crawford; and two pieces of light artillery. About 350 Indian warriors accompanied McDouall's force. When the British reached Dousman's farm, McDouall posted his line and his artillery just north of the Dousman home along a prominent ridge (known as battlefield beach ridge); a commanding position overlooking the open farm fields. McDouall placed his Indian allies in the woods on his flanks.

As the first U.S. troops emerged from the forest at the north edge of the Dousman fields, the British opened fire with both artillery pieces forcing Croghan to withdraw into the woods. Lt. Col. Croghan re-deployed his troops into two lines of battle (Ohio Volunteers in the advance and the regulars in reserve) and again advanced into the clearing. This advance was covered by ineffective U.S. artillery fire and may have utilized several large isolated hills and other features of the natural terrain as cover.[27]

As the U.S. forces crossed the open farm fields, Croghan determined to change his position "by advancing Major Holmes' battalion on the right of the militia" to outflank the British position.[28] This maneuver extended Croghan's formation into a single line of battle that overlapped McDouall's regulars. McDouall reported that his enemy advanced "slowly and cautiously," gradually gaining his left flank. The warriors on McDouall's left, who had yet to open fire, did not oppose these movements. As Holmes's line of U.S. Infantry approached their position, "a fire was opened by Indians in the thick woods near our right." McDouall reports that Chief Thomas led "Fallovine" (Menominee) warriors in an attack on the enemy.[29] It is unclear whether the Indians fired in response or prior to the charge by Holmes's regulars, but it seems clear that Holmes and several other officers were killed or put out of action by the initial blast of gunfire from the previously concealed warriors. The death of these officers "threw the line into confusion" from which they could not recover; but the charge continued forward, driving the enemy back into the woods.[30]

In the meantime, McDouall had withdrawn his regulars and militia in response to a rumored "second landing" to his rear. Apprised that this report was false, McDouall then reversed course and, leaving his regulars behind, led his militia and the bulk of the warriors back to the battlefield. The arrival of this force may have created the "untenable" situation reported by Croghan who ordered his troops to withdraw. McDouall stated that the Indians pursued the Americans until "under the broadsides" of the ships. Heavy firing continued for another 15 minutes but soon firing ceased and the troops were withdrawn to the ships. The battle for Mackinac Island ended in an American defeat.[31]

McDouall reported that the Americans left 17 dead on the field as well as some wounded. Parsons, the U.S. surgeon, reported Holmes and 12 infantry killed, 3 infantry missing, and 39 infantry and 1 Marine wounded.[32] McDouall claims to have "personally superintended the decent interment of the dead, previous to my quitting the field"; however, it is also clear that Holmes went unrecognized as an officer because he had been stripped by the Indians prior to interment.[33] Although Holmes's body was "unmolested"[34] when returned to the American fleet prior to its departure, others, including Elizabeth Davenport, claimed that the dead were scalped and/or dismembered, that cannibalism occurred, and that scalps or body parts were exhibited within the fort following the battle.[35] Decades later, oral tradition claimed the bodies were "gathered up and buried" at the southeast end of Holmes hill, and Van Fleet produced a map indicating the location of a mass grave.[36] In this battle the British forces lost a single Indian chief who was buried with "great military pomp and ceremony."[37]

Mackinac Island's 57-acre Wawashkamo Golf Course lies upon portions of the 1814 Battle for Mackinac Island battlefield. Dousman and others continued to farm the area until development of the golf course began in 1899. This included construction of the greens and tees, collection and re-deposition of boulders to create hazards, and modification of the sand pit. A "road roller" was also utilized to smooth the entire course area, but no widespread grading occurred. Subsequent to the original construction, cast-iron water lines were added in 1907–1908, and additional property was acquired about 1902 and in 1911.[38] The property continues to be operated as the Wawashkamo Golf Course.

The Wawashkamo Golf Club Archaeological Survey

The Heidelberg College CHMA survey of the Wawashkamo Golf Club portion of the Battle for Mackinac Island battlefield was carried out May 15–22, 2002, as part of a larger project designed to develop interpretive signage for battlefield events in the golf course area. The project was funded by the Wawashkamo Preservation and Restoration Fund which had received ABPP support. G. Michael Pratt directed the project, with the assistance of Richard Green and Ernie Humberger of Historic Archaeological Research. The crew included three field assistants and four metal detection specialists. Four volunteers from the Toledo Area Aboriginal Research Society joined the crew for the majority of the survey. The survey was coordinated with an independently organized cadaver dog search that was carried out prior to, but overlapped with, the beginning of the CHMA survey project.[39]

Sandra Anderson and her cadaver dog were contracted to conduct a search of the area prior to the start of the CHMA survey. Ms. Anderson and her crew placed flags at sites where the cadaver dog indicated an interest (presumably decayed human scent). They also placed flags at the site of surface indications of bone, whether or not the dog indicated the presence of decayed human scent. At the completion of her survey, Ms. Anderson indicated that her dog had encountered no areas that were indicative of a grave or a "body." She indicated that the dog "showed interest" in three areas of the golf course, an area including the southeast end of Holmes Hill (Fairway 5 and adjacent rough areas), near the crest of Battlefield Beach Ridge on Fairway 9, and in the edge of the woods east of the 18th tee. Concentrations of marker flags in these three areas showed the dog's apparent interest, and Ms. Anderson interpreted from the dog's behavior that the area southeast of Holmes Hill was the area of greatest interest for the likelihood of former grave sites.

Electromagnetic conductivity survey was carried out in the area southeast of Holmes Hill. The area was selected for its historic reputation as the site of a mass grave of the battlefield dead and Ms. Anderson's assertion that the area was of greatest interest to her cadaver dog. Anderson's survey team placed a number of flags where the dog indicated the possibility of human remains. The 23 × 38 m survey grid was positioned to encompass as many of these flagged locations (21 flags) as was permissible within the scope and budget of this project. The conductivity survey detected no significant anomalies. Several surfacing boulders and small conductive objects were indicated, but no apparent grave feature was noted. Following completion of the EM 38 operations, the survey grid was metal detected using the 2-2-90 method. Pewter fragments, a harmonica reed, a miniature bell, metal can fragments, several machine cut nails, and a rein or line guide from a horse harness were recovered. No battle-related artifacts were encountered.[40]

Sweep surveys were carried out on the nine golf course fairways, exclusive of tees and greens. Sighting poles (the cup flags) were placed at 5-m intervals at the end of each fairway and each detector operator was assigned to a sighting pole. This helped the detector operators to maintain 5-m intervals over the length of each fairway. The sweep survey recovered a total of 136 field specimens.

Four areas of artifact concentrations became apparent during the sweep survey, and at each a series of contiguous 15 × 15 m survey units was established. Subsequently, an additional eight-unit survey area was established at the west end of the golf course (Fairway 3) at the traditional location of the ambush of Holmes's regulars. A 2-2-90 detection was carried out in all five survey areas (totaling 10,350 m^2). An additional 126 field specimens were recovered in this aspect of the survey. The distribution of metal-detected artifacts and the intensive survey areas are depicted in the next figure.

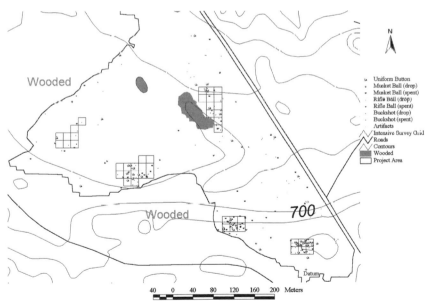

Battle for Mackinac Island Archaeological Survey
Distribution of Artifacts

Wawashkamo survey results. (Heidelberg College)

CASE STUDY 3: THE BATTLE OF BUFFINGTON ISLAND

In the summer of 1863, Confederate General John Hunt Morgan began his "Great Raid" into Northern territory. Morgan, with about 2,000 cavalry and light artillery, crossed Union lines in Kentucky, crossed the Ohio River, and swung eastward through southern Indiana and southern Ohio stealing horses, plundering farms, and creating panic. In Ohio, more than 50,000 militia troops were mustered to defend the state and to impede Morgan's route while over 8,000 Federal soldiers, including cavalry, artillery, infantry, and U.S. Navy gunboats were ordered in pursuit. As Morgan sought to re-cross the Ohio River and escape south, the ford at Buffington Island (Portland, Ohio) became the focus of attention on all sides. General Morgan and most of his 2,000 raiders reached the Portland Bottom late in the evening of July 18 and found the ford guarded by entrenched Ohio militia of unknown strength. The general chose to wait until daylight to attempt a crossing.[41] It was a fatal mistake.

Morgan's second brigade, under the direct command of Col. Basil Duke, appear to have positioned themselves opposite the head of Buffington Island in preparation for an early morning assault on a small Ohio militia earthen fortification placed to guard the approach to the Buffington Island ford. After discovering the Ohio militia position abandoned, elements of Duke's brigade moved south along the river and encountered an advance party of Federals under Gen. Henry Judah. Judah, his staff, and an escort that included a field piece collided unexpectedly with the raiders. A short skirmish ensued in which the Federals were routed with the loss of the artillery piece and a number of prisoners, the loss of several staff officers killed or wounded, and the near capture of Judah himself.[42]

In anticipation of attack by Judah's main force, Duke withdrew and formed a line across the Portland Bottom near the approach to the ford. About this time the Confederates began receiving artillery fire from "Tinclad" gunboats in the river and from Judah's main forces to their south. Shortly thereafter, Duke was attacked by Judah's Federal cavalry and forced from this position with the loss of his two artillery pieces. Duke's account makes reference to his raiders sheltering behind "Indian mounds" during this phase of the battle. The Buffington Island State Memorial Park, which features a mound, is thought to be near the location of Duke's original line of defense.[43]

Further north, near the center of the Portland Bottom, General Morgan anticipated an attack by Federal forces on his first brigade, encamped north of Duke's position. Federal General Hobson, whose cavalry had pursued the Confederates via Chester, was known to be approaching Morgan from the west. Morgan placed a field piece (perhaps the one captured from Judah) south of the Middleswart farmhouse (near the center of the Portland Bottom) and ordered the family to seek shelter from expected Federal artillery fire.[44] Morgan ordered his first brigade, the baggage train, and his remaining artillery to retreat northward along parallel roads on the upper and lower terraces of the bottom. At the northern end of Portland Bottom these roads converged and ran into the deeply entrenched valley of Lauck's Run where the road disappeared into a series of bridal trails climbing the steep, forested hillside across the creek. In attempting to negotiate this road, Morgan's artillery and part of his wagon train fell into the valley of Lauck's Run, while others were abandoned in the road. The stalled wagons also created an impediment to retreating raiders of Duke's and Johnson's brigades.

Col. August Kautz and a "flying column" of about 200 Federal cavalry were the first of Hobson's forces to reach the area. They struck a picket guard in the hills west of the Portland Bottom and drove them through the woods. Strengthened by the arrival of an artillery section and additional troopers under Col. William Sanders, Kautz pushed into the Portland Bottom from the west and confronted regiments of Duke's second brigade under Col. Johnson in a skirmish line along a roughly north-south axis. Fortuitously, Kautz's and Sanders's forces deployed near the apex of an angle formed by the east-west defensive position of Duke's retreating regiments and Johnson's line. Sanders's two Michigan regiments were armed with repeating, seven-shot Spencer carbines, creating an impression of greater numbers of Federals than were actually present. In addition to carbine and artillery fire from the south and west, the raiders also came under naval artillery fire from the Tin-clads on the river to the east.[45]

Under attack from three directions, the Confederate defense collapsed into a precipitous retreat. Kautz's and Sanders's forces pressed after them with a combination of dismounted and mounted charges that turned retreat into rout. Fleeing horsemen became blocked by the stalled wagons and lost their mounts trying to negotiate the steep valley of Lauck's Run. Col. Duke and many of his officers and men were forced to surrender, ending the action in the Portland Bottom.[46] Morgan and about two-thirds of his original force escaped the battlefield and fled north along the Ohio River in search of another crossing; but the capture of over 750 officers and men as well as the expedition's entire baggage and artillery train left the Confederates as fugitives. Within a week, Morgan and those with him were prisoners-of-war.[47]

The Buffington Island battlefield area lies within a large alluvial bottomland along a north-south trending portion of the Ohio River, at Portland, Meigs County, Ohio. The once-important ford has been flooded by the modern Ohio River lock and dam system. The town of Portland was ravaged by the 1913 flood and never recovered. Today the area is less populated than in 1863. At the time of survey, and during the Battle of Buffington Island, the bottomland was mostly cleared of forest and was primarily agricultural in nature.[48] Although efforts to preserve the battlefield continue, much of the battlefield is owned by a gravel operation which plans extensive mining of their battlefield lands.

Buffington Island ABPP and "Bloody Ground" Archaeological Surveys

Unlike Fallen Timbers, the general location of the Buffington Island battlefield was well documented; however, the size and limits of the battlefield were unknown. In the 1990s Shelly Materials, Inc. developed plans to mine gravel on properties in the Portland Bottom and applied for a U.S. Corps of Engineers (USCOE) permit to develop a barge-loading facility on the bank of the Ohio River. The proposed mining area lay within the battlefield and public aspects of the permit process generated widespread interest by regional and local historical societies, Civil War interest groups, and descendants of participants in "saving" the Battle of Buffington Island battlefield.

In a draft Memorandum of Agreement circulated in late 1997, Shelly Materials, Inc. proposed mitigation of adverse effects by temporary burial (for approximately 30 years) of approximately 40 acres of property identified in local oral tradition as the "Bloody Ground" area of the battlefield. The draft MOA excluded the remainder of the Shelly Materials property, some 600 acres, from further survey or mitigation of the archaeological remains of the battlefield.

In an effort to provide information on the location and nature of the actual Buffington Island battlefield site, Heidelberg's CHMA proposed an archaeological reconnaissance survey of the entire Portland Bottom, exclusive of the lands owned by Shelly Materials, Inc. The survey was designed to assess the overall battlefield area without becoming embroiled in the controversy over mitigation issues in the Shelly Materials holdings. By conducting survey on a sample of the overall battlefield area, the project expected to predict the nature and extent of battlefield areas within the Portland Bottom, including the proposed mine area. The project, The Battle of Buffington Island: The End of Morgan's Trail was awarded an ABPP grant, GA 2255-99-013.[49]

Archaeological survey of Buffington Island battlefield was carried out over 16 consecutive days, May 29–June 13, 1999. G. Michael Pratt directed the field crew consisting of Richard Green and Larry Hamilton, metal detection supervisors/operators from HAR; four metal detector technicians; a supervisor of volunteers; a field supervisor; and three undergraduate field assistants. Sixty-five volunteers contributed a total of 1000.37 hours of effort to the field survey aspects of this project, while 18 volunteers contributed a total of 67.25 hours in public participation laboratory sessions on June 24, 1999.[50]

The field survey was carried out on properties belonging to 14 different owners and sampled areas throughout the three-mile length of the Portland Bottom area. Initial sweep surveys were carried out on all properties, followed by the development of grid squares for 2-2-90 survey, where appropriate. About

797,628 square meters (ca. 200 acres) of the battlefield area was investigated out of a total of about 406.5 ha (ca. 1,000 acres) of the Portland Bottom, representing a 19.6 percent sample. Several of the survey areas were located among parcels owned by Shelly Materials, Inc., and these provided an opportunity to sample the battlefield within the area proposed for mining.[51]

In the southern portion of the Portland Bottom, over 100,000 square meters were sampled. Survey efforts were designed to determine the location of the initial contact between Judah and Duke, variously placed south[52] and north[53] of the S-curve in S.R. 124 at its intersection with Dry Run. Survey was conducted in lawn, pasture, fallow, and cultivated fields belonging to six different owners.[54]

The central portion of the Portland Bottom is regarded as the area in which most of the battle events took place: Duke's initial defensive position, Hobson's attack from the west, and the site of Morgan's headquarters. This area also contains the Shelly Materials' properties that were excluded from the ABPP–CHMA survey. Over 287,000 square meters of mostly agricultural lands were sampled in the central portion of the valley. A total of six property owners permitted survey on their lands. One of the survey parcels is adjacent to the southernmost limit of the Shelly Materials property, and seven of the survey areas were located on privately owned property within the outline perimeter of the area proposed for mining. Survey in this area was designed to demonstrate the likelihood that battlefield activities occurred within the proposed mining area as well as to define areas associated with key events of the battle.[55]

The northern portion of the Portland Bottom is associated with the collapse and precipitate retreat of Col. Duke's command, the Federal pursuit of Duke, the abandoned baggage train, and the ultimate surrender of Duke. Shelly Materials, Inc. owns much of this area; however, several parcels of private land lie within and north of their holdings. The results of the survey within 11 areas belonging to two property owners clearly demonstrate that the archaeological remains of the battle, and therefore the battle itself, likely occurred on lands presently scheduled for gravel mining. The archaeological survey was also able to identify traces of the Civil War–era road in and east of the Lauck's Run valley. Archaeological survey along the course of this road yielded concentrations of battlefield materials in densities greater than any of the other sample areas.[56] The figure depicts the artifact distribution within the sweep survey areas and the grid system of 2-2-90 survey squares.

A total of 252 unequivocal battlefield artifacts were recovered by the CHMA–ABPP survey. Of those, 224, or 88 percent, consisted of shot or cartridges dropped or expended in the battle.

Following this survey, CHMA was retained by Shelly Materials, Inc. to conduct a survey on the "Bloody Ground," an area of about 343,000 m^2 planned for "preservation" by burial under the MOA. This area comprised the lower terrace and floodplain of the central area of the Portland Bottom

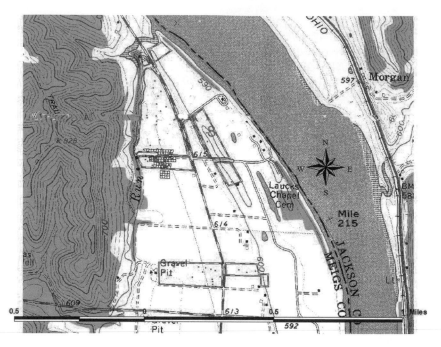

Buffington Island: Survey areas and artifact distribution, northernmost survey areas. (Heidelberg College)

and included the site of the former Tunis Middleswart house, Morgan's head-quarters prior to the battle, and subsequently the Federal HQ. Field survey was carried out during December 10–17, 1999.[57]

Six agricultural field areas were identified, numbered, and subjected to the "sweep" methodology, in order to determine the nature and distribution of battlefield remains within the project area. Survey was facilitated by orienting the survey transect parallel to the most recent furrow or crop row pattern. Survey began in the upland fields which yielded battlefield artifacts and debris associated with the two (Tunis and Franklin) Middleswart residential complexes. Survey was then carried out in the lower terrace area. The lower fields included the area where several Civil War–era shot had been recovered in the early twentieth century and near where two bayonets were reportedly found in a fencerow. Recovery of these materials led to the identification of this area by locals as the "Bloody Ground" and to its "preservation" by the MOA. A total of 116 field specimens were recovered during this aspect of the survey.[58]

First, 2-2-90 survey grids were established utilizing a handheld Brunton compass and tape. These grids were designed to delineate a series of 15 × 15 meter survey areas for the metal detection operators, not as a mapping tool. Then, a 2-2-90 survey was carried out primarily in areas of apparent artifact concentration in order to determine the nature and density of the artifact distribution. Also, a 2-2-90 survey was carried out in areas identified as significant by oral tradition regardless of the results of initial stage survey.

Eight areas of survey units were established; three in the upland portion of the project and five on the lower terrace area. The largest of these, totaling 8,100 square meters (36 grid squares), was located immediately west of the Tunis Middleswart residential complex and was also the location of the largest concentration of Civil War–era military artifacts. Two other survey areas in the upper terrace sampled an additional 4,950 square meters (22 grid squares) and were located based on artifact concentrations. In the lower terrace a total of 8,100 square meters (36 grid squares) were surveyed. Initial stage operations encountered fewer battlefield remains on the lower terrace, but since this area has been declared significant through the Memorandum of Agreement, the majority (61 percent) of the 2-2-90 survey of this part of the project area was devoted to the area identified as the Bloody Ground. A total of 101 additional field specimens were recovered during the second stage survey.[59]

Together, the Buffington Island battlefield surveys explored samples of the battlefield along the entire course of the Portland Bottom. Unfortunately, much of the battlefield remains subject to future gravel mining.

INTERPRETING ARCHAEOLOGICAL BATTLEFIELD REMAINS

Surveys of these three battlefields produced significant numbers of archaeological remains which were accurately mapped by GPS and resulted in the creation of distribution maps that can demonstrate the location and relative density of battlefield artifacts, which in turn define the limits of the site and indicate levels of activity. Identification of artifact types, particularly ammunition, presents the further opportunity to assign artifacts to units or groups of combatants and thereby identify and interpret events or actions that occurred within the larger engagement. The following section provides a means to analyze and classify round shot, the dominant artifact on eighteenth- and early nineteenth-century U.S. battlefields and demonstrates the utility of this artifact in interpreting battlefield action.

ANALYSIS AND DISTRIBUTION OF LEAD SHOT: FALLEN TIMBERS AND MACKINAC ISLAND

The surveys at the Fallen Timbers and Mackinac Island battlefields exemplify interpretations based on analysis and distribution of shot, the predominant battlefield artifact. A total of 535 shot were recovered during two surveys at Fallen Timbers, and 122 were recovered from the Mackinac Island battlefield.[60]

The spherical lead shot were analyzed in terms of the caliber (diameter) of the original ball and by its functional category (dropped or unfired, spent or fired, chewed, or carved) at the time of deposition. Caliber was determined utilizing the following formula derived by Silivich but modified to include the density of lead, rather than lead oxide:[61]

$$D = (V/6)^{1/3} = 1.2407(W/d)^{1/3}$$

D = shot diameter in mm

V = volume in mm^3

W = weight in grams

d = density in grams/mm^3

d_{pb} = 0.011337 g/mm^3

All "dropped" or undeformed shot were also measured in inches at 45°, 90°, and 135° to the mold seam. The average of the three diameters was assigned as the caliber to these balls. As expected on a battlefield site, the majority of the spherical lead shot consist of spent or fired rounds: 81 percent at Fallen Timbers and 73 percent at Mackinac Island. These are indicated by visible deformities to the lead sphere including flattening of the shot, fragmentation, and the presence of cloth patch impressions, bore marks, and other damage to the surface. Dropped (unfired) shot at both sites were indicated by the presence of mold seams and/or sprue scars on undeformed shot and a general lack of damage to the shot.

At Fallen Timbers and Mackinac Island, spherical lead shot were arbitrarily grouped as "buckshot" (.25–.36 cal.), rifle or trade gun shot (37–58 cal.), and musket shot (59–75 cal.). These two battles involved U.S. regulars and militia as well as Indian warriors armed with weapons supplied by the British and the fur trade.

In 1777 American armies received orders that "buckshot are to be put into all cartridges which shall be hereafter made." Termed "buck and ball" loads, a musket ball and buckshot cartridge remained in use in American armies for over 50 years. General Wayne specified "One ball & three heavy buckshot" as the general cartridge for his troops.[62] In the 1995 and 2001 Fallen Timbers surveys, the overall buckshot to musket ball ratio was 2.9:1 and 3.3:1, respectively.[63]

The Legion infantry was armed with French muskets obtained during the American Revolution and with muskets of the same pattern assembled from parts made by American contractors. U.S. production of muskets identical to the French pattern began in 1795, and by 1814 production reached 30,000 per year. The French and American muskets were produced in .69 and .70 caliber. Musket ammunition was issued in the form of paper tubes containing the powder charge, ball, and/or buckshot. Although the size of individual bullets varies, "service loads" issued by the French and Americans for these muskets called for balls sized "19-to-the-pound" (about .64 cal.).[64] At the Fallen Timbers Battlefield site, only three .63–.64 caliber musket shot were recovered in 2001 and only a single ball of this size was found in 1995. The presence of numerous .60–.62 caliber musket shot (n=13 for 2001 and n=17 for 1995) strongly suggests the Legion reduced the weight (and size) of the ball in order to accommodate the added buckshot.[65] However, at the Mackinac Island battlefield, twenty .63 or .64 caliber shot and seventeen .60–.62 caliber shot were recovered (representing 57 percent of the identified musket shot).[66] If, as at Fallen Timbers, the 20 smaller balls represent buck and ball loads and the larger shot are single ball rounds, then the buckshot to ball ratio for this site could be 2.75:1.

The standard British muskets of the era were the second and third pattern Land Muskets, versions of the .75 cal. "Brown Bess." Unlike U.S. troops, British forces fired a single .69–.70 caliber ball. No lead shot of these calibers were recovered at either site.[67]

Calibers between .37 and .58 were designated "rifle," although many appear to have been fired from smooth bore weapons. Rifles and small bore trade guns were commonly supplied to the Native Americans by the British; however, the musket was apparently not a common weapon among the warriors. Both Hamilton and Caldwell agree that the smooth bore fusil or fusee (light musket) was the most popular firearm among Native Americans of the late eighteenth and early nineteenth century.[68] The most well known was the Northwest Gun, which conformed to a specific and identifiable lock, serpent side plate, and trigger guard pattern. Initially produced by the Hudson's Bay Company, the pattern was widely copied and by the late eighteenth century, most trade firearms were called Northwest Guns.[69] The standard Northwest Gun was produced in 24 gauge (about .58 cal.) for single balls or for shot. However, smaller shot is repeatedly found in association with trade gun barrels and these may represent the practice of patching a smaller ball to achieve accuracy at a longer range.[70]

Rifles were apparently less desirable trade weapons. The smooth bore fusil was lighter and more versatile as a hunting weapon; nevertheless, U.S. "factories" distributed "treaty rifles" and private commercial ventures also distributed rifles in the fur trade. These appear to be "Kentucky" or "Pennsylvania" pattern rifles. They were produced in a variety of calibers from .35–.60.[71] Legion rifle companies were issued contract-built rifles. Many of the prominent Pennsylvania gunsmiths built rifles for the army, and therefore contract guns may not have differed significantly from civilian versions.

In addition to "rifle/trade gun" shot from both Fallen Timbers and Mackinac Island, parts of such weapons were also found. The Mackinac Island survey recovered two brass, serpentine side-plates typical of late eighteenth-/early nineteenth-century manufacture, and the 2001 survey at Fallen Timbers recovered 14 metal fragments (representing all but the barrel) from a "Kentucky" style rifle.[72]

THE BATTLE FOR MACKINAC ISLAND: AN ARCHAEOLOGICAL PERSPECTIVE

The archaeological survey of the Wawashkamo Golf Club portion of the Battle for Mackinac Island battlefield was designed to provide additional primary source information by identifying the general area of combat and, perhaps, the location of specific maneuvers or actions. Unfortunately, the discovery of significant numbers of post-battle military artifacts on the 1814 battlefield and therefore the lack of unequivocal association of unidentified or undated buttons and military equipment with the 1814 battle must reduce the confidence level of archaeological interpretations.

In general, the recovery of 1814-era U.S. buttons in association with spent musket, rifle, and buckshot confirm that the Wawashkamo golf course represents part of the battle fought on Mackinac Island. Furthermore, the recovery of infantry and artillery buttons as well as general service "U.S." buttons indicates the presence of Croghan's regulars on this part of the battlefield. Finally, the single iron canister shot found east of Holmes Hill indicates that the artillery fire heard by Parsons throughout the early phase of the battle was indeed ineffectual.[73]

The general distribution of shot and occasional buttons, a U.S. neck stock clasp, and perhaps the compass divider in Fairways 1 and 5 indicate that U.S. forces advanced along the route of present British Landing Road, perhaps supported by at least one of the field pieces. The musket shot from this area consists mostly of military shot (.63–.64 cal.) and trade gun shot (.50–.56 cal.). Only three spent rifle shot and 11 buckshot were recovered from the intensive survey grid in this part of the field. The overall shot density in this area was calculated at $0.004/m^2$.

The Fairway 1 and 5 portions of the Wawashkamo golf course appear to represent part of Croghan's slow and cautious approach toward the British position on the ridge.[74] It is likely that the U.S. musket shot in this area represent rounds fired from skirmishers in advance of Croghan's main force that then advanced over their own spent shot. The light return fire from rifles and trade guns may represent harassing fire directed at Croghan's withdrawal by the Indians and militia that followed the retreat "until under the Broadsides of the ships,"[75] rather than in resistance to the American advance. This interpretation is strengthened by McDouall's statement that the Indians permitted the Americans to gain his left flank "without firing a shot."[76]

As the battle developed, Croghan changed his position by "...advancing Maj. Holmes battalion on the right of the militia, thus to out flank..." the British.[77] Tactical maneuvers of the day indicate that such a move is carried out in line, rather than in a column advance. Previous accounts describe Holmes as making a wide swing around the north end of Holmes Hill and being ambushed near the 8th tee – 7th green and Fairway 3 area[78]; however, there is little evidence of fighting in this part of the field. Rather, the archaeological evidence suggests the westward (right) extension of the line occurred south of Holmes Hill.

Here, relatively high density U.S. military musket shot and buckshot recovered from the base and slope of Battlefield Beach Ridge is intermingled with small musket and rifle shot. Overall shot density in the intensive survey grids in this area was calculated at $0.01/m^2$ in Fairway 8, $0.02/m^2$ at the crest of the ridge in Fairway 9, and $0.008/m^2$ behind the ridge and near the clubhouse. The first two areas lie about 300 m apart and suggest that fighting took place over a wide front. Croghan describes Holmes's death "while beginning the charge" and states his "failure to move left ... led to [a] charge by the regulars towards the front."[79] Croghan also states the death of officers "threw the line into confusion"; as a result, he ordered the regulars to charge to the front. Croghan's use of the terms "line" and "charge" support the archaeological evidence that the attack by the "Fallovine Indians" was made on the front and flank of a U.S. battle line rather than on a column of troops (see figure).[80]

In the confusion following the initial "ambush," the regulars were ordered to charge toward the front. Croghan claims to have driven the enemy into the woods in spite of "annoying fire from Indians" and ordered Lt. Morgan to advance an artillery piece, bringing the "enemy to fire at a longer distance." He then determined his position untenable and ordered his forces to retreat back to the beach.[81] Archaeologically, it is unclear how far the Americans advanced, but U.S. general service, infantry, and artillery buttons were recovered at the crest of the ridge. Since 1815 rifle and infantry buttons also occur in this area, the interpretation of these pre-1815 buttons as the high point of Croghan's attack is equivocal.

Although Croghan does not mention it, his position may have become untenable due to the arrival of McDouall with "the greater part of the Indians and 50 militia."[82] McDouall claims his forces followed the retreating Americans to within the range of their naval guns. Parsons recorded that the direction of gunfire changed at 4:30, but continued until 5:00. Most of the troops had returned to the shore when the gunfire ceased.[83] Together, these statements suggest that warriors and militia kept up a harassing fire while following Croghan's retreat. It is likely that this action generated the small musket shot and rifle balls found opposite Holmes Hill in Fairways 1 and 5, as well as the low density small musket shot from Fairways 2 and 3. Fairway 3 also produced a dropped .63 cal. ball, infantry button, and the silver trade brooch fragment (see figure).

Archaeologically, the British regular forces are almost invisible in this battle. No "ounce"(.69–.70 cal.) balls, the standard musket load of the British Army, were recovered during the survey. McDouall claimed, "a natural breastwork" [crest of Battlefield Beach Ridge] "protected my men from every shot"[84]; but the archaeological evidence indicates that these troops made little or no effort to return the fire. It appears likely that the British regulars withdrew from the ridge before Croghan's forces came within effective musket range.

Archaeologically, the ratio of buckshot to musket shot at this site (0.67:1) does not fit the pattern noted at Fallen Timbers where U.S. forces engaged with "buck and ball." Furthermore, this site produced significant numbers of .63–.64 cal. shot in addition to the .61–.62 cal. shot attributed to the buck and ball load.[85] It is possible that buckshot was under-represented in this survey; however, the same recovery techniques, equipment, and some of the same metal detector operators were used in both surveys.[86] It is also possible, but unlikely, that the American regulars deviated from their standard ammunition in this battle. However, in 1980, Dunnigan proposed that the British militia in this battle were armed and accoutered with U.S. equipment captured in the 1812 invasion of Mackinac Island.[87] Fifty of the militia returned to the field in the late stages of the battle and participated in the fighting. Their use of the 1795 pattern U.S. Musket firing (in the British style) a single ball cartridge could explain the low buckshot to musket ball ratio and account for the presence of the larger caliber shot at this battle. If the .63–.64 shot (n=20) are removed from the equation, the ratio of buckshot to .61–.62 cal. musket shot is 2.75:1.

As the battle came to an end, the warriors turned to the dead. In his letter to Croghan, McDouall states that he "personally superintended the decent interment of the dead previous to my quitting field"; however, the body of Holmes was not recognized as an officer due to "being previously stripped by the Indians."[88] The relative lack of U.S. infantry buttons at a site where 17 regulars were left dead on the field suggests that victorious warriors stripped the dead and carried the uniforms away.

Although given a "decent" burial within hours of their deaths, the bodies may have been disinterred shortly after. Elizabeth Davenport remained on Mackinac Island throughout the British occupation, but was under suspicion as the wife of a "Yankee Rebel." She was detained in the fort's blockhouse from the arrival of the American fleet until after the battle. Mrs. Davenport reports when British and Indians returned to the fort, the Indians carried scalps and other body parts. She claims that hands, hearts, and other pieces of the American dead were cooked and consumed while the scalps were hung on the railings near McDouall's quarters.[89] Van Fleet repeats this story and claims that these remains were later buried in an Indian cemetery. Ground conductivity survey of the "mass grave" reported by Van Fleet and assumed to lie at the foot of Holmes Hill found no evidence of subsurface features. If such a feature ever existed, it is likely to have been destroyed by subsequent agriculture or development of the golf course.

THE BATTLE OF FALLEN TIMBERS: AN ARCHAEOLOGICAL PERSPECTIVE

Two archaeological surveys revealed varying levels of shot and button density (indicative of varying levels of combat) in four distinct areas of the battlefield: (1) east of the forest where the highest concentration of artifacts and virtually all of the uniform buttons were recovered (7200 m²); (2) the northern portion of the NHS property; a field bounded by railroad tracks (2.5 ha);

(3) portions of the northeast section of the forest (1.2 ha); (4) portions of NHS property located between the western edge of the forest and the private homes along the east side of Jerome Road (4.8 ha). Artifact densities from the 2001 survey were calculated for all areas in terms of artifacts/metal detection survey unit (225 m^2) as follows:

1. East field Button Clusters	5.19 artifacts/225 m^2
3. North field	0.75 artifacts/225 m^2
4. Forest	0.57 artifacts/225 m^2
2. Forest to Jerome Road	0.50 artifacts/225 m^2

The relative distribution of battlefield artifacts is consistent with results from the 1995 survey, which identified a much larger area surrounding the button clusters as the area of greatest artifact density (1.12/225 m^2). The 1995 survey interpreted this area as the location of the "fallen timbers" and as the site of the historically documented skirmish between Legion troops and advancing warriors. In the 2001 survey this area produced a greater artifact density than the forest and areas further west, areas interpreted both archaeologically and historically as lying behind the U.S. battle line. To the east of this area, the 1995 survey encountered a drop in artifact density (.47 artifacts/225 m^2). Historically, gunfire dropped precipitously as the U.S. regulars launched a bayonet charge through the fallen timbers area, resulting in the collapse of the Indian position.[90]

All but one of the survey areas that produced multiple (5–23) buttons exhibited buttons from at least two and often three items (coat, vest, or breeches/trousers) of the federal Legion uniform. The single exception yielded "spun back" buttons elsewhere associated with breeches/trousers and a single silver non-military button. The button groups lie within the highest density artifact area and also exhibit high densities of impacted rifle shot within the 2001 survey areas.

Historically, casualties who could not make it off the battlefield on their own or without help from friends were left on the field for two days. When a federal burial party was dispatched, they reported burial of only 19 bodies, well below the most conservative death estimates.[91] The clusters of buttons and lack of grave features in the EM-38 conductivity survey suggest that the casualties interpreted archaeologically were among those " ... left to ferment upon the surface, the prey of Vultures ... "[92]

THE BATTLE OF BUFFINGTON ISLAND: AN ARCHAEOLOGICAL PERSPECTIVE

The ABPP–CHMA archaeological survey demonstrates convincingly that remains of the July 19, 1863, Battle of Buffington Island are present and recoverable in the Portland Bottom. The survey of nearly 797,628 square meters (ca. 200 acres) throughout the Portland Bottom produced a total of 252 battlefield artifacts, primarily spent munitions. An analysis of the distribution pattern of these remains provides new and significant information on the actual location of key events in the Battle of Buffington Island.

The initial engagement of the battle appears to have occurred east of Dry Run and south of the present McCook monument. The former James Williamsen home, which probably received wounded Federals (including Major McCook and Lieut. F. G. Price), has been altered, but remains as a visible battlefield structure.

The first defensive skirmish line established by the 5th and 6th Kentucky Cavalry of Duke's Brigade was not clearly apparent, but likely lies within the mobile home/construction trailer wrecking yard located between the McCook monument and the Buffington Island State Memorial Park. The position of Duke's two Parrot guns may lie in the uplands west of the wrecking yard. The ABPP–CHMA survey did not have permission to work on that property, nor is the land conducive to metal detection survey. The upland areas associated with that property exhibit visible signs of grading and were impacted by early twentieth-century oil production activity. The archaeological potential of this significant part of the battlefield has not been assessed.

The large fields immediately north of the wrecking yard produced scattered remains of pistol fire, artillery shell fragments, and a few carbine rounds. This area may represent Duke's attempt to rally and recover a defensive position after being driven from his first position and losing his artillery or (as Federal officers claim) the beginning of his retreat north. The area of the Buffington Island State Memorial Park and the fields immediately north of it produced only scattered evidence of the battle. It appears that within this portion of the battlefield, Duke's brigades were in the process of repositioning and were producing and receiving little small-arms fire. North and east of the Ohio Historical Society Park, the Portland School and the modern village of Portland have obliterated parts of the battle site. However, the majority of this area of the battlefield is impacted only by agriculture.

The central portion of the battlefield is threatened by impending gravel mining, slated to occur during 2000–2036, which will destroy the archaeological record as well as the viewscape of this part of the Buffington Island battlefield. Recovery of battlefield remains from parcels within the perimeter of the proposed mine area indicate Federal fire, probably resulting from Kautz's skirmishers and Sanders's artillery, was directed into the present Shelly Materials, Inc. properties. This survey, however, was not able to determine which of several possible routes Kautz's forces traveled to the battlefield, nor the location and movements of Duke's and Johnson's regiments once they were engaged by the Federal cavalry regiments and artillery under Kautz and Sanders.

In late 1999 Shelly Materials, Inc. undertook archaeological survey of their holdings east of the intersection of C.R. 31 and S.R. 124, the reputed

"Bloody Ground" area of the battlefield. Survey of this area supported Confederate participant Curtice Burke's description of the area as General Morgan's headquarters of July 19–20 and as the post-battle prisoner-of-war compound. The high proportion of dropped to spent shot in this area indicates relatively little combat occurred in the "Bloody Ground"[93] area slated for preservation by the MOA.

The flanking attack by Hobson's column and the Confederate response to it is the turning point where Duke's measured withdrawal became a rout. Archaeological investigation of this area of the battlefield has the potential to determine the shape and location of Confederate positions, the relative strength of firepower of each, and their response to Kautz's skirmishers and the artillery and cavalry attack by Sanders. Spencer carbine shot and cartridges have the potential to indicate the movements of the 8th and 9th Michigan in their rout of the Confederate forces. The ABPP–CHMA survey and the 1999 survey of the "Bloody Ground" area both indicate relatively little fighting occurred on the T-2 terrace east of S.R. 124 in the central Portland Bottom area. By process of elimination, Duke's and Johnson's formations, the ground over which they retreated, and the route of the Michigan cavalry charge all lie along the crest of the T-3 terrace within the Shelly Materials, Inc. holdings. Thus, though the archaeological record of the central Portland Bottom has the potential to provide information key to understanding the critical moments of the Battle of Buffington Island, under the current MOA, this portion of the battlefield remains under the threat of destruction without mitigation. The Tunis Middleswart house, which stood in the central part of the Portland Bottom, was demolished in the 1970s. The archaeological site (33Ms88) is presently owned by Shelly Materials, Inc. Structural remains and artifacts are visible on the surface; however, the MOA does not include the site in its mitigation measures.

The final events of the Battle of Buffington Island occurred when the fleeing Confederates of Duke's brigade encountered the abandoned wagons and artillery that choked their only road of escape. Federal and Confederate accounts agree that military organization disintegrated and individuals and small parties were left to escape, fight, or surrender under the pressure of Federal cavalry armed with the rapid fire Spencer carbine. The archaeological remains recovered along the visible traces of the 1863 Portland Road west of S.R. 124 document the close-range combat that ended in the death of some and the surrender of most of General Morgan's rear guard regiments. The rapidly shifting stream bottom and the dense vegetation of the Lauck's Run valley have re-deposited and obscured the archaeological record of the valley floor. The upland fields remain agricultural and the trace of the Portland Road represents a battlefield resource little changed since the Civil War. The old roadbed (see figure) remains a visible representation of where the 1863 Portland Road and Morgan's Great Raid came to an end.[94]

CONCLUSIONS

The remote sensing survey methods presented above have proven effective as a means to recover battlefield remains and to interpret battlefield events. At the Fallen Timbers, Mackinac Island, and Buffington Island battlefields, this method demonstrated archaeologically the areas where various battlefield activities occurred. The distribution, density, and type of lead shot recovered identified areas of relatively heavy or light gunfire which, when considered in light of historical and other archaeological information, help to identify troop positions, attacks, and the weaponry utilized at each site. Electromagnetic conductivity survey at the Mackinac Island and Fallen Timbers sites confirmed the treatment of battlefield casualties at the latter site and refuted claims of a mass grave at the former. All three surveys provided "ground truth" information in support of preservation efforts at these sites and all provided local citizens with the opportunity to play a role in uncovering new information about a significant historic event. Finally, all three surveys involved sites which had or would receive support from the American Battlefield Protection Program.

NOTES

1. McKee and Mason 1994.
2. Fox 1993, Scott & Connor 1997, Scott & Fox 1989.
3. Pratt 2000a, b.
4. Pratt 1995a.
5. Pratt 1995a:11–12.
6. Pratt 1995a:15–17.
7. Pratt 1995a:19–21.
8. Pratt 1995a:22–28.
9. Pratt 1995a:28.
10. Smith 1952, *New York Magazine* 1794.
11. Pratt 1995a.
12. Pratt 1997a, b.
13. Pratt 2002.
14. Pratt 1995b.
15. Pratt 1995b.
16. DOrder 2:4.
17. Pratt 2002.
18. Pratt 1995a:25–26.
19. McGrane 1914:30, Lin 1873:339, Smith 1965:8, McKee 1794.
20. Pratt 2002:46.
21. Pratt 2002:46–49.
22. Pratt 2002:49–50.
23. Pratt 2002:50–51.
24. Fredricksen 2000:87.

25. Dunnigan 1980:22.
26. Dunnigan 1980:22.
27. Dunnigan 1980:24.
28. Wood 1918:307.
29. Fredricksen 2000:87, Wood 1918:306–307, MPHC 1894:592.
30. Wood 1918:307.
31. Fredricksen 2000:87–88, Wood 1918:307, MPHC 1894:593.
32. McDouall 1814, MPHC 1894:592, Dunnigan 1980.26, Fredricksen 2000:90.
33. McDouall 1814.
34. Fredricksen 2000:90.
35. Otsego 1845, Van Fleet 1870:118.
36. Van Fleet 1870:142.
37. Otsego 1845.
38. Straus and Dunnigan 2000:31, 40–41.
39. Pratt 2002.
40. Pratt 2002.
41. Miller et al. 1997, Bennett 1998, Horwitz 1999.
42. Miller et al. 1997, Bennett 1998.
43. Duke 1906, Miller et al. 1997, Bennett 1998.
44. Bush n.d., Middleswart n.d.
45. Allen 1903:223–242, Duke 1906:451, Miller et al. 1997, Bennett 1998.
46. Miller et al. 1997, Bennett 1998.
47. Bennett 1998.
48. Hayes 1877.
49. Pratt 2000a.
50. Pratt 2000a:24.
51. Pratt 2000a:29.
52. Horwitz 1999.
53. Miller et al. 1994, Bennett 1998.
54. Pratt 2000a:29.
55. Pratt 2000a:29.
56. Pratt 2000a:29.
57. Pratt 2000b.
58. Pratt 2000b:25.
59. Pratt 2000b:25.
60. Pratt 1995b:17, 2002:54, 2002:35.
61. Sivilich 1995.
62. Lewis 1956:108–110, Knopf 1960:185.
63. Pratt 1995b:23, 2002:57.
64. Lewis 1956:108–110.
65. Pratt 2002:58.
66. Pratt 2002:51.
67. Neumann 2001:49.
68. Caldwell et al. 1982, Hamilton 1980.
69. Caldwell et al. 1982:7.
70. Caldwell et al. 1982:85.
71. Kauffman 1960:19.
72. Pratt 2001:55, 2002:37.

73. Fredricksen 2000:87, MPHC 1894:591.
74. MPHC 1894:591, Wood 1918:306.
75. MPHC 1894:593.
76. MPHC 1894:592.
77. Wood 1918:307.
78. Dunnigan 1980:25.
79. Van Fleet 1870:117.
80. Wood 1918:307.
81. Wood 1918:307.
82. MPHC 1894:592.
83. Fredricksen 2000:88.
84. MPHC 1894:592.
85. Pratt 2002:57.
86. Pratt 2002.
87. Dunnigan 1980:44.
88. McDouall 1814.
89. Otsego 1845.
90. Pratt 1995a, 1995b:26–27, 2002a.
91. Pratt 1995a:26.
92. Quaife 1929:86–87, Smith 1952:302.
93. Burke n.d., Pratt 2000b.
94. Pratt 2000a:46–48.

REFERENCES CITED

Allen, Theodore F. 1903. Pursuit of John Morgan. In *Sketches of War History*, 223–242. Robert Clarke, Cincinnati.

Bennett, B. Kevin. 1998. The Battle of Buffington Island. *Blue & Gray Magazine*, April 1998:7–58.

Burke, Curtice. n.d. Civil War Journal. Photocopy of unpublished manuscript. Archives, US Army Military History Institute, Carlisle Barracks, PA.

Bush, Susann. n.d. Notebook of information and photographs relating to the Tunis Middleswart Homestead. Prepared by Susan Bush, January 24, 2000. Copy in possession of the author.

Caldwell, W. W., Gooding, J. S., Hamilton, T. M., Hanson, C. E. Jr., Huntington, R. T., Russell, C. P., Smith, C. S., Woodward, A., and J. Barsott. 1982. *Indian Trade Guns*. Pioneer Press, Union City, TN.

DOrder 2. 1998. Director's Order #2: Park Planning. National Park Service. Available at http://www.nps.gov/refdesk/Dorders/DOrder2.html.

Duke, Basil. 1906. *Morgan's Cavalry*. Neale Publishing Co., New York.

Dunnigan, Brian Leigh. 1980. *The British Army at Mackinac 1812–1815*. Reports in Mackinac History and Archaeology Number 7. Mackinac Island State Park Commission.

Fox, Richard A. Jr. 1993. *Archaeology, History, and Custer's Last Battle*. University of Oklahoma Press, Norman.

Fredricksen, John C. (ed.). 2000. *Surgeon of the Lakes: The Diary of Dr. Usher Parsons 1812–1814*. Erie County Historical Society, Erie, PA.

Hamilton, T. M. 1980. *Colonial Frontier Guns*. The Fur Press, Chadron, NE.

Hayes, E. L. 1877. *Illustrated Atlas of the Upper Ohio Valley.* On file, Hamilton County Public Library, Cincinnati.

Horwitz, Lester V. 1999. *Longest Raid of the Civil War: Little-Known & Untold Stories of Morgan's Raid into Kentucky, Indiana & Ohio.* James A. Ramage, Publisher.

Kauffman, Henry J. 1960. *The Pennsylvania-Kentucky Rifle.* Stackpole Co., Harrisburg, PA.

Knopf, Richard. 1960. *Anthony Wayne: A Name in Arms.* University of Pittsburgh Press, Pittsburgh.

Lewis, Berkeley R. 1956. *Small Arms and Ammunition in the United States Service 1776–1865.* Smithsonian Miscellaneous Collections Vol. 129. Smithsonian Institution Press, Washington, D.C.

Lin, John B. 1873. General Wayne's Campaign in 1794 & 1795: Captain John Cooke's Journal. *American Historical Record* II (311–316, 339–345).

McDouall, Robert. 1814. McDouall, Robert ALS to George Croghan. Michilimackinac August 5, 1814. (Original letter) Michigan Papers, William Clements Library, Ann Arbor.

McGrane, R C. 1914. A Journal of Major-General Anthony Wayne's Campaign Against the Shawnee Indians in Ohio in 1794–1795. *Mississippi Valley Historical Review* I:419–444.

McKee, Alexander. 1794. Letter to Joseph Chew, 27 August, 1794. RG 8 I "C" Series 247:222–224.

McKee, W. Reid, and M. E. Mason Jr. 1994. *Civil War Projectiles II: Small Arms & Field Artillery with supplement.* Publisher's Press, Orange, VA (reprint).

Miller, Orloff G., Ruth G. Meyers, Krystyna Puc, Rita Walsh, E. Jeanne Harris, Christopher J. Baltz, Mathew E. Bechner, and Kevin Paper. 1997. Phase I Cultural Resources Investigations Above Buffington Island, For Richard & Sons, Inc., Meigs County, OH. Manuscript in possession of Paul Rice, Shelly Materials, Inc.

MPHC (Michigan Pioneer and Historical Collections). 1894. Lt. Col. Robert McDouall to Sir George Prevost, 14 August 1814. *Michigan Pioneer and Historical Collections* 25:591. Robert Smith & Co., Lansing.

Neumann, George C. 2001. The Redcoat's Brown Bess. *American Rifleman Magazine* (April 2001):49.

New York Magazine. 1794. Sketch of the Ground at the Rapids of the Miami of the Lake, showing the Position of General Wayne's Army previous to and after the Action of the 20th of August, 1794. *New York Magazine; or Literary Repository: for October, 1794.* Number X.-Vol.V. Printed and Published by T. and J. Swords, No. 167, William St., New York. (Between 642–643).

Otsego. 1845. Untitled article signed "Otsego" based on personal interview with Ambrose R. and Elizabeth Davenport. *Cleveland Daily Advertiser,* Sept. 27, 1845. Transcribed at http://bailiwick.lib.uiowa.edu/woodrow/Davenport.html.

Pratt, G. Michael. 1995a. The Battle of Fallen Timbers: An Eyewitness Perspective. *Northwest Ohio Quarterly* 67(1):4–34.

Pratt, G. Michael. 1995b. The Archaeology of the Fallen Timbers Battlefield: A Report of the 1995 Field Survey. Ms. on file, The Maumee Valley Heritage Corridor, Inc. and http://www.heidelberg.edu/FallenTimbers/.

Pratt, G. Michael. 1997a. A Report to the Property Owners on Fallen Timbers Lane. Unpublished letter 4/5/97, Center for Historic and Military Archaeology, Heidelberg College, Tiffin, OH.

Pratt, G. Michael. 1997b. A Report to the Director of St Luke's Hospital. Unpublished letter 4/16/97, Center for Historic and Military Archaeology, Heidelberg College, Tiffin, OH.

Pratt, G. Michael. 2000a. The Battle of Buffington Island: The End of Morgan's Trail. A Report on the Archaeological Survey American Battlefield Protection Program Grant No. GA-2255-99-013. Ms. on file, American Battlefield Protection Program, National Park Service, Washington, D.C.

Pratt, G. Michael. 2000b. Assessing the "Bloody Ground": The Archaeological Survey of a Portion of the Buffington Island Battlefield. Prepared for Shelly Materials, Inc. Ms. on file, US Army Corps of Engineers, Huntington District, 502 Eighth Street, Huntington, WV.

Pratt, G. Michael. 2001. The General Management Planning Baseline Archaeological Survey: Fallen Timbers Battlefield NHS. Ms. on file, the Metroparks of the Toledo Area, Toledo, OH.

Pratt, G. Michael. 2002. The Battle for Mackinac Island: The Archaeological Survey of the Wawashkamo Golf Course, Mackinac Island, Michigan. Ms. on file, the Mackinac Island State Park Commission and the Wawashkamo Restoration and Preservation Fund, Mackinac Island.

Quaife, Milo, M. (ed.). 1929. General James Wilkinson's Narrative of the Fallen Timbers Campaign. *Mississippi Valley Historical Review* 14:81–90.

Scott, Douglas D., and Melissa A. Connor. 1997. *Metal Detector Use in Archaeology: An Introduction.* Midwest Archaeological Center, National Park Service. Lincoln, NE.

Scott, D. D., and R. Fox. 1989. *Archaeological Insights into the Custer Battle: An Assessment of the 1984 Field Season.* University of Oklahoma Press, Norman.

Sivilich, Daniel M. 1995. Approximation of Musket Ball Caliber Using Weight Measurements. Unpublished paper presented to the Society for Historical Archaeology Annual Meeting.

Smith, Dwight L. (ed.). 1952. *From Greene Ville to Fallen Timbers: A Journal of the Wayne Campaign July 28–September 14, 1794.* Indiana Historical Society, Indianapolis.

Smith, Dwight L. 1965. *With Captain Edward Miller in the Wayne Campaign of 1794.* The William Clements Library, Ann Arbor.

Straus, Frank, and Brian Leigh Dunnigan. 2000. *Walk a Crooked Trail: A Centennial History of Wawashkamo Golf Club.* Wawashkamo Golf Club, Mackinac Island, Michigan.

Van Fleet, Reverend J. A. 1870. *Old and New Mackinac.* Courier Steam Printing House, Ann Arbor.

Wood, Edwin O. 1918. *Historic Mackinac.* The Macmillan Co., New York.

Mustering Landscapes: What Historic Battlefields Share in Common

John & Patricia Carman

THE BLOODY MEADOWS Project[1] has as one of its goals to develop an understanding of changes in warfare practice and ideology over the long term. In operation, it is an exercise in the comparative study of known battlefields from all periods of history and in all parts of the world: this means the earliest site to be examined would be Megiddo in Syria, from around 1469 BC, and we impose our own limit at 1900 AD, since so many others are engaged in studying the warfare of the twentieth century and beyond.[2] The Bloody Meadows Project is distinctive among battlefield archaeology projects in that it takes an overtly *comparative* approach to such places. The project is interested primarily in the *kinds* of places where people have come together to commit mutual slaughter and how one in this time and region differs from that in another time and region. Over the past five years or so, we have looked at 30 sites, all but two in Europe, from classical Greece, through the medieval period, and into the early nineteenth century. Collectively, the battlefields give insights into the kinds of places where people chose to fight in the past.

APPROACH AND METHODS

As a contribution to archaeology more generally, the project is an attempt to apply some recently developed approaches to landscapes to gain insights into how landscapes, especially particular kinds of landscapes, were *perceived* in the past. For us, the key element is the landscape of the battle itself, which we approach by drawing upon ideas from phenomenology as applied in archaeology. The British archaeologist Christopher Tilley has perhaps given the clearest justification for such a phenomenological approach to studying landscapes:

> The landscape [he writes] is continually being encultured, bringing things into meaning as part of a symbolic process by which human consciousness makes the

physical reality of the natural environment into an intelligible and socialised form. . . . It [is accordingly] evident . . . that the significance of landscape for different populations cannot be simply read off from the local "ecological" characteristics of a "natural" environment.[3]

Cultural markers [such as monuments are used] to create a new sense of place. . . . An already encultured landscape becomes refashioned, its meanings now controlled by the imposition of [a new] cultural form.

These comments by Tilley specifically refer to the relationship of prehistoric monuments to mostly empty rural landscapes in Britain. Following his lead, and that of others, a phenomenological approach to the study of landscapes as taken by archaeologists has generally been limited to the monumental "ritual" landscapes of later European prehistory. The approach is, however, also of more general relevance to any encultured space, especially any marked as a particular kind of space. The typical interpretive device in battlefield research is the battlefield plan, an objective view from above, divorced from the action. But as Tilley also emphasizes, place is not something that can be understood "objectively":

Looking at the two-dimensional plane of the modern topographic map with sites [or artifact scatters] plotted on it, it is quite impossible to envisage the landscape in which these places are embedded. The representation fails, and cannot substitute for being there, being *in place*. [The] process of observation requires time and a feeling for the place.[4]

The primary data source used in the Bloody Meadows Project is the physical landscape of the place where warfare was practiced. Drawing upon the work of previous scholars who have identified the locations of many battlefields from the past, we focus upon the landscape itself to ask specific questions, including:

- How clearly bounded is the battlefield space (does it have clear boundaries, such as impassable ground or a water obstacle)?
- Is it high or low ground relative to the surrounding space?
- What kind of use (other than for war) was the site put to, if any?
- Is it near or distant from settlement?
- Is it visible from settlement?
- Does the ground contain particular types of landscape features—natural or built— which play a part in the battlefield action?
- What features present in the landscape (if any) played no part in the battlefield action?
- Was the battlefield subsequently marked by a monument or memorial in any way?

The answers to these questions can be conveniently set out for each battlefield as follows.

An early medieval site: Assandun 1016 AD. Low open ground by a river.

Parameters for Studying Battlefields

Rules of war	Battlefield architecture
Agreement to fight: Y/N	Features present
Mutual recognition as "legitimate" enemies: Y/N	Type of feature used
Level of violence: High, medium, Low	Type of feature not used
Marking of battle-site:	Use of terrain:
	as cover;
	to impede visibility;
	to impede movement
Participants	Structured formations: Y/N
Functional aspects	
Dysfunctional aspects	

Here, the *rules of war* cover such things as the degree of mutual agreement needed before fighting could commence, whether the two sides were required to see each other as "legitimate" enemies or whether anyone could participate in a battle, some assessment of the level of violence employed, and how (if at all) the battle site was remembered immediately afterward.

These are a measure of how "formal" a battle was regarded and how distinctive it was from other forms of conflict at that time.

The characteristics of the battlefield landscape are addressed in order to identify features present in the battle space and how they were used by combatants. This gives some insight into attitudes to the battlefield as a place. The query as to whether structured formations were present (such as ordered columns or lines of troops) gives a clue to how participants moved through the battlefield space: if the landscape is seen as architecture, so too can the forces engaged be seen as a kind of "mobile architecture." The point is not merely to note those features present and used by combatants, as military historians might, but also and especially those features present but not used, and for purposes of elimination those present today but not on the day of battle.

The two final sections attempt to summarize our expectations as filtered through an understanding of "good military practice" derived from military writings (as in the concept of "inherent military probability" discussed by John Keegan).[5] It is, we believe, the *dysfunctional* behavior (that is, the apparent mistakes or omissions) which can give a clue to cultural attitudes and expectations of the battlefield space which differ from our own. In applying this analysis to examples of warfare from various periods, the differences between periods become evident.

In approaching the landscapes that are our object, we use what we have called "the archaeologist's eye," that is, the capacity of a trained landscape archaeologist to interpret space and to identify (especially manufactured) features in landscapes otherwise unfamiliar to them to reach an understanding of the spaces of battle. By approaching such sites with a structured set of questions and by recording data in a standard format, it becomes possible to recognize what such sites have in common and how they differ from one another. This in turn, by tabulating the results, allows the identification of the types of location favored as battle sites in particular periods of history. Overall, it presents an opportunity to gain a direct insight into the ideological factors guiding warfare practice in that period and to compare them with that guiding warfare practice in a different period.

BATTLEFIELD LANDSCAPE AND TERRAIN

The notion of "terrain" most commonly applied in battlefield studies is perhaps something different from the concept of "landscape" which we apply. Battlefield terrain generally consists of those features considered relevant or important to military purposes. Landscape, by contrast, is all those features present regardless of their military usefulness. This includes the general shape of the area as it presents itself, and all those elements that help to define it, separate it from surrounding land, or bind it together as a more-or-less coherent space. The Bloody Meadows Project is concerned not with terrain but with landscape and so takes a view different from that of conventional military history. In so doing, we distinguish coastal or estuarine places from those further inland; and high places from lower. We also concern ourselves with the relation of the space to urban centers: battles may be fought through, just outside of, within sight of, or completely away from towns and cities. One of the things that are interesting is the different types of space that cluster together as choices for battlefields in different periods of history. Here, all our classical Greek battlefields show the same characteristics, as do all our medieval battlefields; the only battlefields not to fit our patterns are those seventeenth- and eighteenth-century fights at Linton, Fontenoy, and Quebec, all of which were fought within or close to towns. We are frankly surprised there isn't more variation in our sample than this, and we know of only a very few more actual battles of the early modern period fought adjacent to or within urban space.

Apart from the general shape of the land on which battles were fought, we are also interested in the specific features that may be scattered across the battlefield space; some of these are also listed. There may be natural features, the products of geology such as ridges or depressions; or biological entities such as woods, forests, or hedges; or made features, such as ancient burial mounds, earthen banks and ditches, or buildings. Some of these play a part in the battlefield action; many do not. Some may have been noticed on the day, and others not. The presence of some may have been one reason why the place was chosen for battle; that it was considered to be "marked" in some way as significant to those who fought there. To give an indication of how we approach these issues, two examples are used of things that may be present on a battlefield: woodlands, and churches and monasteries.

Woodland can offer a place to hide troops, may be an area to avoid, or may simply provide a source of raw material. At Aljubarotta and at Bosworth the woodland areas were avoided by troops and provided a boundary to the battlefield space. The trees themselves at Aljubarotta were a source for the material used to construct a *chevaux de frise* protecting the defenders' position, and their presence on steeply sloping ground served also to protect the flanks of the position. At Northampton trees provided a boundary to the battlefield space along its southern edge but also provided a modicum of protection from the elements to troops encamped there overnight. At Tewkesbury and at Fontenoy the woods were used to hide the presence of troops from the enemy. Spearmen at Tewkesbury were able to catch a contingent of the enemy by surprise, and artillery at Fontenoy was able to enfilade attacking troops by using woodlands to mask movements and positions. The specifics of particular circumstances seem to determine the role of woodland in battle, as an inconvenience or an asset, as a landscape feature or as merely a number of individual trees. The manner in which woodland is treated by soldiers in different periods may indicate how such features are perceived more generally in that period. These few examples may suggest that trees are more likely to be seen as woodland landscape features in more recent periods, and

Battlefield Landscapes and Features by Period

Classical

Landscape: Low ground *and* visibility from at least
                                        one major settlement

Features: None

Battlefields: Levktra 371 BC

                                        Marathon 490 BC

                                        Philippi 42 BC

                                        Plataea 479 BC

                                        Thermopylae 480 BC

Medieval

Landscape: High ground *or* visible from / within
                                        major settlement *or* both

Features: Near or adjacent to church / monastery

Battlefields: Stamford Bridge 1066

                                        Bouvines 1214

                                        Courtrai 1302

                                        Aljubarotta 1385

                                        St. Albans 1455 & 1461

                                        Northampton 1460

                                        Tewkesbury 1471

                                        Bosworth 1485

                                        Stoke 1487

Seventeenth & Eighteenth centuries

Landscape: Low ground *and* invisible from major
                                        settlement

Features: None

Battlefields: Roundway Down 1643

                                        Cropredy Bridge 1644

                                        Naseby 1645

                                        The Dunes 1658

                                        Sedgemoor 1685

                                        Oudenaarde 1708

A medieval site: Bouvines 1214 AD. High open ground near settlement and monastery, beside a Roman road.

An early modern site: Oudenaarde 1708 AD. Low open ground away from settlement.

more as sources of material in earlier times. There may be scope for more research here.

Churches and chapels are a significant and common feature in any European landscape; accordingly, their presence in the battlefield space may not be remarkable, and also as what are very often the largest stone structures in their area they may inevitably attract attention. The great churches at Tewkesbury and St. Albans dominate the space of and around those towns. Battlefield action bypassed St. Albans Abbey on both occasions, but at Tewkesbury may have penetrated the church itself and certainly reached as far as the doorway where fleeing soldiers were caught and brutally killed. Fighting took place around Linton church and also the church at Fontenoy. At Linton it was sought as refuge for fleeing combatants, while at Fontenoy it was central to the fortified village at the center of the battlefield. Other church buildings are more ancillary to the battlefield action. Sutton Cheney church was the site of devotions prior to the battle of Bosworth and is visible from the battlefield, and the church at Westonzoyland is a few hundred meters only from the site of the action at Sedgemoor but is not visible from it. Stoke church stands off the battlefield across the road, though it is not visible today from the battlefield because of a stand of trees; these may not have been present in 1487 and the church may have been a dominant feature to combatants. By contrast, the chapel at Sorauren, not the village church which may have been fortified, but a small hillside shrine no longer extant, provided a convenient location for scouting enemy dispositions, but no more.

An ancient site: Plataea 479 BC. Low open ground overlooked by settlements.

A nineteenth-century site: Sorauren 1813 AD. Heavily featured space including two rivers, hills, valleys, and settlements.

Where churches are not evident, monastic establishments sometimes are. Monasteries stood just off the battlefield space at Bouvines and Courtrai, and a nunnery was immediately adjacent at Northampton. Battle avoided these places but they provided rescue and medical aid for the wounded once the fighting was over. At the time of the battles, both Tewkesbury and St. Albans Abbeys were the center of monastic activity, and it is possible other battle-fields may also have had monasteries or nunneries nearby. It may be signifi-cant therefore that eight out of our sample of nine medieval battlefields are known to be close to or involve churches and monasteries while only four out of eleven more modern sites do. Fighting penetrates only one such struc-ture in the medieval period while three in the modern period are in the center of the fighting. This suggests a change of attitude toward such places over time: that while churches and church foundations are not to be fought in or over in the medieval period, their presence nearby is desired or expected; while in later times they form merely another part of the battlefield space and no longer command special respect.

CONCLUSIONS

As our title suggests, our work can be seen as the construction of battlefield "typologies" as indicators of what features and type of landscape may be expected to constitute the place chosen for battle in any particular period of history. Rather than taking a top-down approach, based upon our expectations of how people in the past ought to be choosing battlefields, we hope we are taking more of a bottom-up approach, letting the kinds of places they have chosen tell us something about them. We believe we have tapped a source of information about how people in the past perceived the landscape around them.

The modern approach to choosing a battlefield, one that takes root in the late eighteenth or early nineteenth century, is to see it as a source of functional utility; as a set of obstacles to movement, as places to hide troops, as good cover, as dead ground. But in earlier periods this emphasis on usefulness seems to be less evident; instead, ground is chosen because it contains other kinds of value. In the classical and medieval periods, high visibility, especially from a population center, seems to be a key factor; and in the medieval period proximity to a religious foundation also seems to be desirable. In the early modern period sites are chosen that are not overlooked and in general avoid population centers. By the early nineteenth century, sites that contain a number of features, settlements, high and low ground, and woodland, are actively sought as places to do battle. These objects have utilitarian value and are actively used as part of a battle plan. In earlier times, such features are actively avoided or simply ignored.

Our particular approach has, we believe, three distinctive values. First, it represents an approach to battlefields grounded not in military history but in archaeology. We think this matters because it allows us to say things that a military historian cannot by virtue of the inevitable limitations of that field of study (please note: archaeology has its limitations, too, but they are different). Second, we believe that our work may have some predictive value where scholars are seeking to locate a battle from the past. By using our typology for that period some places may appear more likely, others less so. Third, because we highlight not functional rationality in decision making but the unstated assumptions that lie behind choice in the past, we also help to undermine the current myth of war as a rational activity and an appropriate response to perceived threat. The way wars are fought is not grounded in rationality but in cultural beliefs, and these vary across time and across space. Our work reveals some of this variation.

NOTES

1. Carman 1999; Carman & Carman 2001; Carman 2002; Carman & Carman 2006.
2. Schofield et al. 2002; Saunders 2002.
3. Tilley 1994:67, 208.
4. Tilley 1994:75.
5. Keegan 1976:33–34.

REFERENCES CITED

Carman, J. 1999. Bloody Meadows: The places of battle. In S. Tarlow and S. West (eds.), *The Familiar Past?: Archaeologies of Later Historical Britain*, 233–245. Routledge, London.

Carman, J. 2002. Paradox in Places: twentieth century battlefield sites in long-term perspective. In J. Schofield, W. G. Johnson, and C. M. Beck (eds.), *Matériel Culture: The Archaeology of 20th Century Conflict*, 9–21. Routledge, London.

Carman, J., and P. Carman. 2001. Beyond Military Archaeology: Battlefields as a research resource. In P. W. M. Freeman and A. Pollard (eds.), *Fields of Conflict: Progress and Prospect in Battlefield Archaeology*, 275–281. Archaeopress, Oxford. BAR International Series 958.

Carman, J., and P. Carman. 2006. *Bloody Meadows: Investigating Landscapes of Battle*. Stroud Publishers, Sutton, UK.

Keegan, J. 1976. *The Face of Battle*. Jonathan Cape, London.

Saunders, N. 2002. Excavating Memories: Archaeology and the Great War. *Antiquity* 76:101–108.

Schofield, J., W. G. Johnson, and C. M. Beck (eds.). 2002. *Matériel Culture: The Archaeology of 20th Century Conflict*. Routledge, London.

Tilley, C. 1994. *A Phenomenology of Landscape*. Berg, Oxford.

Characteristics of Ancient Battlefields: Battle of Varus (9 AD)

Achim Rost

ANCIENT BATTLES AS A SUBJECT OF BATTLEFIELD ARCHAEOLOGY

Investigating an ancient battlefield by archaeology often depends on interpreting artifact find maps, especially when there are traces of a battle in an open field, without fortifications, and far from a fortified camp or settlement. This type of research requires the preservation of a sufficient number of artifacts. With about 5,000 items from Kalkriese, we have the opportunity to examine an open field battle of the Roman era in detail (compare Wilbers-Rost in this volume).

At an early stage of the research, the percentage of metal objects from military equipment, which is high compared to ceramic remains, as well as bones of men, mules, and horses, allowed identification of the site as a battlefield. However, connection of the archaeologically demonstrated battlefield with events described by Roman historians as the "Battle of Varus" (Tacitus, Annales I 59–62; Cassius Dio 56, 18–23) caused difficulties. Until now, some historians[1] have tried to connect Kalkriese with the 15/16 AD campaigns of Germanicus. Attempting to find indications for a reliable identification by archaeological observations was made more difficult because comparable investigations of ancient battlefields that might aid in understanding the archaeological features of Kalkriese do not exist.

Therefore we have to examine information from finds and features at Kalkriese. We have to clarify whether conclusions can be drawn to better understand the course of the fighting or whether later events, such as plundering, may be identified better than the battle itself. It is possible we will find reasons for the lack of comparable sites during such reflection.

METHODICAL ANALYSIS OF ARCHAEOLOGICAL SOURCES
AS A THEORETICAL MODEL

To judge the quality of preservation on the site discussed in this paper, it is necessary to analyze those factors that had an effect on the archaeological remains of a battlefield over the centuries. The factors are diverse and only some of them can be dealt with here. Landscape, vegetation, and agriculture, for example, will be ignored for the time being, as this chapter focuses on processes of looting expected on all battlefields. These activities manipulated the remains originally lying on the field, meaning, they destroyed, reduced, or moved artifacts.

The amount of archaeological material on battlefields depends on the size of the military units involved in the action as well as on the proportion of the forces of two fighting armies. Only when large units were involved, and one party was clearly defeated, is there a chance for archaeology to find enough remains of equipment after plundering the battlefield.

Even if these requirements are met, later archaeological proof depends on the fact that the dead and wounded soldiers, of which there should be many, remained on the battlefield. If the losers were able, or the winners wanted, to gather those killed in action—to bury them or just despoil them far off the battlefield—this would probably have caused a nearly complete removal of most equipment and weapons attached to the soldiers. For a modern investigation, this would have negative consequences since the potential finds were taken away.

On a concentrated battlefield, plunderers would probably have noticed the bigger pieces of equipment or weapons that were not connected directly to the dead bodies, such as swords, lances, or shields, and were lying about the site as single objects. Thus, most objects usually left on a battlefield may have been pieces of long-range projectile weapons that were scattered widely and were too small and worthless to expend search time.

There are sites that illustrate those aspects. In Olynthos, Northern Greece, for example, where an ancient town was besieged and stormed, almost exclusively slingshots and arrowheads from the attackers were excavated.[2] Find maps of the battlefield of Palo Alto (U.S.–Mexican war) are first of all based on small-arms ammunition.[3] One can easily imagine what remains of military actions if neither firearms, nor slingshots or arrows with iron heads were brought into action. Under such circumstances, very few objects would be left; they would hardly be taken as undoubted proof of a battlefield. Most favorable for an archaeologist investigating a battlesite would be the complete destruction of a large army, with much metal equipment and a large baggage, left to the arbitrary selection of the victors, with no possibility to recover the wounded or dead.

KALKRIESE AS AN EXAMPLE FOR METHODICAL ANALYSES
OF ARCHAEOLOGICAL RESOURCES

Traces of such a battlefield are at Kalkriese. In principle, however, one has to consider that the Germans were not only interested in intact pieces of Roman military equipment for further use. Under the aspect of obtaining raw materials, fragments of gold, silver, bronze, and iron were valuable, and the damage or destruction of objects may have been irrelevant. Bigger pieces might have been destroyed; objects that were less handy, such as long shield edgings, were torn away from the wood and folded several times. Made more compact, they could be more easily carried in baskets or sacks over long distances.

Quite early we noticed artifacts that illustrated the processes of plundering vividly. We often found pieces of military equipment that were once tightly fastened to soldiers, such as buckles and plates from armor, hooks from ring mail shirts, scabbard fittings, belt buckles, and apron fittings. Some might have been lost during the battle; since there are such a large number, most must be interpreted as hints of plundering the dead at the site of their death. These finds can plausibly be explained if we imagine looting as a drastic process. Only a few hours after death, equipment could not be removed except with violence. While collecting booty, the plunderers might fail to notice small pieces and fragments hidden in the grass or under bushes, or that may have been trampled into the earth that preserved them until today.

Roman legionary of Augustan time with equipment (following Horn 1987, Fig. 1). Shading indicates those items that were found in Kalkriese.

In spite of well-developed archaeological fieldwork, no other sites quite like Kalkriese have yet been found. Therefore we have to assume that the battle-field of Kalkriese and the processes of plundering are rather an exceptional case among battlesites of antiquity and not, as we thought in the beginning of the research project, a typical example of a plundered ancient battlefield.

Following these ideas about looting dead soldiers, we also have one reason for the lack of Germanic finds in Kalkriese. The Germans presumably did not have many losses; besides, as victors in their own territory they were able to retrieve their dead, together with their equipment, and bury them according to their cultural rules.

MAPPING ARTIFACTS OF THE BATTLE

Attempts to map artifacts from excavations on the "Oberesch" allow a first check on the above assumptions. Many artifacts were found close to the wall. The reason for this may be destruction of some parts of the wall during the battle or shortly after; therefore the looters may have overlooked the items even when they were the larger objects. This should not be interpreted as an indication of more violent fighting. In the zone near the wall, however, details of some battle activities might be reflected more directly.

More important for methodical reflections about looting is the area a short distance in front of the wall where the Germans had free access to the corpses of the soldiers and the booty. Here we found fragments of military equipment that were not attached to soldiers are rarer than those which were tightly connected.

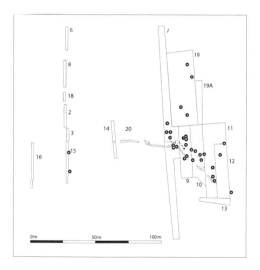

Distribution of pieces of the equipment that were not fixed to the soldier (for example, lances, spears, "pila," blades of swords, shields). (Museum und Park Kalkriese)

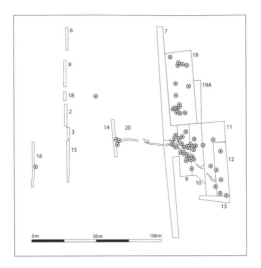

Distribution of pieces of the equipment which was tightly connected to the soldiers. Also shown: drainage ditch and post holes of the wall. The first attempt of mapping such artifacts was made for the trenches No. 1 to 19. (Museum und Park Kalkriese)

A dead legionary lying on the battlefield with his equipment was, as a concentration of objects, easily visible. Only if he were not carried from the battlefield with his equipment but was despoiled at the place where he had been killed would some small objects and fragments be left. In the main activity areas of a battle of annihilation, we should expect many such small pieces of the "fixed" equipment. Places of very violent action must have been strewn with many corpses and equipment. In such concentrations, "not fixed" weapons such as swords, lances, or shields would be noticed, even when lying separated from their owner. Therefore they should be rare in the excavations.

The Kalkriese investigations give the first hints that show the correctness of these theoretical ideas. On the "Oberesch" site, only one fragment of a blade has been found to date that might be part of a sword. Other remnants of this weapon are missing. We found only fragments of the scabbards that were once attached to a soldier's belt. More often, pieces of equipment not fastened to the man, such as lance heads, as well as fragments of pila and shields, were discovered on the "Oberesch" site. One must take into account that some of these artifacts were so badly damaged during the battle, for example when they were run over by baggage carts, that plunderers could not see the small metal points or fittings separated from their wooden parts.

The maps of just a small part of the battlefield at Kalkriese take into consideration only a few groups of Roman finds and cannot give more than a first methodical indication. We have to map the finds over a much larger area. Fragments of equipment carried by legionaries on the march, and of the baggage, including pieces of horse harnesses, carriages, chests, tools, and medical instruments, must be mapped and analyzed in the same way.

Trying to interpret the distribution of finds on a battlefield after considering plundering, it may not be so important to subdivide military equipment fragments according to their original use. Rather, we should think about characteristic criteria that fit those activities and perceptions we expect from battlefield looters. For the different groups of finds, plausible explanations must be developed to help understand why these objects were not taken but, instead, left on the battlefield. Different interpretive models of a group's distribution may exist and must be explained. Only when we are successful in identifying the individual processes of despoiling a battlefield may we have the chance to draw further conclusions about the course of the actions during the battle itself.

For Kalkriese, however, we have to consider that at least the action on the "Oberesch" was a battle in a defilade, fought from on top of the wall. For the relatively restricted area of the "Oberesch," that is the center of the narrow pass between hill and bog, and at the same time the main place of the battle, we have to expect that more and more Roman units reached this place, though no longer in their usual march formation. Therefore we have to assume that many military events continuously overlapped here. Thus, the possibility of reconstructing events of the battle in detail from archaeological observations might be quite restricted.

Mapping artifacts in a larger area, not only on the "Oberesch," may give us even more information. The density and quality of finds in the area of the Battle of Varus (about 50 km^2; see Wilbers-Rost figure in this volume) are in no way uniform. For the "Oberesch," we can infer looting of the dead on the battlefield from the small pieces of the equipment once attached to a soldier. Here we can presume a zone of intensive combat with many dead soldiers. From areas off the main scene, however, we get a different impression. To draw definite conclusions is not yet possible because of the low quantity of finds resulting from field surveys and limited excavations. It is remarkable, however, that a Roman sword scabbard, of which the metal parts were nearly complete and which is a precious silver object ornamented with intaglios, was found at the edge of a bog about 2 km north of the "Oberesch." Concentrations of silver coins are, compared to the "Oberesch," also more often found in this more remote area. Different explanations for this phenomenon have been considered by others including the possibility of war booty sacrifices or that officers might have been involved in the battle here more than at "Oberesch." Those finds, however, were originally connected to a Roman soldier by a belt or they were kept in a leather bag as "pocket money." At sites with many dead soldiers, the plunderers would probably not have failed to notice such pieces. Therefore, I believe that such finds may characterize battle zones with less intensive action that might have left fewer dead soldiers and artifacts. Here, the chance to miss valuable artifacts was much greater because a single object could hardly be seen among grass or bushes by the plunderers. We must now check for further indications that support this assumption. The small fragments of equipment once attached to the soldiers should be fewer in such zones. Someday, maybe, we will be able to distinguish by archaeological methods more intensive, or violent, zones from less important fighting areas or zones of flight.

CONCLUSIONS

The foregoing observations suggest that the distribution of battlefield finds may cause erroneous conclusions if there is no theoretical analysis of the archaeological sources. The retrieval of corpses together with their equipment may cause considerably less finds available on the main sites. In zones on the edges of the battle with fewer casualties, we may expect more striking single objects today, provided that plundering was less thorough on a site with a few bodies and objects. Looting a battlefield usually resulted in a reduction which is not proportionate, but selective, and thus manipulates the later picture of the distribution of artifacts. Archaeological sources may sometimes indicate the opposite of the original proportions.

If these theories are correct, we may also obtain archaeological indications for identifying Kalkriese with the Battle of Varus. The despoiling of many dead Roman soldiers on the battlefield itself, as is highly probable for Kalkriese, can be connected with the complete destruction of three Roman legions in the Battle of Varus known from written tradition. No written Roman sources suggest that during the actions of Germanicus (15/16 AD; Tacitus Annales I, 63–72) Roman units were destroyed to an extent comparable to the Battle of Varus, nor that the remains were left to the arbitrariness of Germanic plunderers so extensively that the victors plundered even the equipment attached to the soldier on a large scale.

The intention of this chapter is to identify the processes of plundering and their effects on the archaeological record by referring to the example of Kalkriese. I also tried to reconstruct patterns of behaviour that might stand behind differing pictures of the distribution of finds on an ancient battlefield. Additional processes that might influence the preservation of finds after the end of the battle, such as religious ceremonies, cannot be discussed in this chapter, nor can the organization of the plundering. A comparison with more recent battlefields, for which more detailed information concerning such post-battle processes might exist, may help to understand events on more ancient battlefields.

NOTES

For helping me with the translation of my text I want to thank Ingrid Recker, Osnabrück, and Lawrence Babits, Greenville, NC.

1. See Wolters 2003; Horn 1987.
2. Lee 2001.
3. Haecker 2001.

REFERENCES CITED

Haecker, Charles M. 2001. The official explanation versus the archaeological record of a US-Mexican War battle. In P. W. M. Freeman and A. Pollard (eds.), *Fields of Conflict: Progress and Prospect in Battlefield Archaeology*, 135–141. Proceedings of a conference held in the Department of Archaeology, University of Glasgow. BAR International Series 958.

Horn, Heinz Günther (ed.). 1987. *Die Römer in Nordrhein-Westfalen*. Theiss, Stuttgart.

Lee, John W. I. 2001. Urban combat at Olynthos, 348 BC. In P. W. M. Freeman and A. Pollard (eds.), *Fields of Conflict: Progress and Prospect in Battlefield Archaeology*, 11–22. Proceedings of a conference held in the Department of Archaeology, University of Glasgow. BAR International Series 958.

Wolters, Reinhard. 2003. Hermeneutik des Hinterhalts: die antiken Berichte zur Varuskatastrophe und der Fundplatz von Kalkriese. *Klio* 85:131–170.

Finding Battery Positions at Wilson's Creek, Missouri

Carl G. Carlson-Drexler

IN NUMEROUS PUBLICATIONS, battlefield archaeologists have likened the archaeological investigation of battlefields to crime scene investigation.[1] As with forensic science, archaeologists consider eyewitness testimony in the form of the historical record as well as the physical evidence (DNA, fingerprints, etc.), a ready analog for archaeologically derived data. The processes of interpretation and reconstruction that are the primary research foci of much of the extant literature on battlefield archaeology are methodologically identical to the reconstruction of a crime based on much fresher evidence. This is fundamentally an apt description of the praxis of historical archaeology, but its sanguinary connotations make it particularly appropriate for battlefields.

Battlefield archaeologists are privileged above almost all other historical archaeologists in that their subjects of interest are much more thoroughly recorded than other kinds of sites. The stress and high excitement of battle make these hours in a soldier's life among the most crisply remembered. Memoirs, letters, diaries, newspaper accounts, and so on, as well as a host of secondary sources, fill innumerable shelves on the history of war. There are numerous sources that we may tap in order to learn the history of any given battle, much more than we may learn about the typical settlement site or privy.

However, this blessing of historical data can be a hindrance as well as an aid to archaeology. If we have so much information on the event in the form of historical data, what more will archaeology tell us? At this point, only a partial answer may be advanced. Archaeology allows us to reconstruct the progress of battle, thereby assessing the veracity of or clearing up ambiguities in historical accounts of the events. The part of the answer that cannot be provided at this time pertains to what archaeology can really tell us about battles. Frequently, battlefield archaeologists cease interpretation at the level of historical reconstruction. This obscures information about not only the battle, but also about the cultures involved in conflict. A number of battlefield archaeologists, notably Scott,[2] Fox,[3] Sterling,[4] Harbison,[5] and Sivilich and

Wheeler-Stone,[6] have attempted analyses of artifacts that go beyond reconstruction to focus on processes encompassing larger subsets of the combatant cultures than only the military.

When we reach the point that we can justly give an answer to the question of what archaeology can tell us about battlefields, we can then create the synthetic, multidisciplinary approach advocated by numerous battlefield archaeologists, though perhaps most explicitly set out by Haecker and Mauck.[7]

This study fits into the development of the epistemological bounds of battlefield archaeology by showing a tiny fraction of the potential that spatial analysis, driven by modern geographic information systems (GIS), holds for the future of this area of research. Using artifacts recovered from the fields around Wilson's Creek, just south of Springfield, Missouri, site of one of the first significant battles of the American Civil War, a GIS is used to identify the locations of certain artillery batteries during several different stages during the battle.

Before we become too thoroughly embroiled in the history and archaeology of Wilson's Creek, a few notes should be made to aid in understanding the complex history of this engagement. The Union army at Wilson's Creek was not pitted solely against the Confederate army. The Missouri State Guard and Arkansas State Troops, those two states' militia units, fought alongside the Louisiana, Texas, and Arkansas men already enrolled in Confederate service. Deeper readings of the history of the battle, particularly the command problems experienced by Southern commanders in attempting to coordinate between these three forces, would find some profit in maintaining this distinction. However, for ease of reading, "Confederate" can be here taken along with "Southern" to denote state militia as well as national units.

HISTORICAL BACKGROUND: THE BATTLE OF WILSON'S CREEK

Wilson's Creek is often referred to as the "second great battle of the Civil War." It was fought a few weeks after First Bull Run, and was the first major battle fought west of the Mississippi River. After a summer of campaigning for control of Missouri, the Union and Confederate armies lay barely a dozen miles apart. After advancing from the rail terminus at Rolla, the Federals had occupied Springfield long enough to deplete the stores they had brought with them.[8] They had to move back to Rolla to stay supplied, but could not do so with the enemy so near to the south. Their commander, General Nathaniel Lyon, had to launch a preemptive attack to stall the Confederates long enough to allow him to withdraw to Rolla.[9]

The Federal army left Springfield on the night of August 13, 1861, in two columns. The larger of the two, a force of 3,300 men under the command of Nathaniel Lyon, was to fall upon the Confederate camps from the north at dawn.[10] Simultaneously, the smaller command, 1,100 men under Franz Sigel, after a march to the east of the Confederate camps, would attack from the south.[11] This pincer move was meant to break up the Confederate force before they could mount an effective resistance, and would allow the Federals to break off and move back to Rolla unmolested.

Initially, the attack proceeded as planned. The Missouri State Guard, who had been joined by a brigade of Arkansas State Troops and a brigade of Confederate army soldiers and now numbered 12,000 men, was completely shocked by the appearance of the Federals, who opened fire on their camps with artillery as the men were cooking breakfast.[12] Lyon and Sigel both capitalized on this confusion by pushing toward each other, squeezing the Southerners between them.

After overcoming the initial shock, the Confederates began to exert their better than two-to-one numerical superiority, halting Lyon on what is now known as Bloody Hill.[13] To the south, Sigel had inexplicably halted his troops in column barely 40 yards from the ravine cut by Wilson's Creek. Confederate soldiers filed into this cover and, at a rush, descended upon the Federals who were, due to their deployment, virtually unable to defend themselves, and therefore fled in confusion.[14]

With the threat posed by Sigel's men neutralized, the Southerners were free to focus on Lyon's men atop Bloody Hill. Repeated attacks had failed to pry the Iowans, Missourians, and Kansans from this position, despite the loss of Lyon, who was struck in the chest by a musket ball.[15] His successor, Major Samuel Sturgis, realized around noon that Sigel was not going to arrive, and that the army had achieved its goal of damaging the Rebels enough to keep them from pursuing, and therefore deemed it time to withdraw. By early afternoon, the battle was over. It had cost the Federals 1,300 men killed, wounded, and missing; 1,200 Southern soldiers were either killed or wounded in the engagement.[16]

Both sides justly claimed victory at Wilson's Creek (known as Oak Hills by some Confederates). The Confederate armies had managed to maintain the field, achieving a tactical victory. On the other hand, the Federals had achieved a strategic victory, as the Southern commanders chose to tend to their damaged army rather than pursue the Yankees back to Rolla. In the following months, the Arkansans and Confederates returned to Arkansas, and the Missouri State Guard did its best to bring Missouri under their control. The Federals remained at Rolla, reeling from the loss of one-quarter of the army as well as their commanding officer. After receiving reinforcements and a new commander that fall, they launched a campaign in January 1862 that culminated in the March battle of Pea Ridge, where they once again faced the combined forces of the Confederate army and the Missouri State Guard.[17]

PATTERNING, RESEARCH QUESTIONS, AND ISSUES OF SCALE

There are literally hundreds of questions that may be posed to the archaeological record of a battlefield. The most obvious questions focus around particularist (i.e., specific to each battle) reconstruction. In essence, these research questions center on the reconstruction of a single battle, linking discrete historical events into a coherent chain through the use of archaeological data. These questions often create ambiguities between the historical and archaeological records, as exemplified by the archaeological investigations of the Little Bighorn.[18]

Reconstruction of historical events is an important component of battlefield archaeology, particularly in cases where the site of conflict has been memorialized in some form of park, as is Wilson's Creek. One of the great services archaeologists can give to the public and to those involved with interpreting a park to that public (i.e., park rangers, historians, tour guides) is bettering our understanding of the event being commemorated.

In pursuing a more nuanced interpretation of a battle, we may follow the gross and dynamic patterning approach developed by the researchers at the Little Bighorn.[19] Gross patterning involves analyzing densities and scarcities of artifacts to arrive at an understanding of where on the battlefield major actions were fought, what ground was most contested.[20] Dynamic patterning, on the other hand, looks at the progress of the battle, using artifact distributions to understand the movement of troops, either individually or in groups, across the landscape.

Archaeological investigations of a number of Indian Wars sites have yielded datasets well suited to dynamic patterning analysis. These sites, where the standard weapons of both warrior and soldier employed metallic cartridges, and generally involved a few hundred troops at the most, allow archaeologists to track individuals through the battle. By comparing the unique marks imparted on both projectile and casing by the discharge of a firearm, the archaeologist may identify numerous shell casings fired by the same weapon at different parts of a single battlefield.[21] By assuming the weapon was held by a single person, we can presume that the dispersal of casings mirrors the movement of that warrior or soldier through the battle.

Unfortunately, American Civil War battles are not nearly so straightforward. Troop strength could vary from a few hundred to nearly 200,000 soldiers on a field at a given time. These staggering numbers of troops could deposit a phenomenal number of projectiles over the course of a single battle, which could last multiple days. Additionally, since most Civil War small arms employed paper cartridges, not metallic ones, we frequently are left only with the bullet, discovered at the point where it fell to earth, with little or no archaeological reference to where it might have been fired from, outside of a limited number of bullets dropped in the haste of reloading.

How, then, would we approach dynamic patterning on a Civil War battlefield? One way would be to look for spent brass percussion caps, used to ignite the powder in a Civil War paper cartridge. Unfortunately, small copper or brass caps are very seldom found. For instance, during archaeological

investigations at Pea Ridge National Military Park, Arkansas, only five percussion caps were collected out of a total artifact count of 2,700. These extant
examples may be detritus from Civil War reenactors performing living history
displays on the site, and are therefore of modern origin.

A second way of approaching dynamic patterning is to identify the cultural
and physical strictures placed on units in battle that affected how they positioned themselves upon the battlefield and how they negotiated it during combat. For instance, Heckman's (this volume) study of the battle of Lookout
Mountain, Tennessee, deals not only with the culturally defined limits placed
on battlefield behavior (i.e., moving men in long lines, two ranks deep), but
also with physical aspects of the battlefield (vegetation, relief, etc.). Her
analysis shows quite compellingly that the surprise suffered by Confederate
troops at the battle was due largely to the approaching Federal force being
masked by local terrain until the Union army had drawn very near to the
Confederate entrenchments. The archaeologists investigating the battlefields
at the Little Bighorn and Palo Alto have employed this approach.[22]

This chapter is similarly focused on dynamic patterning, but instead of
concentrating on the level of the army corps, as does Heckman, two individual artillery batteries have been selected for analysis. Using an analysis of
cultural and physical constraints on artillery fire at the Battle of Wilson's
Creek, we will show how Backof's Missouri Battery, a Union artillery company, and Reid's Arkansas Battery, a Confederate unit, were positioned on
the battlefield during the fight between Sigel's Union troops and Confederates
from Louisiana, Arkansas, and Missouri for control of Sharp's Field.

ARCHAEOLOGY AT WILSON'S CREEK

Beginning in 2001, a team of volunteer metal detector operators and Civil
War enthusiasts, under the supervision of Dr. Douglas Scott, archaeologist for
the National Park Service's Midwest Archaeological Center (MWAC), conducted fieldwork that yielded 1,400 metal artifacts, the bulk of which were
deposited during the battle. The location of each artifact was recorded using a
global positioning system (GPS), allowing MWAC staff to analyze artifact
patterns, of both a gross and dynamic character.[23]

The shell fragments associated with Backof's Battery were recovered in
the southern half of Sharp's Cornfield, in the area where the Confederate cavalry camps were located. During the early stages of the battle, Backof shelled
these camps, and then moved off the surrounding bluffs to join the rest of
Sigel's division as it moved north through Sharp's Field. At no other point in
the battle did a different battery, either Confederate or Federal, report firing
into this area.

Similarly, the artifacts associated with Reid's and Bledsoe's guns were
located along the northern edge of Sharp's Field, in an area where Sigel's

division was posted prior to being surprised and routed by the 3rd Louisiana and elements of the Arkansas State Troops. This area is out of range of the nearest Federal position on Bloody Hill, and from any point where Backof's guns might have been posted.

CIVIL WAR ARTILLERY IN THE FIELD

"In range" is a fairly nebulous concept, and must be considered from two angles. The first of these is what the cannons themselves were capable of. Both Backof and the two Confederate batteries studied here employed 6- and 12-pounder guns. These weapons, antiquated by the time of the Civil War, had maximum effective ranges of 1,532 and 1,072 yards, respectively.[24] Second, we must consider what the battery commanders and soldiers were capable of hitting reliably. One of the main manuals for the artillery, John Gibbon's *Artillerist's Manual*, published in 1860, clearly states that targets more than 1,000 yards from the position of the battery are not usually fired upon, as they are too difficult to see and to take aim upon.[25] Binoculars or telescopes, frequently carried by battery commanders, could ameliorate this shortfall, but, due to the inaccuracy of some field pieces, they were discouraged from attempting such long-range fire.

Battery commanders on both sides were similarly discouraged from employing a firing technique called "indirect fire." Indirect fire involves posting a battery behind some obstacle, shielded from the target's view, making it impossible to see the target from the actual gun position. In order to hit the target, a spotter would have to be posted somewhere in view of the target to observe how the shots were falling, then relay adjustments in aim back to the battery. This kind of fire is predominant in the modern military. Its use was exceedingly rare during the Civil War.[26]

Much more common in the mid-nineteenth century was "direct fire." As the name implies, direct fire involves firing on targets that are directly within the line of site of the battery.[27] References made by members of Reid's, Bledsoe's, and Backof's batteries indicate that both sides could see their targets when they opened fire, indicating that they were indeed firing directly.[28]

Artifact deposition, in most instances, is a process that occurs perpendicularly to the earth's surface, by dint of gravity. Dropping an artifact, sweeping it through the crack in a floorboard, or discarding it are all depositional processes that involve little horizontal displacement of the artifact from its point of use/origin. The deposition of the various kinds of projectiles used on a historic period battle, on the other hand, is typified by great horizontal displacement. Here, the point of deposition, and the point of firing (discard) are widely separated. In many instances, both of these points may be inferred, either historically, through the use of documents, or archaeologically, through the location of, for instance, spent shell casings and associated bullets. With these two batteries, however, we only have one of these points established concretely, the point of deposition. Luckily, we do know the conditions that governed the depositional event (direct artillery fire). Knowing this, we can use the point of deposition to infer the point of origin.

We infer the point of origin by identifying those places from which the artillery could be firing. We know that the batteries were able to see their targets; meaning that those points where shell fragments associated with either Backof's or the two Confederate batteries were recovered must have been viewable from the battery position. This means that the battery position and the location of each associated shell fragment must be "intervisible." This allows us to apply cumulative viewshed analysis (CVA) to identify cannon positions.

CUMULATIVE VIEWSHED ANALYSIS: METHOD AND CASE STUDIES

Cumulative viewshed analysis (CVA) is simply a means to identify those parts of a landscape that are visible from a given set of points. Most studies employing this technique, such as Wheatley's[29] discussion of Neolithic long barrows around Avebury and Stonehenge, England, focus on intervisibility between sites as a means to identify culturally distinct suites of sites in prehistory. This study obviously breaks from this tradition by focusing on intrasite dynamics, not intersite relationships.

In order to perform a CVA on a set of artifacts, the researcher must be able to calculate a viewshed. The term "viewshed" means those areas of a landscape visible from a given point on that landscape.[30]

Viewshed analyses, when calculated on the computer, are facilitated by files known as digital elevation models (DEMs). A standard DEM is essentially the same as a digital image, a matrix of cells containing a given color value, with the important exception that a DEM, instead of storing color information, stores elevation data. This grid of cells is known as a raster dataset. For this analysis, each cell or pixel within the DEM represents the elevation of a 30-meter-square plot of land. The elevation data may then be used by the computer to calculate viewsheds from any point or set of points on the landscape.

When calculating a viewshed from a given point, the computer simply tests each cell in the raster to see if a straight line can be interpolated from the cell to the designated point without being obscured by another cell. If a cell representing a higher elevation value lies between the point and the cell being tested, then that cell being tested is considered invisible from the selected point. However, if no such intervening value is present, than the cell being tested is within the viewshed of the selected point.

So, given a single artifact location, using viewshed analysis we can determine from where on the landscape that location may be seen, which, given the arguments presented above, represents in the case of artillery fragments all the possible positions from which that shell could have been fired. When presented with a number of fragments, however, we must rely on cumulative viewshed analysis, which is only a single conceptual step beyond the individual-point-oriented viewshed analysis.

To perform cumulative viewshed analysis, focusing on multiple locations, one must begin by calculating individual viewsheds for each of the loci selected for study. In this case, individual viewsheds were calculated for each of the shell fragments in the groupings for Backof's, Bledsoe's, and Reid's batteries. The viewshed results are displayed as a raster dataset (same as the DEM or a digital photograph) coded "1" and "0." Cells labeled "1" are those areas visible from the selected point, and those marked "0" are not. In order to identify those areas visible from a number of selected points, we must only sum the viewshed rasters. There are various means of performing this operation, such as the "raster calculator" feature in the ArcGIS program suite offered by ESRI. The raster calculator simply adds the values of the viewshed cells, returning a new raster with the cumulative viewshed information.

For instance, if we had a sample of 21 shell fragments, we would calculate individual viewsheds for each, and then sum them using the raster calculator. The resultant cumulative viewshed would contain values from 0, those areas where no fragment could be seen from, to 21. The cells of the raster containing 21 as a value would be those areas where all of the viewsheds overlapped, and are, therefore, those areas where all of the shell fragments in question could have originated. In a situation like Wilson's Creek or most Civil War battles, where direct fire was the only method of artillery fire employed, those areas that overlook all shell fragment locations are the only areas where the batteries could have stood while firing.

Backof's Missouri Battery Opens the Battle

The first case study presented here focuses on Backof's Missouri Battery, an organization formed in St. Louis during the early struggle for that city's arsenal, primarily from the German immigrant population of the city who made up the area's core Unionist element. At the outbreak of hostilities, the battery was composed of six 6-pounder guns led by Major Franz Backof, a veteran of the 1848 revolution in Germany and an artillerist with considerable experience.[31] By Wilson's Creek, however, many of the battery's experienced men had left and were replaced with infantrymen pulled from the 3rd Missouri Infantry with only "a few days instruction," and four of the guns had been replaced with 12-pounder howitzers.[32]

Sigel positioned two sections (four guns) of Backof's battery on a rise overlooking the camps of Confederate as well as Arkansas and Missouri state cavalrymen posted in Joseph D. Sharp's field. The bombardment opening the southern portion of the battle began at 5:30 in the morning,[33] surprising and greatly disrupting the Southerners, who were cooking their breakfast at the time.

Archaeologically, the location of the Southern camps has been identified as a scatter of 6- and 12-pounder artillery ammunition, as well as a scattering of personal equipment that would be consistent with an encampment. It is the aforementioned scatter of shell fragments that will be the focus of this analysis.

Fourteen shell fragments were recovered from the south end of Sharp's Field during the archaeological investigations there. The majority of them (n = 12) are fragments of 12-pounder howitzer case shot, with the rest (n = 2) being 6-pounder gun case shot pieces. These are consistent with the types of cannon being fired by Backof's men during the engagement. For each, a viewshed was calculated and then summed using the raster calculator. The final cumulative viewshed is shown in the following figure.

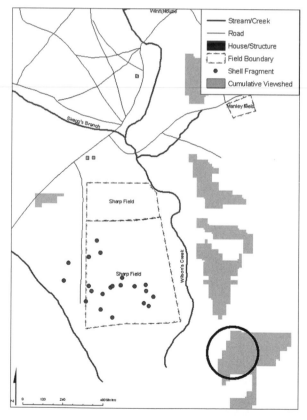

Cumulative viewshed for shell fragments fired by Backof's Missouri Battery (U.S.). Circled area denotes most likely battery position. Courtesy of the National Park Service, Midwest Archeological Center

As the figure shows, based on cumulative viewshed analysis, there are only a few areas along the bluffs overlooking Sharp's Field from which the Federal guns could have fired on the Southern camps.

The history of the early stages of the battle of Wilson's Creek places Backof's battery at the south end of Sharp's Field when they opened fire on the Confederate camps. The figure depicts an area, circled, along the southern margin of the field from which the shell fragments found in the vicinity of the camp could have been fired. This corresponds well with the historical interpretations of the battery's position, and is, based on these two lines of evidence, likely to have been the spot.

In this instance, there is a positive correlation between the position as suggested by historical documents and archaeological data. The next case considered here in part does not enjoy this same correspondence.

Confederate Batteries and the Rout of Sigel's Federals

The rout of Sigel's forces from the north end of Sharp's Field affords us another test of the cumulative viewshed analysis process. In this case, two artillery batteries are known to have shelled Sigel's men in support of Southern troops under the command of General Benjamin McCulloch, who stormed out of a ravine less than 100 yards in front of the Federals, surprising and routing them in a matter of minutes.

The Fort Smith Battery, an Arkansas militia unit under the command of Capt. John B. Reid, fired on Sigel's men from a position in the vicinity of the Ray farmhouse, northeast of the Federals. Simultaneously, Capt. Hiram Bledsoe, commander of a Missouri militia battery placed north of the Federal position, opened fire on Sigel's men.[34] This fire corresponded with the charge of the 3rd Louisiana against Sigel's troops, who believed the onrushing Confederates to be the 1st Iowa, who also wore gray uniforms. Sigel, mistakenly believing that the artillery fire was coming from friendly batteries, was heard to shout, "*Sie haben gegen Uns geshossen!*" (They have fired against us!).[35]

Two viewshed analyses can be performed here. First, both batteries report being able to see the Federal force when they opened fire, so calculating a cumulative viewshed for the shell fragments in the northern portion of Sharp's Field and between the field boundary and the banks of Skegg's Branch should result in a viewshed that suggests possible battery positions for both.

Additionally, archaeological work at Wilson's Creek yielded a number of projectiles that are directly associable with Bledsoe's battery. Prior to Wilson's Creek, the Missouri State Guard, the state militia of whom Bledsoe's unit was a member, found itself woefully short of ammunition. The gunners in the guard were particularly destitute of canister rounds. In order to fill this need, men from the Missouri batteries contracted with local blacksmiths while camped at Cowskin Prairie, near Sarcoxie, to cold cut iron bars and rods into inch-long segments.[36] The use of bar and rod canister by the guard at both Wilson's Creek and later at Pea Ridge has been documented both historically and archaeologically. Three pieces of rod shot were found in the vicinity of the rout of Sigel's forces. These were almost certainly fired by Bledsoe's battery. Not only are such rounds not documented as being used by Arkansas troops (i.e., Reid's battery), the Fort Smith battery was posted at a great enough distance that they had to use long-range shells, the first rounds of which accidentally fell among the Louisianans as they attacked.[37] These three pieces of rod canister can therefore be used as a basis for a cumulative viewshed analysis to identify, in tandem with the analysis of shell fragments, the position of Bledsoe's battery alone.

Rod Canister Viewshed

As stated above, three pieces of rod canister were recovered just south of Skegg's Branch, and can be attributed to Bledsoe's Missouri gunners. Using the locations of these three artifacts, we calculated a cumulative viewshed raster. The next figure shows the raster placed over the Wilson's Creek battlefield. The area of interest in this raster is the region just north of the points of recovery (circled). Canister rounds are only effective at short range, ideally at less than 400 yards. The distance between the nearest area within the viewshed and the points of recovery is greater than that distance, but, since Bledsoe's men were firing downhill at the Federals, the effective range of their projectiles was somewhat greater.

It should be reiterated that outside of the above-mentioned area of interest, no other points on the battlefield are very close to the points of recovery for these canister slugs, meaning that it is unlikely that another battery, such as Reid's Fort Smith unit, fired their own scratch-built ammunition at the Federals. The cumulative viewshed analysis for these canister slugs, then, reliably displays the possible locations of Bledsoe's cannons. The above-mentioned area is, then, the best archaeological guess at where these guns stood during the brief fight for Sharp's Field.

Shell Fragment Viewshed

Calculating a cumulative viewshed for the shell fragments that were found mixed with the rod canister slugs in Sharp's Field, as mentioned above, will provide possible locations for both Bledsoe's and Reid's batteries. In all, four shell fragments were used in conducting this stage of analysis, the results of which appear in the figure below.

Several things should be noted in the outcome of the shell fragment viewshed. First, the area north of Skegg's Branch where the rod canister analysis suggests Bledsoe's battery stood is replicated by the shell fragment

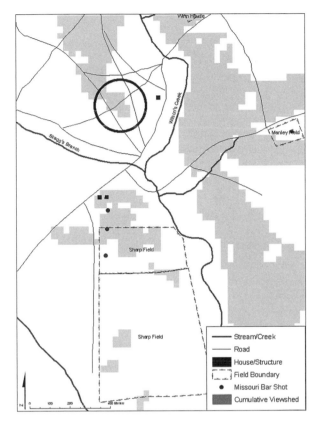

Cumulative viewshed for Missouri bar shot recovered at Wilson's Creek. Circled area denotes possible position of Bledsoe's Missouri Battery (C.S.). Courtesy of the National Park Service, Midwest Archeological Center

analysis. This strengthens the position for Bledsoe's battery suggested by the rod canister viewshed analysis.

Second, the areas west of Wilson's Creek, where many historians have placed Reid's Fort Smith battery during the engagement, are not visible from the sites of the shell fragment finds. This suggests that the actual position of Reid's battery was farther to the north, near the Telegraph Road. The position of this battery is not easily established historically, and, in this case, it may have been positioned too far to the south.

Based on this analysis, then, we can suggest positions for both Bledsoe's battery and Reid's Fort Smith gunners. Bledsoe's men stood roughly where most historical sources document their position as being, but Reid's battery appears to have been placed farther north, closer to the Telegraph Road than was previously believed.

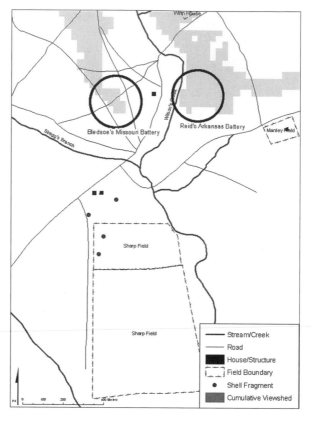

Cumulative viewshed for Confederate shell fragments. Circled areas denote possible positions of Bledsoe's Missouri Battery (C.S.) and Reid's Fort Smith Battery (C.S.). Courtesy of the National Park Service, Midwest Archeological Center

CONCLUSIONS

Using cumulative viewshed analysis has, therefore, allowed us to use archaeologically derived data (artifact locations), coupled with spatial analytical procedures, historical data, and ethnohistoric information (firing methodologies), to construct an interpretation of the locations of some of the units involved in the fighting at Wilson's Creek during different stages of the battle. These suggested locations are approximations only, however, and should not necessarily be considered highly precise, hyper-accurate analyses. There are a few potential confounds that should be noted at this point because of their potential to alter the outcomes of the cumulative viewshed analysis.

The first of these considerations is the actual location of the artifacts. Two factors should be highlighted, one depositional and one taphonomic. The first of these is the fact that shell fragments stem from cannonballs that explode in the air, dispersing fragments over a wide area. This dispersing effect could theoretically deposit a shell fragment in an area not visible from the battery position, thereby creating a measure of error in any attempted cumulative viewshed analysis. The same cannot be said, however, for canister, which was deposited as it fell, within the viewshed of the firing position.

The second consideration, the taphonomic one, is that Sharp's Field was an agricultural field both prior to and subsequent to the battle. Over time, repeated plowing and other land use practices could move artifacts around under the soil. The extent of the effect of this process on artifact locations has not been extensively studied. This source of error is one that needs to be studied more in future.

One final error vector should be mentioned, and this is a flaw inherent to all viewshed analyses. Digital elevation models, the files containing the elevation data for a region, consider only topographic information, neglecting vegetation and cultural elements of the landscape. Stands of trees and housing communities will naturally affect what can be seen from a given location. While suburban sprawl did not begin to encroach on the Wilson's Creek battlefield until recently, ground cover could have an effect on this analysis. Until field and forest areas have been identified through archaeological (soil analysis) and historical methods, an ongoing effort by the University of Arkansas, we cannot gauge the effect on the cumulative viewsheds that vegetation cover poses.

This chapter set out to achieve two tasks. First, it sought to aid the staff and volunteers of the National Park Service in the interpretation of Wilson's Creek to the public who visit the site each year. Through the above-described methods, we have offered an artifact-driven idea of where Backof's, Bledsoe's, and Reid's batteries fired from during salient parts of the engagement. To return to the criminalistic analogy mentioned in the introduction, this analysis has combined the physical evidence (artifact locations) with eyewitness testimony (historical information) to arrive at an interpretation of aspects of the event under study.

The second goal of this chapter is to show how battlefield archaeologists can incorporate spatial analytical procedures into their analyses of battlefield assemblages to refine and expand our historical-archaeological understanding of a past event. Battlefield archaeology possesses great potential for epistemological fluorescence, the bulk of which remains to be fully tapped. There are currently some flaws with this methodology as here presented. None of them are fatal to the effort, however, and can be ameliorated through further, ongoing fieldwork.

It is hoped that by showing how cumulative viewshed analyses can be used to identify battery positions, other archaeologists will explore other ways of asking for more information from their assemblages. Heckman's chapter in this book is another illustration of the suitability of using GIS-based spatial analyses for battlefield interpretation. By exploring a wider range of methods and approaches when studying battlefields archaeologically, not only will battlefield archaeology be able to extend itself beyond the particularist reconstruction focus that currently dominates the field, it will be able to contribute to a growing body of anthropological, sociological, and political science literature focusing on warfare as a cultural process, thereby making battlefield archaeology relevant to historical archaeology as a much-refined approach to interpreting the past and building archaeological theory, and also to understanding processes currently at play in the modern world.

NOTES

1. Gould (2005) reports this analogy as being first published by Collingwood (1946).
2. Scott et al. 1989, Scott and Fox 1987, Scott and Hunt 1998.
3. Fox 1993, Fox and Scott 1991.
4. Sterling 2000.
5. Harbison 2000.
6. Stone and Sivilich 2003.
7. Haecker and Mauck 1997:6.
8. Cutrer 1993:231.
9. Ibid.
10. Piston and Hatcher 2000:185.
11. Ibid., 190.
12. Cutrer 1993:231.
13. Ibid., 236.
14. Ibid., 234.
15. Piston and Hatcher 2000:268.
16. Ibid., 337–338; Confederate casualty totals are estimates due to the lack of existing documentation on the true extent of the losses sustained by the Confederate Army, Missouri State Guard, and Arkansas State Troops.
17. Shea and Hess 1992.
18. Scott et al. 1989, Fox 1993, and other publications on the archaeology of the Little Bighorn deal extensively with the discrepancies between the popular vision of Custer and his men engaged in a valiant "last stand" and the progress of the battle that an analysis of the artifacts suggested.
19. Scott et al. 1989:146.
20. Ibid., 147.
21. Ibid.
22. Scott et al. (1989), and Fox (1993) heavily rely on this approach in their analysis of the Little Bighorn. Haecker and Mauck (1997) employ the same approach in studying Palo Alto.
23. This data is currently being readied for publication by Drexler, Scott, and Roeker.
24. Drury and Gibbons 1993:77–78.

25. Gibbon 1860.
26. Griffith 1989.
27. Haecker and Mauck 1997:77.
28. Piston and Hatcher 2000:222; a private in Backof's battery recalls seeing the Confederates running around in confusion when the battery opened on them. On page 254, Piston and Hatcher clearly note that both Reid and Bledsoe could see Sigel's men from their positions.
29. Wheatley 1995.
30. Wheatley and Gillings 2002.
31. Piston and Hatcher 2000:34.
32. Ibid., 189.
33. Holcombe and Adams 1961[1883]:40.
34. Piston and Hatcher 2000.
35. Holcombe and Adams 1961[1883]:42.
36. Patrick 1997.
37. Piston and Hatcher 2000:254.

REFERENCES CITED

Collingwood, R. G. 1946. *The Idea of History*. Oxford University Press, New York.

Cutrer, Thomas W. 1993. *Ben McCulloch and the Frontier Military Tradition*. University of North Carolina Press, Chapel Hill.

Drury, Ian, and Tony Gibbons. 1993. *The Civil War Military Machine: Weapons and Tactics of the Union and Confederate Armed Forces*. Smithmark Publishers, London.

Fox, Richard A. Jr. 1993. *Archaeology, History, and Custer's Last Battle*. University of Oklahoma Press, Norman.

Fox, Richard A. Jr., and Douglas D. Scott. 1991. The Post-Civil War Battlefield Pattern: An Example from the Custer Battlefield. *Historical Archaeology* 25(2):92–103.

Gibbon, John. 1860. *The Artillerist's Manual*. Morningside Publishers, Dayton.

Gould, Richard. 2005. The Wreck of the Barque *North Carolina*: An Historic Crime Scene? *American Antiquity* 70(1):107–128.

Griffith, Paddy. 1989. *Battle Tactics of the American Civil War*. Yale University Press, New Haven.

Haecker, Charles M., and Jeffrey G. Mauck. 1997. *On the Prairie of Palo Alto: Historical Archaeology of the U.S.-Mexican War Battlefield*. Texas A&M University Press, College Station.

Harbison, Jeffrey. 2000. "Double the Canister and Give 'Em Hell": Artillery at Antietam. In C. R. Geier and S. R. Potter (eds.), *Archaeological Perspectives on the American Civil War*. University Press of Florida, Gainesville.

Holcombe, Return I., and Adams (first name not given). 1961[1883]. *An Account of the Battle of Wilson's Creek or Oak Hills*. Dow & Adams, Springfield.

Patrick, Jeffrey L. 1997. Remembering the Missouri Campaign of 1861: The Memoirs of Lieutenant William P. Barlow, Guibor's Battery, Missouri State Guard. *Civil War Regiments* 5(4):20–60.

Piston, William G., and Richard W. Hatcher III. 2000. *Wilson's Creek: The Second Battle of the Civil War and the Men Who Fought It*. University of North Carolina Press, Chapel Hill.

Scott, Douglas D., and Richard A. Fox. 1987. *Archaeological Insights into the Custer Battle: A Preliminary Assessment*. University of Oklahoma Press, Norman.

Scott, Douglas D., Richard A. Fox, Melissa A. Connor, and Dick Harmon. 1989. *Archaeological Perspectives on the Battle of Little Bighorn*. University of Oklahoma Press, Norman.

Scott, Douglas D., and William J. Hunt Jr. 1998. The Civil War Battle of Monroe's Crossroads, Fort Bragg, North Carolina. Prepared for the U.S. Army, XVIII Airborne Corps and Fort Bragg, Fort Bragg, North Carolina by the U.D. Department of the Interior, National Park Service, Technical Assistance and Partnerships Section, Southeast Archeological Center, Tallahassee, FL.

Shea, William L., and Earl J. Hess. 1992. *Pea Ridge: Civil War Campaign in the West*. University of North Carolina Press, Chapel Hill.

Sterling, Bruce B. 2000. Archaeological Interpretations of the Battle of Antietam through Analysis of Small Arms Projectiles. In C. R. Geier and S. R. Potter (eds.), *Archaeological Perspectives on the American Civil War*. University Press of Florida, Gainesville.

Stone, Gary W. and Daniel M. Sivilich. 2003. The Battle of Monmouth: The Archaeology of Molly Pitcher, the Royal Highlanders, and Colonel Cilly's Light Infantry. Paper presented at the 36th Annual Conference of the Society for Historical Archaeology, Providence, RI.

Wheatley, David S. 1995. Cumulative Viewshed Analysis: A GIS-based Method for Investigating Intervisibility, and Its Archaeological Application. In G. Lock and Z. Stancic (eds.), *Archaeology and Geographic Information Systems: A European Perspective*, 171–186. Taylor and Francis, London.

Wheatley, David, and Mark Gillings. 2002. *Spatial Technology and Archaeology: The Archaeological Applications of GIS*. Taylor and Francis, New York.

Battlefield Viewsheds, or What the General Saw: Lookout Mountain Battlefield, Chattanooga, Tennessee

Elsa Heckman

SOUTHWEST OF DOWNTOWN Chattanooga, Tennessee, Confederate forces occupied Lookout Mountain from September to November 1863; the mountain was considered impregnable by its rebel defenders, who dubbed it "the Gibraltar of America."[1] To their astonishment, it was captured by Federal troops on November 24, 1863. Without closer examination of the terrain and circumstances of the battle, it is difficult to understand how Federal troops were able to overwhelm entrenched Confederate forces on the side of the mountain and effectively rout the startled rebels. By utilizing historic maps and written documents to determine troop placement on the day of the battle and incorporating that data into a series of viewshed displays from key Confederate and Federal positions on the lower slopes of Lookout Mountain, this study draws conclusions about the visibility of attacking and defending forces on the morning of the battle. Given the spotty accounts of the extent of mountainside vegetation at the time of the battle, this is meant only as a cursory evaluation of viewsheds on the battlefield, assuming best possible visibility scenarios.

A viewshed is simply the area that is visible from a particular point of view. It exists in "real space" or three dimensions and is the same in two directions. For example, any point that can be *seen* from point "A" can also *see* point "A". Most post-battle (modern) analyses of troop positions and approach tactics are approached in a two-dimensional context accompanied by written accounts such as historic maps, personal accounts, and official records. With two-dimensional maps it is possible to draw arrows and make inferences about troop locations and paths of movement, but without much discussion of actual visibility and the reality of being a soldier on the ground at these locations.

Once troop placement and movements are established on a three-dimensional map or digital elevation model, advanced analysis can be performed. Computer-generated viewsheds are one of the easiest ways to determine what could be seen by soldiers on the ground. Once generated, these viewsheds can aid in interpretation of troop movements and battlefield positioning based on terrain.

At Lookout Mountain it is easy to assume that attacking Federal troops were marching along the mountainside on a steep slope that rose only to their right and fell to their left. This is the impression that one gets from studying two-dimensional historic maps. In reality, that march was even more difficult than it seems at first glance because the side of Lookout Mountain is undulating and the slope that the soldiers had to contend with was not just to their right and left, but *also* to their front. With this undulating terrain on the Federal approach, it becomes clear from generating multiple viewsheds that their visibility was greatly restricted, as was their detection by Confederates to their front.

BACKGROUND

Although the prospect of taking Lookout Mountain, "... with its high palisaded crest and its steep rugged, rocky, and deeply furrowed slopes" seemed foolish, Union Commander Major General Joseph Hooker was charged with the task of doing just that.[2] With a force of about 15,000 men, the massive body of Federal troops under the leadership of General John White Geary crossed Lookout Creek about two miles upstream from the major Confederate entrenchments and ascended the mountainside. Unexpected aid came in the form of "drifting clouds [that] enveloped the whole ridge of the mountain top and heavy mists and fogs [that] obscured the slope from lengthened vision."[3] General Geary's command stretched from the sandstone cliffs, near the top of Lookout Mountain, to the banks of Lookout Creek. Sweeping northward in formation, perpendicular to the slope of the mountain and crossing large areas of rough terrain, the troops made steady forward progress (see figure).[4]

There are many existing accounts detailing the difficult march by the Federal troops to the northern end of the mountain that day. Lt. John R. Boyle of the Pennsylvania Infantry wrote that " ... the mountain sloped downward at an angle of nearly forty-five degrees, and was covered with underbrush and heavy boulders, and broken by yawning ravines from fifty to one hundred feet deep."[5] Private David Mouat, also of the Pennsylvania Infantry, complained of "traveling over the rocks and fallen trees & up and down gullies ... "[6] Based on these accounts, historical photographs, and two paintings by James Walker, it is likely that the lower slopes of Lookout Mountain and the Lookout Creek floodplain were partially wooded at the time of the battle with interspersed areas denuded of vegetation. It is, however, impossible to determine exactly which areas were wooded and which were not in 1863. This is why the viewshed data must be interpreted strictly upon ground relief.

Western slope of Lookout Mountain with highlighted troop positions.

As the main Federal body was working its way north, swiftly encroaching upon the Confederate left and contained earthworks, Major General Edward C. Walthall's 34th Mississippi was contending with a diversionary force across Lookout Creek to their immediate front. At this same time, portions of General Wood's and Grose's Brigade had just successfully forded Lookout Creek approximately 1 kilometer southwest of the 34th's position with full intention of reinforcing Geary's already substantial force on the middle and upper slopes of the mountain. The only obstacle standing between Wood and his goal of linking with Geary's left flank was the battered 34th Mississippi. The Official Records describe this action as follows:

> General Walthall's 34th Mississippi, was cut off, along with the center and right of the picket line, from the rest of the brigade by the swift movement of the Union assault on its flank. As Captain H. J. Bowen of the 34th Mississippi attempted to meet the attack of Wood's brigade head-on, a portion of Grose's Illinois regiments, who were across the burnt out bridge on the west side of the creek, poured enfilading fire into the 34th's ranks.[7]

The Union artillery also effectively raked the ground behind and around the disintegrating Confederate regiment, blocking their only route of retreat. Nearly all of the soldiers in the 34th Mississippi surrendered or were killed.[8]

METHODS AND ANALYSIS

The primary goal was to generate viewsheds along General Geary's route of advance, from Wood's and Grose's river crossing, and from the doomed 34th Mississippi's stationary position on the lower slope of Lookout Mountain. This analysis was conducted using Idrisi raster GIS software but one can achieve similar results with ArcMap spatial analyst. A digital elevation model, or DEM, was obtained from the United States Geological Society (USGS) website in the form of a BIL file. It was necessary to convert the BIL file into ASCII before attempting to import it into Idrisi. Once this was successfully accomplished, a vector contour map was generated from the DEM and the hill shading module was employed. The contour map was created in order to ease identification of details in the landscape. It is from these details that viewpoints could be established. The hill shade module enhanced the visual relief of the landscape.

Next, vector files of both the Tennessee River and Lookout Creek were created for topographical reference purposes. Historic maps of troop placements on the day of the battle as well as historic documents aided in the generation of an approximate Confederate picket line and appropriately placed "points of view." The "viewing" locations were chosen for their strategic value on the battlefield to reconstruct what could actually be seen by soldiers from key positions on the ground.

The southernmost line of three (3) viewsheds (representing Geary's line of sight) was generated from the east bank of Lookout Creek and is representative of the initial Federal line's position immediately after their successful river crossing. The second line of three (3) viewpoints, located approximately one mile north on the mountainside, represents the approximate midpoint between Geary's river crossing and initial contact with Confederate forces. A solitary (1) viewshed was generated from the point where portions of Wood's and Grose's Brigades crossed Lookout Creek and began their thrust toward the 34th Mississippi's entrenched position. And finally, three (3) closely spaced viewshed points were generated from the position held by the 34th Mississippi. Separate viewsheds were generated for each individual viewpoint using a viewer height of 1.6 m, to simulate the height of a man on the ground, and a 4-km viewing distance. To more clearly demonstrate viewsheds from large groups of viewers like Geary's entire line and the 34th Mississippi's stationary position, viewsheds in the same general vicinity were combined to achieve comprehensive views from these more diffuse locations.

Viewshed 1

The combined viewshed from the initial Federal position on the mountain shows the visibility to the north on the western slope of the mountain to be fairly minimal due to the deep furrows running perpendicular to the

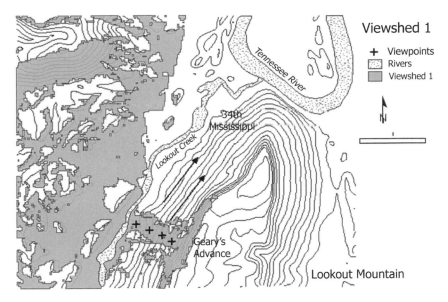

Viewshed from General Geary's initial position on Lookout Mountain.

mountainside (see figure). These gullies are responsible for long linear gaps in visibility to the north, along the entire Federal approach. This somewhat poor visibility could have been further lessened depending on the presence of trees and the dense fog on the upper elevations of the mountain. At this point, the Federal troops would not be in sight of Rebel forces located on the lower slopes of the mountain and due to the reported fog, the Confederates on top of Lookout Mountain would not have been able to detect their presence either.

Viewshed 2

The second viewshed depicts visibility of the advancing Federal forces midway between their Light's Mill river crossing and the Confederate line (see figure). At this point, portions of the Confederate Picket line would have been in sight as well as earthworks present at the 34th Mississippi's battlefield position. This suggests that the Federal troops on their northward march would have been in full view of Confederate forces on the lower slopes of Lookout Mountain within approximately 1 km of actual contact. As the bulk of this Federal command became engaged with the Confederate forces higher up on the mountain, the troops of Generals Wood and Grose were pouring across Lookout Creek approximately 700 meters to the rear of the 34th Mississippi.

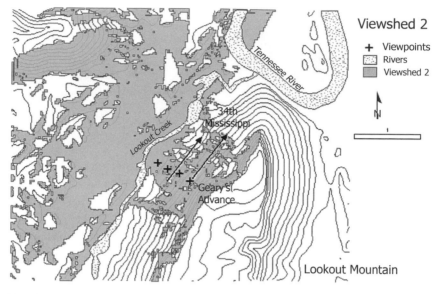

Viewshed from the midpoint of General Geary's advance.

Viewshed 3

This viewshed was generated from Wood's and Grose's river crossing. From this vantage, the soldiers of Wood's and Grose's Brigade had a direct route, with clear line of sight, to close in on the 34th Mississippi (see figure). The attack was a success and the 34th Mississippi's regimental battle flag was captured in this engagement.[9]

Viewshed 4

Finally, the perspective of the 34th Mississippi's position must be examined in light of the previous discussion. This final viewshed was generated from a northward pointing finger ridge at the base of Lookout Mountain which was occupied by troops from the 34th Mississippi (see figure).

A generally circular range of view is apparent around the entrenched 34th Mississippi's battlefield position. Based upon this viewshed, the Federal body of soldiers roaring across the western slope of Lookout Mountain would have been virtually undetectable from their stationary position. By the time that the 34th knew that an enormous body of Federal troops was gaining the Confederate left flank, it would have been too late to request reinforcements. Also, considering that the 34th Mississippi was occupied with fire to its front, its attention would have been diverted away from Wood's and Grose's river crossing. By the time the 34th turned to meet the onslaught of Wood's and Grose's brigades, they were taking fire from their left *and* their front.

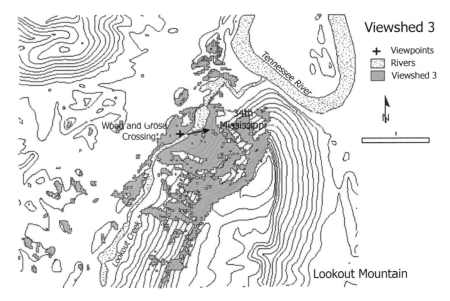

Viewshed from perspective of Wood and Grose's troops.

Although in retrospect it is simple to say that this position could not be held, it is obvious, based on this viewshed, why this particular landform was chosen for manning by the Confederate army. This small ridge afforded a prominent view of the railroad bridge spanning Lookout Creek below and

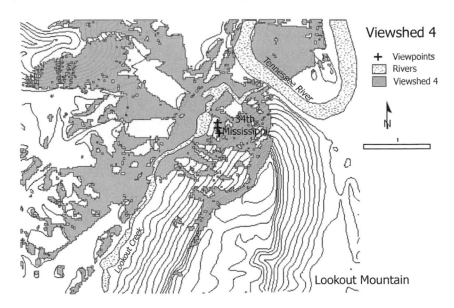

Viewshed from the 34th Mississippi's position.

also provided a good vantage for observing enemy behavior across Lookout Creek.

CONCLUSIONS

By implementing viewshed analysis on the lower slopes of the Lookout Mountain Battlefield, a comprehensive spatial understanding of troop movements and visual reality on the day of the battle can be further explored. An attack from the rear left flank was likely the last place that the Confederates were expecting an advance due to the unbelievably harsh terrain and the Federal demonstration to the Confederate front. This study suggests that the likely way Confederate forces on the lower western slopes of Lookout Mountain could have been alerted to the imminent attack would have been from their own forces on top of the mountain. With the extreme fog hovering over the crest and upper slopes of the hill this was not to be. The extreme furrowing and slight bend in the western slope of Lookout Mountain (apparent in the viewshed analyses) effectively hid the attackers from widespread Confederate observation.

An understanding of the physical environment at Lookout Mountain is best achieved by actually being there, but unfortunately, a trip to the study site is not always practical. Digital landscapes offer the investigator and the curious citizen, alike, a means of exploring the peaks and valleys of the area, without the hike. We have seen here that a first-person perspective in this virtual landscape has much to reveal about the battle of Lookout Mountain, and illustrates how digital technologies can be employed in furthering our understanding of the "reality" of battle situations. Additional research could allow the investigator to approach a complete environmental reconstruction of the site, re-creating field boundaries and forest cover of the landscape as it was in 1863. A three-dimensional representation of troop movements along a landscape, as seen from a soldier's point of view, can also provide visitors with a good and accurate understanding of what this particular engagement may have felt like. Using the Lookout Mountain Battlefield as a test case, this study demonstrates the contribution that viewshed analyses can make in understanding the perspectives of both attacking and defending forces on battlefields.

NOTES

1. Official Records of the War of the Rebellion [O.R], 1890: XXXI, 2: 437.
2. Official Records of the War of the Rebellion [O.R], 1890: XXXI, 2: 315.
3. Official Records of the War of the Rebellion [O.R], 1890: XXXI, 2: 391.
4. Taken from "The Civil War in Lookout Valley" by Harry M. Hays with contributions by Doug Cubbison, found in Alexander and Heckman 2005.

5. Boyle 1903:176.
6. Mouat n.d.
7. Official Records of the War of the Rebellion [O.R], 1890: XXXI, 2: 170, 181.
8. Alexander and Heckman 2005; Official Records of the War of the Rebellion [O.R], 1890: XXXI, 2: 703.
9. Rowland, Dunbar 1978.

REFERENCES CITED

Anonymous. 2001. Muster Roll of the 34th Miss. Infantry. http://www.rootseb.com. Military History of Mississippi by Roland Dunbar was referenced within the site (13 Nov. 2001).

Alexander, L. S., and E. Heckman. 2005. *Archaeological and Historical Survey of the Western Perimeter of the Lookout Mountain Battlefield.* Report submitted to the National Park Service, American Battlefield Protection Association. On file at Alexander Archaeological Consultants, Chattanooga, Tennessee.

Boyle, Lt. J. R. 1903. *Soldiers True, The Story of the 111th Pennsylvania Veteran Volunteer Infantry, 1861–1865.* New York, and Cincinnati, OH.

Mouat, Priv. D. n.d. Unpublished Reminiscences, Historical Society of Pennsylvania, Philadelphia, PA.

Official Records of the War of the Rebellion [O.R]. 1880–1901. War of the Rebellion: a Compilation of the Official Records of the Union and Confederate Armies. 129 Volumes. United States War Department, Washington, D.C.

What the Musket Ball Can Tell: Monmouth Battlefield State Park, New Jersey

Daniel M. Sivilich

A MUSKET BALL is not always a small lead sphere designed to be fired from a musket, pistol, or rifle at a specific target with deadly force. Musket balls were not always made of lead, spherical, or used with small arms. So how does one identify lead artifacts found at early military sites? This chapter will examine that question and develop a typology for spherical balls starting with basic lead balls that did begin as spheres and were designed for use with musket, rifle, or pistol, and then examine variations.

Musket balls are manufactured by pouring molten lead or another alloy into a two-part single or a multiple cavity mold. After the lead cools, the mold is separated and the musket ball removed. The casting sprue is cut close to the ball and any flashing around the mold seam is removed. Usually the musket ball would be put into a paper cartridge with a pre-measured charge of black powder. Eighteenth-century molds were made of iron or brass, but crude molds made of soapstone and brownstone are known.[1] The figure below shows a steatite (soapstone) mold on display at the Monmouth County Historical Association, Freehold, New Jersey. As can be seen, two different musket ball sizes and several sizes of buckshot could be cast with this mold. Seven buckshot cavities are ganged together to maximize the mold's available capacity. The different ball sizes suggest that the owner had two weapons, possibly a Brown Bess smooth bore musket or large bore pistol and a smaller bore rifle. Note the side of the mold is inscribed "1776."

The following terminology (see lower figure on page 85) is used here to describe weapons and musket balls.

> *Mold Seam*: a thin, often raised, line around the ball's circumference. Some molds were crude and the two halves would not match exactly when closed, allowing molten lead to seep out and resulting in musket balls that have two slightly offset or misaligned halves.

 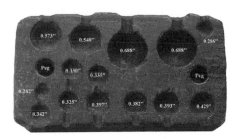

Steatite musket ball and buckshot mold. (Monmouth County Historical Association, Freehold, NJ)

Casting Sprue: a small raised cylinder from the mold's inlet channel. This is usually clipped off close to the surface of the musket ball.

Patina: lead carbonate/oxide. Musket balls buried in the ground for some time develop a white lead carbonate and lead oxide coating.[2] However, iron or other chemicals in the soil can change the color from white to tan to brown. Pine and oak trees produce high levels of tannic acid that can change the color of the patina to a dark reddish-brown.

Diameter: the size of a musket ball (usually measured in inches). This is not the caliber of the gun.

Caliber: the diameter of the gun barrel bore, also known as nominal caliber.

Windage: the difference between the gun caliber and the ball diameter. Typically the windage is approximately 0.05–0.10 inches.[3]

If an excavated musket ball is round, and has a mold seam and a casting sprue, then it probably was dropped and not fired. However, not all dropped musket balls have a mold seam or casting sprue. Some unfired musket balls excavated at Revolutionary War British occupation sites do not have these two features. It is possible that the musket balls were processed by pressing in England to remove surface irregularities. Another possibility is that the musket balls were made in England, packed tightly in crates or barrels, and transported

Musket ball.

by ship and over land by wagons. The rough modes of transportation could cause the balls to bang together many times, causing mold seams or casting sprues to be erased.[4] However, this is most likely not the case for pre-made cartridges. The paper wrapping tends to keep the ball from moving or rotating and also provides protective insulation.

What type of gun was a ball used with? To determine the weapon a ball came from, the diameter of the ball needs to be established (see figure). Diameter can be measured using a good set of calipers. When the diameter is known, the bore of the gun can be estimated. As an example a military British Brown Bess musket has a bore of 0.75 inches or is 75 caliber, but would take a 0.693-inch diameter musket ball. A .69 caliber French Charleville musket usually took a 0.63-inch ball. However, during the seventeenth and eighteenth centuries, musket balls were categorized not by diameter, but as to how many musket balls weighed a pound. For example a service British Brown Bess musket took musket balls that were 29 per two pounds.[5]

Examples of musket balls with different diameters.

If one size of spherical musket balls is found in quantities in areas not known to have a conflict, then this may be an indication of a campsite where musket balls were either cast or cartridges were being rolled. If found in a battle area, unfired balls may indicate a position where soldiers stood and fired. Sometimes during the heat of battle, a soldier would remove more than one cartridge from his cartridge box and inadvertently drop one. Dropped or unfired balls could also indicate where a soldier fell and cartridges spilled from the cartridge box.

By knowing a musket ball's diameter, one can estimate the bore of the gun it came from. However, what if the musket ball was fired, hit something, and is no longer round? The diameter cannot be measured directly. Another method was developed to estimate the diameter of deformed musket balls. Lead has a specific gravity of 11.4. This can be used to calculate the diameter of a musket ball based on its weight in grams. However, eighteenth-century lead contained air and impurities. This can be compensated for by using the Sivilich Formula:

$$\text{Diameter in inches} = 0.223204 \times (\text{Weight in grams})^{1/3}$$

The diameters of 781 musket balls excavated at Monmouth Battlefield State Park and surrounding associated areas were measured and/or calculated. The next figure is a histogram of the distribution of the diameters. There are two very distinct peaks: 0.63- and 0.69-inch diameters. Both the British and Americans were using standardized munitions, and the Brown Bess musket took a 0.693-inch diameter ball. Therefore, musket balls with diameters greater than 0.66 inch were most likely associated with that weapon. The center peak is between 0.60- and 0.66-inch diameter with a peak at 0.63 inch. This size ball was used in a variety of muskets, including two of the most common: the French Charleville, supplied to the Americans prior to Monmouth, and the British fusil.

The Americans used a number of riflemen at Monmouth. Rifles typically took musket balls with diameters less than 0.60 inch. The distribution confirms that the rifles had a wide distribution of calibers rather than being standardized.

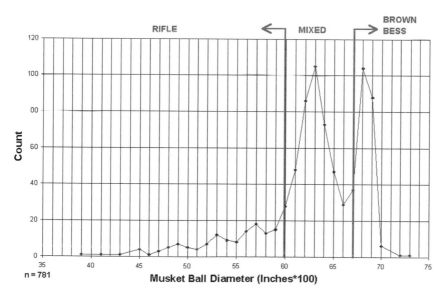

Diameter distribution of musket balls associated with the Battle of Monmouth.

Buck and ball.

A Phase I archaeological survey was conducted as part of the proposed road widening at the site. The archaeologist confirmed that they had found a musket ball. He had not formally measured it but estimated it to be just over a quarter of an inch. It had no visible sprue. This was not a musket ball. Notice that the lowest value on the chart in the above figure was 0.39-inch diameter for a musket ball. Smaller lead projectiles excavated at Monmouth are classified as buckshot. In 1776, George Washington issued a general order that a standard cartridge shall have one musket ball and 3 or 4 buckshot. The figure above shows a typical load and the relative size differences between buckshot and ball. Buckshot has changed little in the past two centuries and standard 00 buckshot today has a diameter of 0.33 inch and 000 buck has a diameter of 0.36 inch. Shot excavated at Monmouth ranges from 0.27- to 0.38-inch diameter. It is very difficult to tell eighteenth-century buckshot from modern buckshot that has been in the ground for only a few years and developed a patina. The most significant difference is that eighteenth-century shot was made in a gang mold and usually has a sprue visible if it is not too flattened from impact.

Ramrod marks on a musket ball.

Some musket balls excavated at Monmouth have shallow circular depressions as shown in the next figure. Based on the author's personal experiences firing black powder flintlock muskets, these appear to be ramrod marks. Even though a ball may sit loosely in the breech of a musket, it is still rammed several times to seat the ball. If the ball is loose, it will rotate slightly with each strike. This ball has three blows from a ramrod.

Impacted musket balls can take many different shapes. One of the most common is a hemisphere. This

(a) Hemispherical-shaped, impacted musket ball; (b) Reproduction musket ball fired into tree.

form usually occurs when a ball strikes a compressible material such as wood or bone as replicated in the figures above.

Sometimes the shape can be used as a diagnostic tool. The musket ball shown in the figure hit a very smooth, uniformly curved object. The curvature present on this musket ball matches the outside diameter of a Brown Bess musket barrel. It may have hit a Brown Bess musket barrel.

If a musket ball traveling at a relatively high velocity hits a solid object such as a tree, a rock, a fence rail, and so on, at a shallow angle, it can ricochet or glance off. The force of this action will usually deform the musket ball and create a sweeping tail of metal as seen in the first figure on page 90.

After repeated firing, muskets begin to foul, building up a residue of unburnt powder in the barrel. This fouling can cause a musket ball to jam in a barrel. A steel screw commonly called a ball puller can be attached to one end of a ramrod and be drilled into a stuck musket ball to remove it. Distinctive thread marks are left in the musket balls similar to those

Musket ball that appears to have hit the barrel of another musket.

Ricocheted musket ball.

Pulled musket balls with extraction screw marks.

shown in the figure above. These have been excavated both at campsites and on battlefields. The balls were usually discarded after being pulled and are usually still round. Therefore the diameters can be measured.

Occasionally unusual artifacts are excavated that can evoke one's imagination. The musket ball, shown in the top figure on page 91, is hemispherical and probably hit and imbedded in a tree. It appears that it was then hit by two more musket balls. This suggests all three shots were being aimed at a specific target, possibly someone standing behind a tree.

There are the grim realities of war. The musket ball in the lower figure has what appears to be a human front incisor impression in it but is hemispherical in shape. It is hypothesized that this musket ball hit a soldier's front tooth and proceeded through the back of the head.

Anesthetics were not available during the Revolutionary War. If you were an officer and some rum or wine was available, you might dull the pain of surgery a little by getting drunk. However, the average soldier was simply given a stick or a piece of leather or a musket ball to bear down on to keep from biting his tongue or cracking his teeth from the pain of having a limb removed or having a musket ball extracted. This is how the phrase "bite the bullet" may

Impacted musket ball that appears to also have been hit by two musket balls.

have originated. Chewed musket balls may be an indication where wounded soldiers fell or the location of a field surgery. Thirty-five musket balls excavated at Monmouth have evidence of teeth impressions. These were examined by Henry M. Miller of Historic St. Mary's City, Maryland. A basic question of how much deformation a human can impart to a lead sphere with his teeth was first addressed. The author obtained reagent grade (99.9 percent pure)

Musket ball with front incisor impression.

Modern musket balls with human chewing marks.

lead from a chemical supply company and had it cast into 0.69-inch musket balls. The author and Henry Miller proceeded to chew several musket balls using molar and canine teeth with as much force as could be tolerated. The results are shown in the figure above.

234-3-669

Musket ball with human canine and incisor teeth impressions.

This test showed that it was not possible to flatten a spherical musket ball. However, this does not preclude the use of flattened lead as a biting object during surgery. Seven musket balls were identified as being likely human chewed from the Monmouth Battlefield sample.[6]

It is unlikely that all human-chewed musket balls are associated with pain and/or surgery. The musket ball in the figure is a lightly chewed musket ball that has human canine and incisor teeth marks. Incisors are not used as bearing teeth like molars, so these musket balls were probably not chewed to ease pain. These were most likely chewed to promote salivation. The Battle of Monmouth took place on June 28, 1778. It is reported that temperatures reached 96° in the shade. Many soldiers from both sides fell to heat exhaustion. This has been documented at other battles as well. Thomas Mellen, a soldier at the Battle of Walloomsac, stated:

> I soon started for a brook I saw a few rods behind, for I had drank nothing all day, and should have died of thirst if I had not chewed a bullet all that time.[7]

One must be careful in analyzing chewed musket balls. Musket balls can also be chewed by animals. Pigs root up objects and chew on them while looking for nuts, edible roots, and tubers. A number of pig-chewed musket balls

Musket ball chewed by a pig.

excavated at Monmouth were identified by Henry Miller. The impressions on these musket balls are usually long deep scrape marks and lack any molar crowns.

However, pigs are not necessarily the only animal to chew musket balls. In his analysis, Dr. Miller also noted a musket ball that a rodent chewed (see figure). It is possible that this musket ball had blood or bits of flesh attached or the sugar of lead (oxidized lead) that attracted a rodent.[8]

Artifact 90M16RP4 with possible rodent gnawing marks.

It can be concluded that spherical lead balls can be used as diagnostic tools because:

- Diameters suggest the weapon type used.
- Round, dropped, or pulled balls indicate either a campsite or where soldiers may have stood.
- Impacted musket balls indicate target areas.
- Deformation of impacted musket balls may suggest target types and potentially landscape features of the time period.
- Human molar-chewed musket balls suggest locations of wounded soldiers and possible field surgery sites.
- Lightly chewed (human canine and incisors) musket balls might indicate dry or hot weather.
- Animal-chewed musket balls suggest post-battle farm activities such as hog ranging.

We have reviewed lead musket balls that were originally spherical and used with muskets, rifles, or pistols. Returning to the original question, are musket balls always made of lead? The answer is no. A number of "pewter" musket balls were excavated at Monmouth. Pewter has many different formulae depending on its end use, but it is primarily a tin alloy. "Tin was generally alloyed with small amounts of lead and sometimes also copper to obtain better casting properties. ..."[9]

Some musket balls found at Monmouth have a lower specific gravity than lead and therefore do not exactly fit the diameter formula. These musket balls are rarely flattened from impact, suggesting they are harder than lead. They have a very poor and flaky patina that blisters (see figure). The overall color is grayish. Lead was in short supply in the colonies so other materials may have been used to produce musket balls. There is the story of the gilded leaden statue of King George III that was pulled down in Bowling Green Park, New York City, in 1776 and cast into 42,088 musket balls.[10] Since lead is much too soft for a statue, likely it was hardened with tin and was possibly a pewter statue. Since these "pewter" musket balls do not flatten very much on impact, their approximate diameter can be measured with calipers.

Not all musket balls are spherical (before firing). The musket

"Pewter" musket ball.

balls shown in the next figure were excavated in Zboriv, Ukraine, the site of a 1649 battle between Cossacks and Polish nobility. As can be seen, early musket balls were slightly cylindrical and had a lipped sprue used to secure the musket ball in the paper cartridge by tying the cartridge off with string around the sprue to keep the projectile from separating from the cartridge.

Seventeenth-century musket balls from Zboriv, Ukraine. (Adrian Mandzy, Ph.D., More-head State University, Morehead, Kentucky)

A variety of cylindrically shaped shot have been excavated at Monmouth and are shown in the figure below. Most of these shot have faceted faces from being hammered.

Cylinder-shaped shot.

Soldiers occasionally altered round balls by hammering them into cylinders or "Sluggs" as they were called in the eighteenth century. This shot type would tumble after firing and rip through human targets, causing massive injury. The use of cylindrical shot is not unique to Monmouth and appears to have a long history. Five specimens recovered from the pirate ship *Whydah* that sank off Cape Cod in 1717 are currently on display in the museum in Provincetown, Rhode Island.

Musket balls were sometimes quartered and halved to fire a spray pattern at the enemy, creating, in effect, a dum-dum bullet. The ball was cut partially through so it would fragment after exiting the muzzle (see figure). Although

Intentionally mutilated musket balls.

not very accurate, one has to wonder if this was done more for psychological purposes. Calver and Bolton reported excavated musket balls with nails driven through them. This was so common a practice that the British General Lord Howe wrote to General Washington in September 1777, complaining about the use of mutilated shot by the Continentals. "My aid-de-camp will present to you a ball cut and fixed to the end of a nail, taken from a number of the same kind, found in the encampment quitted by your troops on the 15th inst. I do not make any comment upon such unwarrantable and malicious practices, being well assured that the contrivance has not come to your knowledge." From his headquarters on Harlem Heights, on September 23, 1776, Washington replied, "Your aid-de-camp delivered to me the ball you mention, which was the first of the kind I ever saw or heard of. You may depend the contrivance is highly abhorred by me and every measure shall be taken to prevent so wicked and infamous a practice being adopted in this Army." It is interesting that Calver and Bolton note that the specimens they found were at the British camp at Inwood. A variety of mutilated musket balls have been excavated at Monmouth, examples of which are shown in the figure (white color). Calculated values of the original diameters suggest that both sides engaged in this practice.

Although we have not found any musket balls with nails in them, a musket ball with a fragment of an iron wire through its axis was found in Burlington County, New Jersey, by metal detectorist Robert Campbell (see figure on page 97).

It is interesting to note that the pair of gang-molded musket balls was found in the same area as the musket ball in the next figure. It is unknown whether they were lost before being separated or were specifically cast as

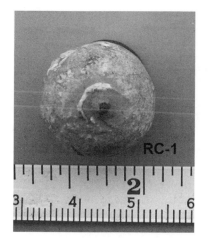

Musket ball with imbedded iron wire.

Musket balls molded together.

double shot. I suspect the latter since the joining sprue was so short as to make separation difficult.

Are musket balls always fired from small arms or shoulder arms? The answer is no.

Quantities of wedge-shaped and cubic-shaped "musket balls" were excavated at Monmouth in one specific location. These had multiple concave depressions. Lead will assume the shape of the object it hits upon contact.

(a) Wedge-shaped; (b) Cubic-shaped artillery canister shot.

Fused musket balls (canister shot).

A pair of fused "musket balls" were also excavated in the same area. These fused shot also had the same multiple concave depressions.

Numerous fused musket ball pairs were found. All had multiple facets with concave depressions. These were not musket balls, per se, but lead canister shot. Major-General William Alexander, Lord Sterling, wrote about firing grape and canister shot at the British.[11] Canister shot is a tin can filled with lead balls. It is often fired at the ground at a glancing angle about 75 yards in front of the enemy. The can ruptures on firing and the shot skips off the ground and rips through the enemy ranks. Canister is an excellent anti-personnel round. The effect of firing causes the balls in the can to compress. The lead balls get concave depressions from neighboring balls and take on wedge and square shapes. Some shot compresses to the point of fusing together.

Several fused artillery canister shot.

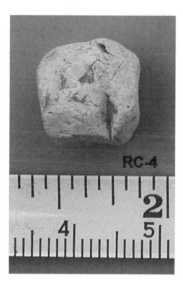

(a) Reproduction lead dice and lead cube; (b) Possible lead dice in the making.

Finally there are the non-projectile uses of musket balls such as gaming pieces. A few examples are shown.

Musket balls were occasionally used to make gun flint wraps. Clamping a gun flint in the steel jaws of a musket hammer without a wrap will either give a poor grip or crack the flint. The flint is wrapped in leather or lead to hold it in place and act as a shock absorber.

Gun flint wrap and "French honey" gun flint.

CONCLUSION

These are but a few examples of musket balls, artillery shot, and other lead artifacts found at Monmouth Battlefield. Next time you excavate a piece of lead at a military site, ask yourself ... was this a musket ball?

ACKNOWLEDGMENTS

The author would like to acknowledge the many people responsible for making this paper possible. Foremost is Garry Wheeler Stone, Ph.D., who had the courage to work with volunteer metal detectorists in a time when many archaeologists had a dim view of metal detecting. His wisdom and knowledge has kept the projects on a professional level. Thanks to the many members of the Battlefield Restoration and Archaeological Volunteer Organization (BRAVO) who spent countless hours excavating in the field and cleaning, measuring, and cataloging artifacts in the lab. Henry Miller, Ph.D., of Historic St. Mary's City in Maryland was kind enough to identify the teeth impressions in a number of "chewed" musket balls as being from pigs. Henry even identified which teeth made the impressions and the approximate ages of the animals. Eric Sivilich and Michael Smith did outstanding work in photographing the re-enactors and the artifacts for this presentation. Monmouth County Historical Association graciously allowed the author to measure and photograph the "1776" steatite musket ball mold. Finally thank you to Russ Balliet and Robert Campbell for allowing the author to photograph artifacts from their collections.

NOTES

1. Neumann and Kravic 1989:190–193.
2. Roberge 2005.
3. Neumann 1967.
4. Sivilich 1996.
5. Muller 1977:14.
6. Miller 2004.
7. Lord 1989.
8. Miller 2004.
9. Petersen 2002.
10. CTSSAR 2002.
11. *Proceedings of the New Jersey Historical Society*, Vol 60, No. 3 (July 1942):173–175.

REFERENCES CITED

(CTSSAR). The Connecticut Society of the Sons of the American Revolution. 2002. *Where is King George's Head*. Internet paper, http://www.ctssar.org/articles/ling_georges_head.htm.

Lord, Phillip. 1989. *War Over Walloomscoick*. New York State Education Department, Albany, NY.

Miller, Henry M. 2004. An Analysis of Marks on Musket Balls Recovered from the Revolutionary War Battlefield of Monmouth, New Jersey. Historic St. Mary's City, St. Mary's City, MD. Not published.

Muller, John. 1977. *A Treatise of Artillery 1780*. Museum Restoration Services, Bloomfield, Ontario, Canada.

Neumann, George C. 1967. *The History of Weapons of the American Revolution*. Bonanza Books, New York.

Neumann, George C., and Frank J. Kravic. 1989. *Collector's Illustrated Encyclopedia of the American Revolution*. Rebel Publishing Company, Texarkana, TX.

Petersen, Karen Steman. 2002. *Preservation of Historical Pewter in Church and Museum Collections*. Internet paper, http://www.natmus.dk/cons/reports/2002/tinbevaring/pewter.htm.

Roberge, Pierre R. 2005. *Lead Corrosion*. Internet paper on the Corrosion Doctors Web Site, http://www.corrosiondoctors.org/MatSelect/corrlead.htm.

Sivilich, Daniel M. 1996. Analyzing Musket Balls to Interpret a Revolutionary War Site. *Historical Archaeology* 30(2):101–109.

"Listen to the Minié Balls": Identifying Firearms in Battlefield Archaeology

Douglas Scott & Lucien Haag

THE IDENTIFICATION OF guns or gun parts found on archaeological sites is a relatively straightforward process. Most archaeologists are aware of expert literature on the subject and can readily use existing references to identify, type, and date guns or gun parts. Archaeologists are also reasonably adept at using available references to identify cartridge case headstamps, allowing them to identify a caliber, and usually a date range, for the use ammunition. However, researchers often overlook a wealth of other information contained in archaeologically recovered ammunition components. Bullets, cartridge cases, cartridges, artillery shot and shell fragments, canister shot, primers, and percussion caps can also provide a range of information on dating, types of firearms present, minimum numbers of firearms, and activities of the site's occupants as they related to the firearms. Our intent is to introduce archaeologists studying sites of conflict, or other sites containing evidence of firearms, to potential of firearms identification procedures. This chapter is not intended to be a ''how to''; rather our purpose is to provide a background to firearms identification and to introduce a variety of analytical firearms identification procedures adaptable to archaeological investigations.

The comparative study of ammunition components is known as firearms identification analysis. Firearms, in their discharge, leave behind telltale signatures or markings on the ammunition components (see figure on page 103). These signatures, more properly termed class and individual characteristics, allow the determination of the firearm type (i.e., model or brand) in which a given cartridge or bullet was fired, including artillery. This identification then allows determination of the number of different gun types at a given site. Further, individualized characteristics allow the identification of individual weapons or grouping of fired bullets or fired cartridge cases as having been fired in a common firearm. This last capability is very important because coupled with precise artifact locations, matching individual characteristics can identify activity loci. With this information, patterns of movement can be established and sequences of activity more precisely interpreted.

FIREARM-GENERATED
MARKINGS ON CARTRIDGE CASES
[SEMI-AUTOMATIC PISTOL CARTRIDGE]

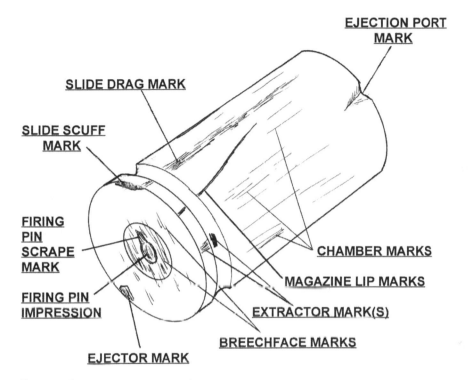

Features that remain on a cartridge case after firing aid in the identification of the firearm type.

The means to this analytical end requires some explanation. When a cartridge weapon is fired the firing pin strikes the cartridge primer, often leaving a distinctive imprint on the case. The primer ignites the powder, thus forcing the bullet out the barrel. Rifling in the barrel imprints the lands and grooves on the bullet in mirror image. The extractor frequently marks the fired case as it is extracted from the gun's chamber. These imprints are called class and individual characteristics. Class and individual characteristics are also present on projectiles fired from muzzle-loading firearms like flintlocks and percussion weapons including some smooth-bore guns.

FIREARMS IDENTIFICATION: HISTORY AND THEORY

Law enforcement agencies have long used firearms identification as an aid in solving crimes. A method commonly used by police departments includes comparison of bullets and cartridge cases to identify weapon types from which they were fired.[1] Law enforcement criminalists and firearms examiners are routinely successful in matching bullets and/or cartridge case characteristics to a crime weapon simply by demonstrating that the firing pin, breechface, ejector, chamber, and extractor marks on fired cartridge cases, or the land and groove marks on fired bullets, could only have been made by a specific weapon. In the event that weapons used in a crime are not recovered, the law enforcement laboratory can say with certainty, on the basis of class and individual characteristics found on recovered bullets and cartridge cases, that specific types and numbers of weapons were used.

Firearms identification procedures, often erroneously called forensic ballistics, are analogous to the archaeological wear pattern analysis. Like wear pattern analysis, firearms identification did not spring up overnight, but has an evolutionary history. Firearms identification had its earliest known beginnings in an 1835 London murder case.[2] A London policeman helped secure a conviction by proving a bullet (ball) with a peculiar flaw could have only been cast in the defendant's mold which had the same flaw. Another case of incipient firearms identification occurred in determining who caused the death of Confederate General Stonewall Jackson on May 2, 1863. An examination of the recovered bullet proved it to be a type and caliber used by the Confederate Army. Jackson was killed by one of his own pickets—a probable friendly fire fatality.

Other cases followed in ensuing years with each building on earlier conclusions. In 1900 Dr. Albert Hall published the first truly scientific treatment on forensic ballistics and began its advancement as a common law enforcement tool. Firearms identification, as it has become known, was used to establish guilt in the 1907 Brownsville, Texas, race riots.[3] The examination resulted in cashiering three entire companies of the all-black 25th U.S. Infantry. By 1925 the field was becoming well established, and in that year the greatest single advancement occurred to ensure a solid footing for its future. The comparison microscope was used for the first time and became the firearm examiner's standard tool. With publication of several textbooks in 1935, the field was firmly established and now nearly every major law enforcement agency has one or more firearms examiners in its laboratory.[4]

THE COMPARISON MICROSCOPE

The comparison microscope is critical to analyzing ammunition components. The microscope is constructed so that two separate microscope tubes are joined by a bridge with prisms mounted over the tubes. Two separate images are transmitted to the center of the bridge, where another set of prisms transmits the images to a central eyepiece. The eyepiece is divided so that each image appears on one-half of the eyepiece. Movable stages allow the object under scrutiny to be manipulated so that it can be directly compared for class and individual characteristics.

CLASS AND INDIVIDUAL CHARACTERISTICS

Class Characteristics[5]

The number of land and groove impressions on a bullet or the size and depth of a firing pin impression are termed "class characteristics." These gross details are common to a type, model, or brand of firearm (see figure). As an example, the Smith & Wesson company designs and builds their revolver barrels with a five land and groove, right-hand twist of specific dimensions. The Colt Company manufactures its barrels with a six land and groove, left-hand twist of slightly different dimensions. An archaeologically recovered fired bullet with five land and groove impressions with a right-hand twist to the rifling was not fired from a Colt. If the bullet's land and groove dimensions are the same as the Smith & Wesson revolver, then it can be assumed the bullet was fired from a Smith & Wesson gun. By knowing caliber and researching the models made by Smith & Wesson in that caliber, it is possible to narrow the bullet down to a specific model and have a firm date for when that model or caliber was introduced on the market, and thus determine an *ante quem* date for the archaeological specimen.

The cartridge case firing pin signature can also be characteristic of the gun type in which it was fired. This is important because many types of ammunition can be fired in a variety of different firearms. By way of example, .44 caliber Henry cartridge could be fired not only in the Henry repeating rifle (for which the cartridge was designed) but also in the Model 1866 Winchester, the .44 rimfire Colt pistol, and the .44 rimfire Remington revolver, among others. The class characteristics for each weapon type's firing pin are distinctive, and it is possible to identify the weapon type in which a given .44 Henry cartridge was fired. These data allow the archaeologist to determine the *ante quem* date and the number of different firearm types present on a site.

Individual Characteristics

Macroscopically, firing pin impressions often appear identical from weapon to weapon within a single type. However, minute variations, unique to each firing pin, allow identification of individual weapons if they survive the ravages of time in buried contexts. Such features are visible only via the

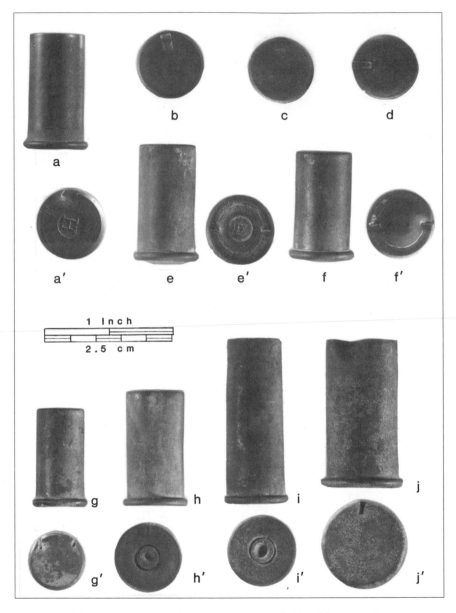

A variety of firing pin imprints shown on .38, .44, and .50 caliber cartridge cases.

microscope. The unique characteristics result from the manufacturing process and subsequent wear, degradation, damage over time, and general use. Because class and individual characteristics are left on the most durable metallic substances—brass, copper, and lead—most ammunition components at archaeological sites are amenable to firearms identification procedures even after a century or more in the ground. In essence, the markings are a metallic fingerprint.

Fired bullets also retain an individual fingerprint. The barrel of rifled guns has a series of lands and grooves that impart spin to the bullet as it travels out the barrel. This spin gives the bullet greater aerodynamic stability and accuracy in its trajectory. The bullet is lead and the barrel is steel. Since the bullet fits tightly in the barrel, the barrel leaves its land and groove impressions, in reverse, on the softer bullet. As with a firing pin, each barrel manufactured for a certain weapon type has individually recognizable characteristics due to wear on the rifling tool during the manufacturing process as well as wear to the weapon during its use. The individual and unique striations left on any given bullet when it is fired will match the striations on any other bullet fired in that same gun. Even though a bullet may be deformed on impact, it may retain sufficient individual and unique striations to permit multiple bullets to be associated with a single firearm or to be matched to a specific firearm in the present-day situation.

ANALYTICAL PROCEDURES

The first step in the analysis is cleaning the artifact. Bullets are made of lead and are sometimes jacketed with copper or other metals. Cartridge cases are made of brass or copper (more properly Bloomfield Gilding Metal), although some are tinned and shotgun hulls usually have a paper or plastic upper body. Lead, brass, and copper oxidize upon prolonged environmental exposure. Oxidation obscures details of the individual characteristics and must be removed before analysis. Very careful sonic cleaning and chemical removal of the oxides mixed with gentle scrubbing are the only satisfactory means to completely clean ammunition components.

Step two of the analysis is identifying class characteristics, and sorting artifacts into like groups. A low power hand lens or microscope (7–40x) is used to identify class characteristics. The process involves handling each bullet to determine the presence or absence of rifling marks, and when present, direction of twist and number of land and groove impressions. Measuring the bullet's diameter and weight as well as the widths of its land and groove marks allows further class segregation.

A similar procedure is followed with cartridge cases or percussion caps. Caliber or size is determined, then the size and depth of firing pin marks, and the location and type of extractor marks. Headstamps are generally not helpful in the class segregation process since many manufacturers loaded cartridges for specific firearms. Percussion caps retain marks, in reverse, of the hammer that fired it. These can also be sorted and identified. At the completion of the class segregation, the investigator will be able to determine the minimum number of weapon types (models, brands, calibers, etc.) present at a site.

Identifying class characteristics is aided by a comparative collection of bore molds and fired cartridge cases from a variety of firearms. Many firearms investigators maintain such collections for firearms manufactured since 1910. Modern firearms investigators have very little experience or reference material on pre-1910 firearm characteristics. Unfortunately most cartridge collectors and antique firearms collectors have little or no knowledge of fired ammunition. At present only a limited number of individuals have direct experience of firing or collecting data on class characteristics of pre-1910 firearms.

Once artifacts are identified as to class the third analytical step begins. The comparison microscope is brought into play. The microscope usually has objectives with a range of 10x to 150x. The analytic procedure is a tedious one, but as yet no means other than comparing each case or bullet against every other case or bullet from the same class has been found satisfactory. Individual characteristics are located and compared under magnification. Striations, flaws, scratches, unusual wear, etc. are the individual characteristics that aid in making a match between two or more cases, bullets, or percussion caps. At the completion of this process the investigator will be able to determine the minimum number of individual firearms represented.

PERCUSSION CAPS

The percussion cap is an external priming device used on a muzzle-loading firearm to ignite and detonate the powder charge and bullet situated in the bore of a gun.[6] Percussion caps were developed in the early nineteenth century and, like other percussion primers, served to improve upon the flintlock system of ignition. Flintlocks were plagued by a high rate of ignition failure due to chronic powder dampness and lack of an adequate spark. Research being conducted on explosive materials around the turn of the nineteenth century soon moved the flintlock system into retirement.

It is generally agreed that the method of using an explosive compound to ignite gun charges can be attributed to the Rev. Alexander Forsyth of Scotland. His experiments and success at using fulminates and chlorate of potash in the early 1800s gave rise to dozens of patents, some of them his own, as inventors experimented with different methods of harnessing this new ignition material. The wave of innovation resulted in the creation of many varieties of percussion primers in the form of tubes, pellets, pills, and caps, as inventors vied for distinction in what was recognized as a significant transition in firearms use and manufacture.[7]

A popular and widely accepted design of that era was the percussion cap, consisting of a small open-ended cup containing a small quantity of igniting compound sealed in place with varnish or another waterproof sealer. The percussion cap was more reliable and easier to use than earlier attempts at percussion primers, and thus began to solidify the movement toward a reliable ignition system. Percussion cap design is most often attributed to British painter Joshua Shaw based on his claims of inventing reloadable iron caps in 1814 or earlier. Shaw received a U.S. patent for his idea in 1822, but claims of percussion cap conception by European inventors around the same period make it difficult to determine who deserves true credit for this innovation.[8]

There was no shortage of patents for variations on percussion six cap design. In terms of function, most variations were negligible, focusing mostly on differences in size and material. Caps with ribbed or corrugated sides became popular as a way of lessening the chance of cap fragmentation upon ignition. These primers became known as "common caps," but are also called "pistol caps" due to their smaller size and lighter ignition charge being more suitable for pistol or small rifle operation. Another accepted design was the "top hat" cap, also called the "military" or "musket" cap. This cap was developed with wings or protruding sides for easier handling by soldiers wearing gloves. Top hat caps were not exclusively military-issue, however, as sporting versions were also manufactured and are still in production today.[9]

Manufacture of percussion caps varied slightly depending on individual design, but most required, at a minimum, nine basic steps: (1) rolling copper sheets to a proper thickness, excluding those areas with imperfections; (2) an annealing process to ensure malleability; (3) cleaning to eliminate effects of fire or heat during the annealing process; (4) cutting and/or punching sheets of copper into the proper forms; (5) oiling of cut-outs to promote ease of machining; (6) formation into the desired shape, using a tool and die process; (7) removal of oil by using sawdust; (8) insertion of the ignition compound; and (9) varnishing to seal the ignition compound. By the mid to late nineteenth century, steps 1 through 8 were accomplished at a rate of 31,000 caps per day per machine or workstation, with the finishing touches of varnishing (step 9) accomplished at the rate of 7,000 caps per hour per laborer. A manufacturer's stamp was sometimes included in the formation process, further documenting the company, country, or region of manufacture.[10]

Percussion caps are a well-known artifact type from pre-1870 sites where firearms were used. Many archaeologists mention finding percussion caps, and several provide measurements of the artifacts, but little archaeological study has been made of this artifact type. One exception is an analysis of percussion caps from Fort Union Trading Post National Historic Site, North Dakota.[11] William Hunt used measurements of cap size to predict potential weapon type: pistol, small caliber rifle, or musket.

The Fort Union study notes that there are currently four manufacturers making common or pistol caps today. The modern caps range in diameter from 0.17 to 0.18 inch (0.43–0.46 cm) with lengths of 0.17 to 0.24 inch (0.43–0.61 cm). There are also five manufacturers producing six types of musket or top hat caps that range in diameter from 0.22 to 0.24 inch (0.56–0.61 cm) and in length from 0.22 to 0.25 inch (0.56–0.64 cm). The study found that diameter is a greater predictor of cap/firearm correlation than length. The Fort Union (1829–1868) archaeological percussion caps fell into two size modes similar to modern percussion cap diameters. The smaller or common straight-sided cap from Fort Union ranged in diameter from 0.16 to 0.21 inch (0.42 to 0.53 cm) and the larger top hat or musket cap ranged in diameter from 0.21 to 0.26 inch (0.53 to 0.65 cm).

Baker and Harrison are among the few archaeologists who attempted to identify percussion caps by using measurements. Unfortunately, they equated their measurements to modern percussion caps sizes cited in Barnes[12] without realizing that there is significant variation in cap dimensions through time by manufacturer and even within a manufacturer's lot. Measurements taken from modern and historic percussion caps demonstrate that sizes are not quantifiable by precise measurements, rather that percussion caps can be sorted by measurement into three or four gross types: musket, large rifle/pistol, small rifle/pistol, and shotgun. Individual measurements of percussion caps show statistically significant variation in dimensions by as much as several thousandths of an inch in a single container holding a purported specific cap size, for example, Remington No. 11 caps vary by 3–4 thousandths of an inch in each dimension—length, head diameter, and inside mouth diameter—from a container of 100 caps.

As with modern-day cartridge cases, percussion caps come into contact with parts of the firearm that have both class and individual characteristics due to imperfections and machining techniques used during their manufacturing process coupled with random changes during use. On muzzle-loading firearms, percussion caps come into contact with both the nipple, or cone, and the hammer. The force of the hammer striking the percussion cap, coupled with the explosive force of the igniting compound, cause any imperfections and unique characteristics of the hammer, the nipple, or both, to be imparted to the cap. These markings allow the firearm examiner to make determinations that multiple percussion caps were fired on the same firearm, even without the firearm being present (see figure on page 111). The more unique the markings present, the greater likelihood of being able to single out a specific firearm.

Additional identifying characteristics may be attributed to the black powder shooting process itself. Black powder firearms are easily dirtied or "fouled" during shooting. Fouling can provide additional characteristics for making an identification on percussion caps. Incompletely burned powder and metal particles from the projectile coat the barrel and associated components of the firearm with a sooty residue.[13] The same powder and residue, as well as additional residue and metal particles from the percussion cap, can manifest itself on the firearm's nipple or cone and its hammer. When this occurs, fouling can add to the unique set of impressions and striations created by the hammer and nipple, thus transferring to the percussion cap as well. Fouling

Photomicrograph of two different percussion caps with identical toolmarks indicating they were fired on the same gun.

may remain a part of the hammer and nipple impression for a lengthy period of time as a reproducing mark, or may vanish after the next firing.

Another factor to be considered upon examining percussion caps is the manufacturing process of the caps themselves. At any point during the manufacturing or storage process, it is possible for machined parts, storage receptacles, or even other caps, to impart markings onto a percussion cap. These markings tend to be subtle, but can be confusing if interpreted improperly. Order of placement may need to be determined in order to decide which markings are more critical for examination. One method of determining whether an impression or striation is more recent than another is to look for overlapping or even continuous patterns. If a striation or impression appears to cut off or otherwise obscure another marking, it is probable that the overlapping striation or impression occurred after the interrupted mark. Likewise, if a set of markings are apparent on either side of an impression, and also can be seen throughout the contoured impression, those markings may be a pre-existing set of characteristics incurred during the manufacturing process.

Not all percussion caps retain markings with enough individualization to show that a cap came from a specific firearm. Due to overall consistency in the firearm manufacturing process, individual hammers or nipples installed on a firearm may transfer markings to caps that are similar to other firearms. When markings are not individualized to the extent necessary for identification, it is only possible to say that the cap displays class characteristics consistent with having been fired in a black powder firearm.

In one study, well-preserved percussion caps dating back 150 years were found to yield hammer face and nipple marks that are unique and reproducible, thus expanding our capability to identify minimum numbers of firearms used at an event. Analysis of modern fired percussion caps from 11 different antique and reproduction firearms used as a validation study confirms our ability to identify individual characteristics that define a specific firearm used in an event.[14] Percussion cap analysis demonstrates that these seemingly inconsequential artifacts are a dataset that can be measured, sorted, and studied microscopically and will yield information that can expand our knowledge about an event and the role that firearms played in creating the event under study.

SMALL-ARMS CARTRIDGE CASES

Aside from determining model and brand of firearms at a site, cartridge cases hold other information valuable to the archaeologist. Headstamps on cartridge case bases are the most commonly used temporal indicator.[15] In addition to the headstamp, the primer type, case composition (brass, copper, tinned, rubber, etc.), caliber, and case type (rimmed, semi-rimmed, rimless, rebated, or belted) provide information on the date of that cartridge case's introduction. Each model has a date of introduction, and in most cases, a date for the cessation of manufacture. Combining all this information can provide an archaeologist with some very restricted date ranges for the cartridges.

SMALL-ARMS BULLETS

Likewise bullets can provide some datable information. Like other diagnostic artifacts, some are more temporally sensitive than others. Bullet composition (lead, lead alloy, jacketed, etc.), number and type of cannelures, and shape have date ranges associated with their introduction and, in some situations, last date of manufacture. As was noted, firing pin impressions land and groove marks can identify a firearm type, brand, and model.

Bullets also contain other information depending on their preservation. An analyst can determine if the bullet was cast in a mold or pressed (also sometimes called swaging) in a machine. The introduction of bullet pressing machines is known, occurring in the 1850s with the rise of the industrial revolution. The presence of pressed bullets can serve as a rough dating criteria in some sites.

Lead bullets fired from a black powder firearm usually have one end or side, if a spherical ball, with a rough texture. This stippling effect is the direct result of powder burning behind the bullet during its initial travel down the barrel of the weapon. Likewise the nose of the bullet or other side of the spherical ball, if loaded with the aid of a ramrod, may have distinctive marks that can be associated with a firearm type.[16] For example, the loading mark left by a U.S. Model 1816 "button-tip" ramrod is decidedly different from the mark left by a Model 1855 or 1861 "tulip-shaped" ramrod.

Fired and impacted bullets are often deformed in the process of impact. Conical bullets are more amenable to impact analysis than spherical balls, but the analysis can be applied in some cases to both types. Spin stabilized conical bullets strike their target nose first. Depending on the hardness of the object struck a conical bullet will deform by expanding outward from the nose, the so-called mushroom effect. The amount of nose deformation or mushrooming is a rough indicator of the bullet's velocity on impact, and can be used to aid a rough approximation of range in some situations.

Bullets that were deflected in flight, or are in yaw (not spin stabilized), will strike an object at any number of angles off the bullet centerline. The resulting impact deformation can tell an examiner something of the bullet's stability when it struck and the nature of its yaw. Bullets in yaw can have impact scars ranging from flattened on one side to slight basal deformation, or simple scarring on one side, but all are witness to whether the bullet was tumbling, in slight yaw, or near its terminal velocity. Bullets in yaw reflect an improper sized bullet, a dirty gun barrel, or the fact the bullet hit an intervening object prior to coming to rest.

Bullet impact scars can remain on very hard surfaces such as stone, brick, and other masonry for literally hundreds of years. The direction of impact and thus, the general direction from which the firearm was fired, can be determined using criminalists' shooting scene reconstruction techniques. Even after 100 or more years, it may be possible to lift traces of the lead bullet from an impact scar. The technique requires training to make the lift, but it is possible to do in the field with relatively simple materials.

The trace lead from a lift, or for that matter a bullet, can be analyzed to determine its source and association with other bullets from the site in some cases. Chemical and spectrographic analyses can determine the lead source from any number of mines. A technique used in law enforcement criminal investigations, and employing a variety of spectrographic analyses, identifies trace elements in bullet composition which allow comparisons between bullets to ascertain if they have a different origin or if a common source is indicated. While this level of finite analysis is probably not necessary on many sites, the fact that it can be done is worth knowing as some research questions could be answered using these examination procedures.

ARTILLERY PROJECTILES

Like small-arms bullets and cartridge cases, artillery projectiles and cartridge cases are amenable to firearms identification analysis. Artillery projectiles fired from guns or mortars, whether spherical or conical, are manufactured of iron or steel, and sometimes, in expedient situations, other materials like copper. Standard metallurgical analyses can yield information regarding the iron, steel, or copper, or other base metal and trace element content of a projectile or projectile fragment that may aid in identifying its origin, such as Mexican or American for the Mexican–American War, or Russian or British or Turkish for the Crimean War, and so on Utilizing fracture mechanics in studying artillery fragments, the physical properties involved in their manufacture and use such as failure analysis can be determined.

Resistance offered by a shell (including case shot) to the force of the powder increases with side thickness. When a shell bursts while stationary, the pieces are dispersed in almost every direction with more or less force according to the resistance of the sides. The number of fragments is directly related to the brittleness of the material.[17] Theoretical and experimental evidence shows that the least amount of resistance and crack initiation propagates through the fuse ring. If the projectile is in motion, the fragments projected forward will continue with an increase in velocity and those in the rear with a decrease in velocity. If the shell is moving very slowly, the fragment velocity may be overcome for the rear parts of the explosion and the pieces may drop to the ground or be thrown backward.

Most artillery projectiles manufactured prior to the beginning of the twentieth century were constructed of gray cast iron. All gray irons fail in a brittle manner. Fracture occurs along the lamellar graphite plates, exhibiting a "gray" fracture surface. The compressive strength of gray cast iron is roughly three to four times its tensile strength. Fracture occurs at the maximum compressive load.[18] Think of a cannon ball as a thick-walled spherical pressure vessel and the failure as an impact overload exceeding the compressive strength. It appears that the mode of failure can be attributed to thermal stress overload wherein the stress from a thermal change (the charge) demands a specific change of dimension. As the gray cast iron cannot expand plastically, the yield strength is exceeded, causing fracture. Spherical shell and case shot fracture in a predictable manner, usually large trapezoidal fragments. Individual fragments can be analyzed to determine if pieces have the same iron and trace element content, thus suggesting they are from either the same projectile or same lot of projectile manufacturing. Gray cast iron conical projectiles exhibit similar fracture patterns and are amenable to similar analyses as are gray cast iron hand grenades.

Steel bodied conical artillery projectiles have more advanced metallurgical theory behind their manufacture. Depending on the era of production, steel artillery projectiles are designed to burst into long, thin splinter-like fragments that may be razor sharp and are intended to make horrific wounds. The transition from gray cast iron projectiles to steel based projectiles occurred during World War I and has seen a number of technological advances since. Steel bodied hand grenades likewise saw similar and concomitant development as to the lethality of the fragments. The presence of iron or iron and steel projectile fragments in a site can aid in dating the site or feature since the introduction of artillery shell types is reasonably well documented.

It is also possible to use spatial attributes to associate fired artillery fragments with specific combatants or even in some cases to specific artillery batteries, by employing the historic record and documentary resources. Another analytical tool uses differences in standardization and formalization to better understand production practices, well developed or exhibiting shortages, among the home cultures that supplied the combatants.[19] In doing so, it provides an example of how battlefield assemblages may be studied in a more anthropological way to assess the logistic and supply networks available to combatant groups, or how stressed the home culture was to provide war materials to the front, such as the greater the diversity in war materials the less able the supply base to provide adequate munitions or greater deviation from the norm in desired quality of artillery projectiles suggesting reliance on dispersed and cottage industries to produce munitions among other possibilities.

ARTILLERY AND MORTAR CRATER ANALYSIS

In some battlefield situations where conical artillery projectiles were fired, there may be impact craters remaining in the archaeological record. If the crater is reasonably well preserved it may be possible to apply a field of military field analysis called crater analysis.[20] A well-preserved impact crater, whether still observable on the surface or a filled-in crater (see figure on page 116), may allow the researcher to determine the approximate bearing from which the projectile originated, determine the type, whether it is an artillery round or a mortar round, potentially determine the caliber of the weapon, and possibly the shell or bomb type.

If shell fragments and/or fuse parts are present in the crater, then it is possible to determine the shell or bomb type and caliber. Measuring the radius of a shell or bomb fragment, compared against a template, will give the approximate caliber. Distinctive body features, such as fins, driving bands, fuse types, and so on may aid in identifying the shell or bomb type.

Crater shape provides some indication of the type of projectile fired (see figure). Shell craters are slightly elliptical in shape, often with two wing-like grooves in the soil on either side of the main crater. The crater often has a smaller and deeper depression, or an undercut within the larger crater. Since a shell strikes the ground at a relatively shallow angle, then bursts, the shell creates a depression. The deeper depression or undercut often found in the

A World War I artillery impact crater at Crossroads near Ieper, Belgium.

center is created by the impact explosion. Shell splinters are thrown to the sides creating the wing-like extension grooves; if the shell was nose fused, then the fuse usually is thrown forward and creates a small trench or track. The wings are usually at a slight acute angle relative to the fuse track. The wings and fuse track define the reverse angle of the gun's orientation.

Mortars are fired at a high angle, are relatively short range devices, and create a high angle trajectory that causes the mortar bomb to strike at a steep angle. The resultant crater usually has the farthest edge away from the weapon undercut and the mortar fuse is often buried in the slightly forward deeper undercut in the crater. The crater edge opposite the fuse usually shows a ragged, almost serrated, series of grooves or trenches. These trenches are a result of splinters from the bomb fragmentation and they point in the direction of the mortar tube's location.

SUMMARY AND CONCLUSIONS

Multidisciplinary studies are not new to archaeology, and the application of firearms identification to archaeology is another example of the utility of multidisciplinary interaction. Archaeologists can expect modern firearms identification techniques to produce additional data for the dating of sites, details

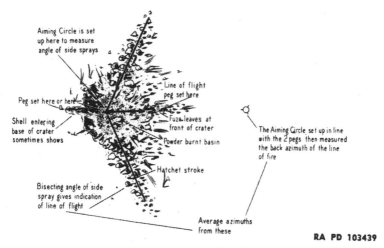

RA PD 103439

Figure 4—Typical Shell Crater, FQ (Small Angle of Fall)

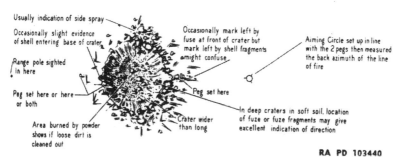

RA PD 103440

Figure 5—Typical Shell Crater, FQ (Larger Angle of Fall)

Method of artillery crater analysis as portrayed in a World War II manual and still used today. (1945 identification of Japanese shells and shell fragments; location of enemy batteries. War Department Technical Manual TM E9-1901. Washington, DC)

concerning the weapon types utilized and the minimum number of firearms present, and identifying patterns of firearms utilization at a site. One of the more desirable and unique aspects of firearms identification is its ability to pinpoint individual patterns or behavior related to firearms use. There are very few techniques that enable the archaeologist to identify and study the individual in the context of a site. While firearms identification cannot answer all the details of individual idiosyncratic behavior, it does bring us closer to the ability to study specific individual behavioral patterns, and that is an opportunity seldom achieved in most archaeological studies.

NOTES

1. Firearms identification concepts and methods are described by Harris 1980, Hatcher, Jury, and Weller 1977, and Heard 1997.
2. Berg 1977:535–537.
3. Doughtery 1969.
4. Gunther and Gunther 1935.
5. The basic descriptions of class and individual characteristics are taken from Wilhelm 1980:202–215.
6. Lucas 1985.
7. Dickens 2003, Bailey 2003, Gooding 1966a.
8. Gooding 2004, Gooding 1974, Anon. 1869:90, and Coates and Thomas 1990.
9. Gooding 1966b, 1975.
10. Whittemore and Heath 1878:20–22, Benton 1867:350, Gooding 1966a, Thomas 2003.
11. Herskovitz 1978, Hunt 2003, Jensen 1998, Mainfort 1980, Oakes 1990, Reynolds 1983, Ziegler 2001. See also Hunt 1989.
12. Baker and Harrison 1986. See Barnes 1980 for modern percussion cap measurements.
13. Coggins 1990.
14. Weber and Scott, in press.
15. White and Munhall 1977, Datig 1956, 1958, 1967.
16. Bishop 1995:310–313.
17. Gibbon 1860:163, 250.
18. Davis 1996:4, Angus 1976:46.
19. Drexler 2004.
20. War Department 1945, United Nations 2003.

REFERENCES CITED

Angus, H. T. 1976. *Cast Iron: Physical and Engineering Properties.* Butterworths, London.

Anonymous. 1869. Joshua Shaw, Artist and Inventor, The Early History of the Copper Percussion Cap. *Scientific American* 21(6):90.

Bailey, D. W. 2003. Who Invented the Percussion Cap? Joseph Egg, Joseph Manton and the Board of Ordnance Trials of 1820. *Man at Arms* 25(4):41–45.

Baker, T. Lindsey, and Billy R. Harrison. 1986. *Adobe Walls: The History and Archeology of the 1875 Trading Post.* Texas A&M University Press, College Station.

Barnes, Frank C. 1980. *Cartridges of the World 4th Edition.* DBI Books, Northbrook, IL.

Benton, J. G. 1867. *Course of Instruction in Ordnance and Gunnery.* D. Van Nostrand, New York.

Berg, Stanton O. 1977. The Forensic Ballistic Laboratory. In C. G. Tedeschi, William G. Eckert, and Luke G. Tedeschi, *Forensic Medicine Volume I Mechanical Trauma*, 527–569. W. B. Saunders Company, Philadelphia.

Bishop, Eugene E. 1995. Tool Mark Identification on a Black Powder Revolver. *Association of Firearms and Toolmark Examiners Journal* 27(4):310–313.

Coates, Earl J., and Dean S. Thomas. 1990. *An Introduction to Civil War Small Arms*. Thomas Publications, Gettysburg, PA.

Coggins, Jack. 1990. *Arms and Equipment of the Civil War*. Barnes & Noble, New York.

Datig, Fred A. 1956. *Cartridges for Collectors, Volume I*. Borden Publishing, Los Angeles, CA.

Datig, Fred A. 1958. *Cartridges for Collectors, Volume II*. Borden Publishing, Los Angeles, CA.

Datig, Fred A. 1967. *Cartridges for Collectors, Volume III*. Borden Publishing, Los Angeles, CA.

Davis, J. R. (ed.). 1996. *ASM Specialty Handbook: Cast Irons*. ASM International, Materials Park, OH.

Dickens, B. 2003. Forsyth & Co.: An Unrecorded Ignition System. *Man at Arms* 25(6):19–24.

Dougherty, Paul M. 1969. Report on Two Early United States Firearms Identification Cases. *Journal of Forensic Sciences* 14(4):453–59.

Drexler, Carl G. 2004. Identifying Culturally-Based Variability in Artillery Ammunition Fragments Recovered from the Battlefield of Pea Ridge, Arkansas. Master's Thesis, Department of Anthropology and Geography, University of Nebraska, Lincoln.

Gibbon, John. 1860. *The Artillerist's Manual*. Reprint by Benchmark Publishing Company Inc., Glendale.

Gooding, S. James. 1966a. The Top-Hat Cap. *The Canadian Journal of Arms Collecting* 4(1): 26 27.

Gooding, S. James. 1966b. The Percussion Primer. *The Canadian Journal of Arms Collecting* 4(4): 127–149.

Gooding, S. James. 1974. The Development of Percussion Primers. *The Canadian Journal of Arms Collecting* 12(4):283–297.

Gooding, S. James. 1975. Pellets, Tubes, and Caps: The Percussion Primer, Part II. *The Canadian Journal of Arms Collecting* 13(1):107–125.

Gooding, S. James. 2004. Joshua Shaw—Landscape Artist...Con Artist? Or Inventor of the Percussion Cap? *Man at Arms* 26(2):34–43.

Gunther, Jack Disbrow, and Charles O. Gunther. 1935. *The Identification of Firearms*. John Wiley and Sons, London.

Hall, Albert. 1900. The Missile and the Weapon. *Buffalo Medical Journal* (June):37–49.

Harris, C. E. 1980. Sherlock Holmes Would Be Impressed. *American Rifleman* 128(5):36–39, 82.

Hatcher, Julian, Frank J. Jury, and Jac Weller. 1977. *Firearms Investigation, Identification and Evidence*. Stackpole Books, Harrisburg, PA.

Heard, Brian. 1997. *Handbook of Firearms and Ballistics: Examining and Interpreting Forensic Evidence*. John Wiley Sons, New York.

Herskovitz, Robert M. 1978. Fort Bowie material culture. *Anthropological Papers of the University of Arizona Number 31*.

Hunt, William J. Jr. 1989. Firearms and the Upper Missouri Fur Trade Frontier: Weapons and Related Materials from Fort Union Trading Post National Historic

Site (23 WI 17), North Dakota. Ph.D. Dissertation, Department of American Civilization, University of Pennsylvania.

Hunt, William J. Jr. 2003. Archaeological Investigations at Fort Clark State Historic Site, North Dakota: 1973–2003, Studies at the Fort Clark and Primeau Trading Posts. PaleoCultural Research Group, Flagstaff, AZ.

Jensen, Richard E. 1998. The Fontenelle & Cabanne Trading Posts: The History and Archeology of Two Missouri River Sites: 1822–1838. Publications in Anthropology, No. 11, Nebraska State Historical Society, Lincoln.

Lucas, A. 1985. Forensic Chemistry and Scientific Criminal Investigation. *Association of Firearms and Tool Mark Examiners Journal* 17(4):57–90.

Mainfort, Robert C., Jr. 1980 Archaeological Investigations at Fort Pillow State Historic Area: 1976–1978. Division of Archaeology, Tennessee Department of Conservation.

Oakes, Yvonne R. 1990. The Glorieta Burials: Report to the Board of Regents Museum of New Mexico. Office of Archaeological Studies, Museum of New Mexico, Santa Fe.

Reynolds, John D. 1983. Archeological Investigations at Old Fort Scott, 14BO302, Fort Scott, Kansas 1968–1972. National Park Service, Midwest Region, Omaha.

Thomas, Dean S. 2003. *Round Ball to Rimfire: A History of Civil War Small Arms Ammunition, Part Three, Federal Pistols, Revolvers, and Miscellaneous Essays.* Thomas Publications, Gettysburg, PA.

United Nations. 2003. Crater Analysis. School for Peace Support Operations Training Manual, New York.

War Department. 1945. Identification of Japanese Shells and Shell Fragments; Location of Enemy Batteries. War Department Technical Manual TM E9-1901. Washington, DC.

Weber, Kent L., and Douglas D. Scott. 2006. Applying Firearms Identification Procedures in the Analysis of Percussion Caps. *Journal of the Association of Firearms and Toolmark Examiners* 37(1):34–44.

White, Henry P., and Burton D. Munhall. 1977. *Cartridge Headstamp Guide.* H. P. White Laboratory, Street, MD.

Whittemore, James M., and F. Heath. 1878. Ordnance Memoranda, No. 21: Ammunition, Fuses, Primers, Military Pyrotechny, etc. Ordnance Board, U.S. Army, Government Printing Office, Washington, DC.

Wilhelm, Russell M. 1980. General Considerations of Firearms Identification and Ballistics. In Werner U. Spitz and Russell S. Fisher, *Medicolegal Investigation of Death*, 202–215. Charles C. Thomas, Springfield, IL.

Ziegler, Robert J. 2001. Historical Archaeology at Locality 6 of Fort Ellsworth Site (14WE26), Kanopolis Lake, Ellsworth County, Kansas. U.S. Corps of Engineers, Kansas City District, Kansas City, MO.

Total Roman Defeat at the Battle of Varus (9 AD)

Susanne Wilbers-Rost

HISTORY OF RESEARCH

Five hundred years ago written accounts by Roman historian Tacitus that told about the so-called "Battle of the Teutoburg Forest," or "Battle of Varus," between Germans and Romans in 9 AD, were found in the northern Germany monastery of Corvey. Since then, many people have tried to find the battle-field where three Roman legions were destroyed by German tribes. Most searchers were unsuccessful because Tacitus (Annales I 59 62), as well as Velleius Paterculus (2, 117–119) or Cassius Dio (56, 18–23), described the situation differently and were not quite exact. Therefore more than 700 theories concerning the battlefield were developed. Theodor Mommsen, a special-ist on Roman history, had the right idea as we know today. In the 1880s, Mommsen thought that the hundreds of Roman silver and gold coins found by farmers on their fields north of Osnabrück indicated the battle's site.[1] Since there were no remains of military equipment, not many people believed Mommsen.

It took about 100 years until more details were discovered—not by pur-poseful research, but by an unexpected discovery. An amateur archaeologist, British Major Tony Clunn, found a hoard of Roman silver coins.[2] During a follow-up metal detector field survey by the Osnabrück Museum, pieces of military equipment were found as well. At that time in 1987/1988, no one thought the battlefield had been discovered; we had the impression that these few Roman equipment fragments had been lost, perhaps by Roman soldiers or merchants, who passed through the area at the time of the battle. In 1989, archaeological excavations started on one interesting site, the field "Oberesch." Apart from many Roman finds, a wall was excavated, and ini-tially it was thought to be part of a Roman fort. After some months, however, we realized that most of the finds lay in front of the wall, not behind it. Together with the nearly complete lack of Roman pottery, the deduction was possible that all the artifacts, coins, military pieces, and the wall itself,

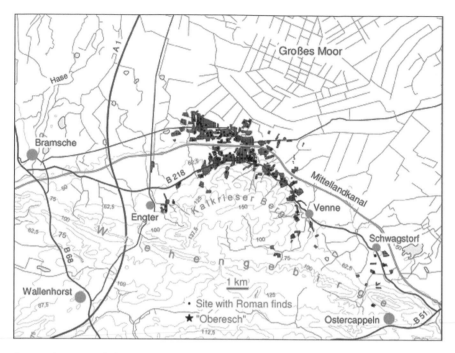

Research area of the "Kalkriese-Project" with surveyed fields, sites with Roman finds, and the field "Oberesch." (Museum und Park Kalkriese)

showed that Romans had been attacked by Germans from on top of the wall and that they had obviously been beaten. In combination with field research in surrounding areas, the idea that the site of the Battle of Varus was now located was one conclusion of these excavations. Other sites with Roman finds indicated that engagements must have taken place in an area of more than 50 km^2 (see figure). Coins of the time before 10 AD and copper coins with countermark VAR of Publius Quinctilius Varus helped date this event to 9 AD.[3]

TOPOGRAPHICAL SITUATION AND HISTORICAL BACKGROUND

The "Oberesch" wall was apparently built by Germans who had obviously planned this ambush perfectly. It was constructed at the narrowest place between the Kalkriese Hill, a part of the Wiehengebirge, and the Great Bog, a few kilometers to the north. Between hill and bog, the land was wet, sandy, and nearly impassable. The topography worked like a fish trap, and when the Romans arrived, coming from the east, perhaps from a summer camp on the Weser as Roman historians reported, they had no chance to fight in a normal formation or to flee once the German attacks began. Two thousand years ago, the land was occupied by Germans in single farmsteads or very small villages.[4] Paleobotanical analysis indicates that there was a wood on the hill, but it was a cultivated forest, not a natural growth.[5] Near the farms, there were fields; small roads connected the settlements. The roads were not comparable to Roman roads, so the legions of Varus would have had difficulties passing through this area even without being attacked.

Until Varus started to integrate northern Germany into the Roman Empire, Romans had not settled east of the Rhine. The nearest Roman camps, at the rivers Lippe and Rhine, were about 100 km to the south and southwest and too far to get help in case of a fight. Therefore, the place for the ambush was tactically well chosen by the Germans. The German leader was Arminius, a young nobleman, who had been educated by the Romans and had led Germanic auxiliaries in the Roman army. He was well prepared because he knew the strong and the weak points of the Roman army as well as the northern German landscape. We do not know how many Germans were involved in preparing the battlefield and the battle itself. The local native population was not enough, and we have to presume that soldiers from other Germanic tribes helped.

THE WALL

Excavations of the last 15 years, together with botanical and soil analyses, revealed many details of the wall construction that were not expected at the beginning of research (see figures on page 124).[6] After two years of excavation, we thought the wall was shaped as a semicircle. Later we saw that the form was much more complex; the wall bent several times, with salient and rentrant angles similar to a fort's bastions. It had a length of about 400 m, parallel to the hillside. This shape was advantageous for the Germans: there was room for more soldiers on top of such a wall than on a straight line. The Germans could attack Roman legionaries from more than one side if the Romans tried to assault the wall.

Among others, these observations led to a conclusion that the Germans had built the wall some time before the Romans arrived. Other details show that the wall was built in a very short time, perhaps only one or two weeks, before the legions came. Different materials were used for the wall: in the western part, grass sods were taken from a deserted pre-Roman Iron Age settlement just in front of the wall. The material of the eastern half consisted of more sand. The archaeological interpretations were proved by soil scientists who analyzed samples collected during excavation. At the western end of the wall, chalk stones stabilized the wall where sand or grass sods were not enough. All the materials were taken from very nearby. It seems as if different groups worked together in a very pragmatic way. The rampart was

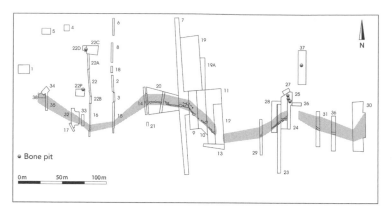

Excavated trenches, wall with drainage ditch, and bone pits at the "Oberesch."
(Museum und Park Kalkriese)

probably sufficient for a short time, but was not stable for long-term use. On one side, part of the wall was strengthened by a palisade, probably to protect the most prominent part against the attacks. Many narrow gates through the wall allowed the Germans to sally from cover and engage the Romans in front of the wall, then to retreat into the wall's shelter if pressed too hard. The gates and the shape of the wall demonstrate that the structure is a

Rest of the wall and v-shaped drainage ditch under a thick layer of "Plaggenesch"
during the excavation. (Museum und Park Kalkriese)

Germanic construction, not Roman. The Romans would have built a closed fortification to be secure when they were in enemy territory.

Only in one short section was there a ditch in front of the wall. This provided sand for the wall's construction. In different parts, long narrow pits or ditches were discovered behind the wall; they apparently served to prevent water, which could not seep through the impermeable loam, from washing away the wall before the Roman troops arrived. The Germans seemingly realized the necessity of the drainage after they had nearly finished the wall as field observations show; they had to reduce the wall on the inner side to dig the ditch. This caused instability, and during the battle this wall section may have been destroyed, a conclusion drawn from the hundreds of Roman finds concentrated in a small zone in front of the wall. Drainage was restricted to a wall section that was clearly in danger of being destroyed by water, showing that the Germans did only what was absolutely necessary. The Germans also chose a type of flat sandridge to put the wall on with as little expenditure as possible. These details show that the wall could be built in a short time; nevertheless, it was very effective for attacking the Roman legions that went past.

VEGETATION

The investigations and botanical analysis changed our concept of the landscape and vegetation around the wall. The western zone in front of the rampart was open since a former pre-Roman Iron Age settlement may have been used as a pasture. The eastern part, however, must have had different vegetation. The excavation results, soil borings, and analysis by soil scientists provided a picture of the surface, indicating the area in front of the eastern wall had an uneven relief with wet hollows; hints of prehistoric settlement were very rare. Here we suppose were more trees or bushes, but not pasture or open fields. Surface and vegetation must have caused problems for the Romans walking through or trying to fight. Differences in the vegetation also caused different possibilities for the later discovery of objects during post-battle plundering. Dense vegetation might have hidden more objects than open landscape. Therefore, more finds do not necessarily mean more intensive fights.

ARTIFACTS

More than 4,000 iron and bronze artifacts were unearthed on the "Oberesch," in addition to about 400 silver and copper coins. Since these artifact descriptions are published,[7] I will only give a short summary. Most items are only very small fragments, and without a metal detector we would hardly find them; nevertheless, they show the complete equipment of a Roman legion. Besides, we get unique information about Roman legions on the march in Augustan times.

We believe that the large number of objects belonging to fighting units and baggage show that many Roman soldiers must have taken part in the actions. We found fragments of swords, daggers, pila, spears, and lances (see figure), even catapult bolt points, shield bosses, harnesses, medical instruments, tools, personal equipment, pieces of horses equipment. Many items, especially edgings from shields, exhibit damage. They were not only torn from the original artifact's organic material, such as wood or leather, but were then purposely folded, perhaps to carry them away more easily after post-battle plundering.

The distribution of finds on the "Oberesch" is not homogeneous (compare Rost in this volume). Many pieces are from immediately in front of the wall; among them are the bigger finds, including the famous face mask of a Roman helmet, a pioneer's axe, and tools. This concentration resulted from the wall's destruction during the battle and soon after. A few finds lay in the drainage ditch behind the rampart. Some may have been lost there during the fight, but concentrations near the gates may possibly have been caused by Germans plundering the battlefield and trying to hide the booty behind the wall before distributing it.

Iron weapons (lance-head, lance shoe, catapult bolts). (Christian Grovermann for Museum und Park Kalkriese)

BONES

Another category of battlefield finds that is important for interpreting what happened during and after the battle are human and animal bones. Because the sand in the subsoil usually does not preserve bones very long, we did not expect many bones when beginning the research. Therefore, we were quite surprised when we found half a skeleton of a Roman mule with many metal harness pieces.[8] It had died just in front of the wall and must have been covered with material from the wall very quickly. If this had not happened, Germans would have taken the metal, including pendants, an iron chain, and a bronze bell, while the bones would not have remained in anatomical position. Preservation of a nearly complete mule skeleton with iron bit and a small bell at the neck can be explained the same way. Wild animals would have torn up the dead mules and scattered the bones over a larger area. This indicates that the wall was partly destroyed during the battle or a short time after. This should not be surprising if one considers the short term and weak construction. These features and single finds of animal bones which zoologists identified as only mules and horses—there are no bones from remains of meals—confirm what metal finds tell us; the Romans were here with their baggage.

Isotope analyses of the mules' teeth may provide another chance to learn some battle details. Archaeozoologists try to determine the time of the death and the region where animals came from. This research is somewhat difficult because comparative material is rare, but we already know that the mules died in late summer or early autumn. The time of death confirms research on plant remains by botanists that demonstrates some plants in the bell worn by a mule were cut in late summer.[9] Another experiment was made by soil scientists; using phosphate analyses, they try finding spots where bodies once lay. It looks as though this may be possible in some places, even when there are no bone fragments left.

During the last years of excavations, we did not only find bones on the old ground surface. We also have six pits where bones of men, mules, and horses were deposed (see figure).[10] The interment was not done immediately after the battle. Since only disarticulated bone fragments were found, one must conclude that some time passed until the bodies were buried. Flesh and sinews had already disappeared completely, and specialists for zoology and anthropology think that the bones had been lying on the surface for 2 to 10 years before burial. These pits are mass graves because all of them contain remains of more than one individual. Human bones, of which some exhibit damage from swords, were mixed with bones of horses and mules; among them were Roman artifacts comparable to those we found on the surface. Some human bones, especially skulls, show careful treatment during the interment. We think that they were buried by Roman troops under the leadership of Germanicus who visited the battlefield six years later (Tacitus Annales I, 62).

Bone pit with fragments of animal and human bones. In the center of the pit is a human skull. (Museum und Park Kalkriese)

Nobody expected such mass graves on the Varus battlefield, because Tacitus described construction of a grave mound. No traces of a mound have been located yet; maybe there was one somewhere in the larger area as a symbol for the whole burial. The bones in the pits, however, clearly show that the bodies of fallen soldiers and animals were left on the battlefield for some time. The Germans plundered them, but they did not bury them. Burial was done some years after most bones were destroyed naturally, by weather and animals, not by burning the bodies as there are no traces of charcoal. For interpreting the battlefield remains, this means that at least two post-battle human activities manipulated the material: plundering and burial.

AGRICULTURE ON THE "OBERESCH" IN EARLIER TIMES

Together with soil scientists we try to get information about the use of the "Oberesch" after the battle. Traces of settlements were not found. More than 1,000 years later, farmers put grass sods as a natural fertilization on the fields.[11] This method, the so-called "Esch" or "Plaggenesch," was used for several hundred years and it probably helped preserve not only the Roman finds but also rampart remnants. Without the "Esch," the plough would have destroyed the remaining wall and many finds would be more fragmentary than they are now. Different kinds of agricultural techniques applied in the area of the battlefield influenced the preservation of finds differently. Though the "Esch" helps archaeological investigations, it causes difficulties because modern survey techniques such as aerial photography or magnetic measurements can seldom be used to support the research.

THE BATTLE AREA

In the beginning, the "Oberesch" was just one place among the sites we discovered during the initial investigation. When excavations started, nobody thought that this place would become the most important site. We did not imagine that the large number of artifacts, the wall, and the mass graves would be the exception in the Battle of Varus area. The field survey continued all the time, and many more sites are now known.[12] None of them, however, compare with the "Oberesch." More than 1,000 coins were found, but the numerous pieces of military equipment, some 400 items, are much less than on the "Oberesch." We have to analyze the differing quality of finds at the different places in the battle zone.

Though excavations were made at other sites, no structures comparable to the wall or other features that might be connected with the battle were found. Besides, there are no other bone fragments or bone pits. This means that the "Oberesch" is not only a very important site, but perhaps the main fighting place. Such a special function is not surprising; the wall was built at the narrowest place where all Romans had to pass when they marched from east to west.

Other sites in the area of more than 50 km^2 demonstrate that the battle did not take place only on the "Oberesch," and that it must have lasted for more than one day. Germans must have attacked the long column of Roman troops at different places and different times. It is possible that they hid in the woods or behind a brush barrier that left no archaeological traces. One aspect, however, seems to be certain after 15 years of research: the number of Romans must have been fewer than was expected earlier. The written sources mention three legions, cavalry, and auxiliaries that were involved in the battle. Theoretically this could mean about 20,000 persons. This large number of people on the Roman side, however, seems too many. Maybe only about 10,000 Romans took part in this engagement. Others may have stayed in the winter camps. Besides, there would have been great logistical problems for the Roman army to get enough rations for men and animals as they moved through this thinly settled Germanic territory.

Finally, it should be mentioned that Roman items with signs of processing and melting drops were found at contemporary native settlements sites in the battle area. They show that the battlefield was plundered and that Germans living nearby used at least a small part of the war booty to make products of their own.

ARCHAEOLOGY AND WRITTEN SOURCES

The information we got from Roman written sources did not really help identify the battle of the Teutoburg Forest site. The results obtained from the archaeological investigations now show a picture which differs in some parts from what one would have expected whilst interpreting the ancient descriptions. Roman historians, for example, did not write that the Germans built a wall to ambush the troops of Varus; they only mention walls of Roman camps, one of them seemingly built by the remaining, diminished Roman legions. Perhaps the new archaeological sources allow us a modified interpretation of the written sources today.

Further reflections are possible if the bone pits can actually be connected with the burial ceremony of Germanicus in 15 AD.[13] Those who buried the dead soldiers six years after the battle must have seen the wall. It is only a short distance from the pits; in 15 AD it was without a doubt visible, though partly demolished. Could this rampart that, according to the archaeological interpretation, was built by Germans, be identical with the fortification which the Roman sources claim, by mistake, was the camp of Varus's legions? Could the wall on the "Oberesch" be the structure described by Tacitus as a flat wall with a shallow ditch, perhaps constructed as a camp for the night by the rest of the three legions of Varus during the battle? Though this is still a thesis, it helps understand how archaeology can augment the interpretation of ancient written sources.

PLANS FOR THE FUTURE

Our plans for the following years are, if we get money to continue our work, to find out more about what happened on the "Oberesch," and on other sites in the surrounding countryside. Excavations, natural sciences, and settlement archaeology will be necessary to get a picture of the battle's landscape, as well as the settlement patterns that were responsible for the Roman march route and the battle's course.

One important approach for understanding the battle's events will be the theoretical analysis of finds and their distribution. The first ideas were described in the chapter by Achim Rost in this volume.

For helping me with the translation of my text I want to thank Ingrid Recker, Osnabrück, and Lawrence Babits, Greenville, NC.

NOTES

1. Mommsen 1885.
2. Clunn 1999, Schlüter 1999.
3. Berger 1996, Chantraine 2002.
4. Rost and Wilbers-Rost 1992.

5. Dieckmann 1998:111–113.
6. Wilbers-Rost 2003.
7. Franzius 1996, Schlüter 1999, Wells 2003.
8. Rost and Wilbers-Rost 1993.
9. Dieckmann 1998:110.
10 Wilbers-Rost 1999.
11 Lienemann and Tolksdort-Lienemann 1992:335–339
12. Harnecker and Tolksdort-Lienemann 2004.
13. Rost 2003.

REFERENCES CITED

Berger, Frank. 1996. *Kalkriese 1. Die römischen Fundmünzen.* Römisch-Germanische Forschungen, Bd. 55, Mainz.

Chantraine, Heinrich. 2002. Varus oder Germanicus? Zu den Fundmünzen von Kalkriese. *Thetis* 9:81–93.

Clunn, Tony. 1999. *In Quest of the Lost Legions.* Minerva Press, London.

Dieckmann, Ursula. 1998. *Paläoökologische Untersuchungen zur Entwicklung von Natur- und Kulturlandschaft am Nordrand des Wiehengebirges.* Abhandlungen aus dem Westfälischen Museum für Naturkunde 60 (4), Münster.

Franzius, Georgia. 1996. Die Römischen Funde aus Kalkriese 1987–1995 und ihre Bedeutung für die Interpretation und Datierung militärischer Fundplätze der augusteischen Zeit im nordwesteuropäischen Raum. In Carol Van Driel-Murray (ed.), Roman Military Equipment: Experiment and Reality. Proceedings of the IXth International Roman Military Equipment Conference (Leiden, 15th–17th September 1994), Vol. 2. *Journal of Roman Military Equipment Studies 6*, pp. 69–88.

Harnecker, Joachim, and Eva Tolksdorf-Lienemann. 2004. Kalkriese 2 – Sondierungen in der Kalkrieser-Niewedder Senke, Mainz.

Lienemann, Jörg, and Eva Tolksdorf-Lienemann. 1992. Bodenkundliche Untersuchungen im Zusammenhang mit den Ausgrabungen auf dem Oberesch in Kalkriese, Stadt Bramsche, Landkreis Osnabrück. In W. Schlüter, Archäologische Zeugnisse zur Varusschlacht? Die Untersuchungen in der Kalkrieser-Niewedder Senke bei Osnabrück. *Germania*, 70(2):335–344.

Mommsen, Theodor. 1885. *Die Örtlichkeit der Varusschlacht.* Berlin.

Rost, Achim. 2003. Kalkriese – Archäologische Befunde und antike Schriftquellen. – *Archäologie in Niedersachsen*, 25–29.

Rost, Achim, and Susanne Wilbers-Rost. 1992. Die vorgeschichtliche Besiedlung am Kalkrieser Berg zwischen Engter und Schwagstorf. In W. Schlüter, Archäologische Zeugnisse zur Varusschlacht? Die Untersuchungen in der Kalkrieser-Niewedder Senke bei Osnabrück. *Germania* 70(2):344–349.

Rost, Achim, and Susanne Wilbers-Rost. 1993. Fragmente eines römischen Zugtieres mit Resten der Anschirrung. In W. Schlüter (ed.), Kalkriese – Römer im Osnabrücker Land. Archäologische Forschungen zur Varusschlacht, Bramsche, 199–209.

Schlüter, Wolfgang (ed.). 1993. Kalkriese – *Römer im Osnabrücker Land. Archäologische Forschungen zur Varusschlacht*, Bramsche.

Schlüter, Wolfgang. 1999. The Battle of the Teutoburg Forest: Archaeological Research at Kalkriese Near Osnabrück. In John Douglas Creighton and Roder John Anthony Willson (eds.), Roman Germany. Studies in Cultural Interaction. *Journal of Roman Archaeology, Supplementary Series No. 32*:125–159.

Wells, Peter. 2003. *The Battle that Stopped Rome*. W. W. Norton and Co., New York.

Wilbers-Rost, Susanne. 1992. Grabungsbefunde auf dem "Oberesch" in Kalkriese, Stadt Bramsche, Landkreis Osnabrück. In W. Schlüter, Archäologische Zeugnisse zur Varusschlacht? Die Untersuchungen in der Kalkrieser-Niewedder Senke bei Osnabrück. *Germania* 70(2):332–335.

Wilbers-Rost, Susanne. 1999. Die Ausgrabungen auf dem "Oberesch" in Kalkriese: Deponierungen von Menschen- und Tierknochen auf dem Schlachtfeld. In R. Wiegels, W. Schlüter (eds.), *Rom, Germanien und die Ausgrabungen von Kalkriese*. Akten des Internationalen Kongresses vom 2. bis 5. September 1996 an der Universität Osnabrück. Osnabrücker Forschungen zu Altertum und Antikerezeption, Bd. 1, 61–89.

Wilbers-Rost, Susanne. 2002. Kalkriese und die Varusschlacht – Archäologische Nachweise einer militärischen Auseinandersetzung zwischen Römern und Germanen. In P. Freeman (ed.), Limes XVIII. Proceedings of the XVIIIth International Congress of Roman Frontier Studies Held in Amman, Jordan (September 2000). *British Archaeological Reports. International Series 1084* (I):515–526.

Wilbers-Rost, Susanne. 2003. Der Hinterhalt gegen Varus. Zur Konstruktion und Funktion der germanischen Wallanlage auf dem "Oberesch" in Kalkriese. *Die Kunde N.F.* 54, 123–142.

Wilbers-Rost, Susanne. In press. *Kalkriese 3 – Ergebnisse archäologischer und naturwissenschaftlicher Untersuchungen auf dem "Oberesch" in Kalkriese.*

English Battlefields 991–1685: A Review of Problems and Potentials

Glenn Foard

THIS CHAPTER REVIEWS the problems and potentials in the investigation of battles and battlefields across England over the last millennium, from the earliest apparently securely related battle, that of Maldon (Essex, 991), through to the last major field engagement, Sedgemoor (Somerset, 1685).

If one examines the period range of papers given in the past Fields of Conflict conferences, one finds a very heavy bias to the postmedieval and especially to the industrial era. This is mirrored in period distribution of papers at other conferences held in England, such as the battlefields session at the Institute of Field Archaeologists Conference in 2004 and the three National Army Museum conferences on battlefield archaeology in 2001–2003. It demonstrates the way in which the industrial period dominates battlefields research both in England and worldwide. This runs completely contrary to the chronological distribution of battles in England and shows the degree to which especially medieval and earlier battles are being largely ignored, with the notable exception of the late medieval battle of Towton (Yorkshire, 1461).[1] This chapter explores this far wider resource and considers the problems and potentials that we face if we are to deal effectively with the full chronological range of battlefields in England.

The methodology, which must be applicable across the full time span, can be defined under five main headings:

- Locating the battlefield
- Reconstructing its historic terrain on the day of the battle
- Characterizing the armies that fought there
- Using documentary evidence to position their preliminary maneuvers, initial deployments, and subsequent action within the reconstructed terrain
- Validating and refining the interpretation using the wholly independent evidence of battle archaeology

This requires the application of a range of evidence and techniques, each of which bring their own distinctive problems that also vary, sometimes dramatically, depending on where and when the battle was fought.

Location and Chronology

The general location of very few early battles is as clearly and specifically located as Bosworth (Leicestershire, 1485). Christopher Saxton, England's first great national cartographer, depicted the location of the Bosworth battlefield almost within living memory of the battle.[2] The battlefield appeared on his 1576 map of Leicestershire, published in his national Atlas, which was produced specifically for the Tudor government. Bosworth was the only battlefield identified in the Atlas and this was the battle which had brought the Tudors to the throne, so it would be highly unlikely that Saxton would have wrongly placed the action, especially given the consistently high level of accuracy of his work. Despite this and other almost irrefutable evidence, there has recently been a suggestion that the battle was actually fought some six miles to the west, near Atherstone.[3] It is a mark of the difficulty that exists in the location of historic battles that one of the best known and most important of English battles can be open to such dispute by reputable scholars. For lesser battles and especially those of an earlier period the problems are far greater.

Thus the first task of locating the battlefield is for most early battles the hurdle at which we fail. More than 100 documented battles as well as many lesser actions have been fought in England over the last two millennia, from the Roman Conquest of AD 43 through to the skirmishes of the Jacobite Risings and other minor engagements of the eighteenth century. Forty-three of the most securely located, best understood, and best preserved of these battlefields have been identified by English Heritage on their Register of Historic Battlefields.[4] While some were excluded from the Register because they were poorly preserved, many were omitted because their sites were too poorly understood to be able to define reasonable boundaries for conservation purposes. However, the greatest number of battles was excluded because their battlefields are wholly unlocated, with in some cases various alternative sites many miles apart being suggested for the same action. Almost all of the more than 70 battles and other actions from before 1066 are as yet unlocated. The resolution of such major problems of location, if possible at all, must await the effective application of a methodology for the investigation of the battlefields of the last millennium, most of which are at least located in general terms. Perhaps when we understand the archaeology of these battles we will then be able to tackle with more confidence the problem of those from before the Norman Conquest.

In order to effectively manage the resource for its research values it is essential to have a comprehensive record of all fields of conflict, including information on the scale and character of the action. Only then will it be possible to assess, with any confidence, a site's relative potential. Given the rarity of fields of conflict, compared to many other components of the historic environment, the resource can only be effectively assessed at a national scale.[5] The present analysis is based upon the Battlefields Trust's *UK Fields of Conflict* database.[6] Though as yet incomplete, with skirmishes and other lesser actions very inconsistently represented and sieges wholly absent, it provides the best starting point for an assessment of battlefields. In collaboration with Historic Scotland, the database is currently (winter 2004–2005) being enhanced for Scotland from secondary sources and enhancement for England is planned to follow.

Using the current dataset, broad trends can already be discerned. There is a fairly steep decline in the number of actions as one moves back in time from the seventeenth to the twelfth century, when numbers increase once more. The one exception is the sixteenth century where only a handful of battles are recorded. It would appear from the graph (see figure) that the Register provides a relatively representative selection of English battlefields in terms of their chronological spread, that is of course until one gets back to the eleventh century, when the problems of battlefield location really begin to dominate. The Register also gives a relatively good geographical spread in terms of the national distribution of located battles. The Registered battlefields may thus provide a reasonable sample with which to examine many of the problems of investigating battles over the last millennium and across the varied historic landscapes of England. However, the very reason of their Registration, that they are the best documented and located of our battlefields, and as a result the most intensively studied, means that they do not give us a fully representative view of the problems that must be faced in the study of

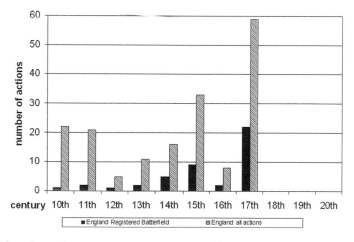

Graph of numbers of registered versus unregistered battlefields in England by century.

battlefields. Therefore it will be essential also to sample from other, poorly preserved and currently poorly located or unlocated battles, to assess their potential.

In any assessment we must also take account of the degree to which our chronological distribution of battles is skewed by the Wars of the Roses in the fifteenth century and the Civil Wars in the mid-seventeenth century. If we are to use battlefields as a major resource for the investigation of warfare in the UK over the last millennium and as an example of a wider tradition of warfare in Europe in that period, then it is important to pay particular attention to those periods where far fewer actions are recorded. Indeed it would be far more effective to sample from the whole of the UK in order to maximize the sample, especially for the less well represented periods, such as the sixteenth century.

Historic Terrain

Understanding the terrain of a battlefield as it was at the time of the action is critical to the understanding of any battle. It has long been known that the English landscape has been transformed a number of times and in very different ways in different regions over the last millennium or so. Despite this one typically finds that, even today, historic battles are discussed and mapped in relation to the modern landscape.

The realization that terrain is a key to the understanding of historic battles can be traced through battlefield studies over the last 300 years, right back to the contemporary military manuals that guided the commanders in the fighting of the actions themselves.[7] Hutton wrote in 1788: "By carefully comparing the writers, the field, and the traditions, I have attempted to remove some absurdities and place truth on firmer ground."[8] In this he was followed by many others, such as Brooke in 1857 in his study of battlefields of the fifteenth century: "the fields of battle, and the positions of the hostile armies, may in several instances, be clearly identified, after a perusal of the statements of the old chroniclers, and a comparison of their descriptions with the present aspect of the localities where the battles were fought."[9] Most students of battlefields in England over the last two centuries have had to independently rediscover this reality rather than follow in a clear tradition of battlefield study. This is because most of the really effective investigations were conducted by people who approached the subject incidentally, not from the subdiscipline of military history. The earliest examples include Scatcherd's study in the 1830s of Adwalton Moor (Yorkshire, 1643) and Fitzgerald's investigation of Naseby (Northamptonshire, 1645) in the 1840s.[10] In the case of Bosworth and Naseby, part of the landscape had only been transformed within living memory from open field to hedged enclosures and thus both Hutton and Fitzgerald were well aware of landscape change. Despite this realization by at least some antiquaries, most battles were largely interpreted in the light of the terrain of the antiquaries' own day.

This is where Twemlow's 1912 study of Blore Heath (Staffordshire, 1459) represents a significant departure, for he attempted to produce a map of the battlefield as it had been in the fifteenth century.[11] Burne, working in the late 1940s and 1950s understood the need for such reconstruction of historic terrain but lacked the expertise to achieve this.[12] Thanks to the work over the last 50 years within the English Landscape tradition, which developed out of the work of Hoskins in the 1940s and 1950s, we are now in a position to reconstruct historic landscapes to a very high standard of accuracy.[13] As a result we can see the inadequacies of Twemlow's work and the degree to which Burne's investigations were undermined by his lack of access to techniques of landscape study that we take for granted today. But we should still acknowledge the pioneering nature of their work.

Some of the shortcomings in battlefield studies can be explained by the way in which the study of the past has evolved over the last century or more. While in the eighteenth and nineteenth centuries antiquaries covered the full range of historical themes, in the later nineteenth and especially twentieth centuries the divergence of the disciplines of archaeology, military history, and historical geography have meant that advances in one field have not effectively fed through into the investigation of the other, at least as far as the study of historic battles is concerned.

Remarkably, the tradition of local historians and historical geographers stumbling upon a valuable application in battlefield studies for their specialist skills in historic landscape reconstruction continued in the second half of the twentieth century. For example, in the 1970s Pannett, while mapping the historic landscape of Warwickshire, realized the implications of his work for the interpretation of the battle of Edgehill (Warwickshire, 1642).[14] It was, however, only with the work of Newman in the late 1970s, in his study of Marston Moor (Yorkshire, 1644), that the next major step was taken.[15] Newman consciously built upon the important base provided by Burne, and wished to extend and develop Burne's method through a coherent approach to the problem of historic terrain. While work such as that by Fitzgerald and Pannett remained unpublished and inaccessible, even the well-known published work of Newman failed to lead to a coherent school of battlefield study.

The failures are best exemplified in the case of Bosworth, where in the 1970s Williams failed to apply the most basic principles of historic landscape reconstruction, with the result that key terrain features were placed where they could never have existed.[16] Again it was only when a local historian, Peter Foss, conducted careful work with key landscape and documentary sources, to establish the basic structure of the terrain as it was in the later fifteenth century, that the difficulties at Bosworth began to be resolved.[17] Yet neither the work of Newman nor Foss has managed to take center stage in the methodology of battlefield study, despite the major advances that it offered.

What seems to lie at the heart of the problem in battlefield studies in the UK is the lack of sufficient critical mass to be able to build, enhance, and

sustain a coherent methodology and body of expertise. The problem is compounded by the fact that effective integration of the techniques of different
disciplines is essential to battlefield studies, not just in the reconstruction of
the historic terrain but in all its other aspects. This remains the most important challenge for the current development of battlefield studies in the UK.
What is required is a secure cross-disciplinary base in both an academic and
a professional context, and an adequate level of work in battlefield research
and conservation to sustain it.

What then of the application of a methodology of historic terrain reconstruction right across the chronological range of our battles? The problem of
reconstructing a day in the life of a landscape is far from simple, even given
the major advances in the investigation of the English landscape that have
been achieved in the last half century. For the earliest battles in particular
one may find that even the most basic elements of physical geography have
been transformed. This is most clearly exhibited at Maldon (Essex, 991),
which is recorded in an epic poem composed within a short time of the battle.[18] The location of the battlefield and the accurate positioning of the events
within the landscape are dependent upon the way in which the two armies
were initially separated by a tidal stream in the Blackwater Estuary near the
burh at Maldon. This was a channel which was impassable at high tide yet
was narrow enough to enable a shouted exchange and where there was a cause-
way which joined the two sides at low tide. This and other related information on the topography of the battlefield led in the 1930s to the identification
of the battlefield as lying on the mainland immediately adjacent to Northey
Island, less than two miles to the east of the burh at Maldon. But objections
were made by various scholars that the channel separating the island from the
mainland is too wide at high tide to shout across. Work by Petty and Petty in
the 1970s, revised in 1993, demonstrated that the present character of the area
and width of the channel had been determined by rises in sea level in this
region of England over the last 1,000 years.[19] In the later tenth century the
channel had been much narrower than today. Also, while today it is flanked
by salt flats, at the time of the battle there had been solid land to the water's
edge. Their analysis provides a reconstruction of the physical geography
which enables the action to be played out as described in the famous contemporary poem *The Battle of Maldon*. This is a major step forward but, as with
all battles, such work on the terrain only provides a context. Whether this
was indeed the site of the battle and, if so, how the action fitted within the
terrain requires a quite separate study, particularly of our surviving battle
archaeology.

For most of the battles of the last millennium it is not naturally induced
changes but rather those resulting from exploitation of the landscape that
have to be investigated to recover the contemporary battlefield terrain. It
might be assumed that in such work there is a simple correlation between the
length of time that has passed since the battle and the difficulty of

reconstructing the battlefield terrain. In reality this is not the case. It depends to a considerable degree within which historic landscape zone within England the battlefield lay and thus the nature of that historic landscape and the chronology of its evolution. This is best demonstrated in the "central province" of planned open field landscapes and nucleated villages, identified by Roberts.[20] The landscape of the high medieval in the central province was largely an open one which had a high degree of stability for many centuries. In contrast, when enclosure began in earnest in the fifteenth century, gaining pace in the sixteenth century but not completed until the nineteenth century, for a long period it resulted in a continually evolving patchwork landscape, part enclosed and part open. Most of the landscape remained open through the period of the Wars of the Roses, and so for the investigation of those battles the potential for reconstruction of the terrain can be very high. In contrast, for the student of Civil Wars of the seventeenth century it can require considerable effort to establish what remained open field, what was enclosed, and in what form at a particular time.[21] Indeed for some battlefields the fine detail of the landscape as it was on the particular day of the battle may always remain elusive.

However, when one moves out of the central province or, as at Northallerton (Yorkshire, 1135), goes back beyond the period when the open fields had reached their maximum extent, then the problems are multiplied. Determining the character of the terrain for a battlefield as early as 1135, even in the central province, poses great challenges. Yet application of even the most basic of analysis can yield important evidence, as at Northallerton with the identification of areas of former marsh from the evidence of the British Geological Survey 1:50,000 scale mapping of alluvial and peat deposits, together with the mapping of Roman and major medieval roads.[22] The resultant crude reconstruction suggests very clearly why the English commander chose this location at which to try to halt the Scottish advance south. Here he could control the major north–south road where areas of marsh and open water provided a very narrow constriction and also enabled him to anchor his left wing, secure in the knowledge that he could not be outflanked. However, to understand the finer detail of this terrain as it was in 1135, which is so important to the reconstruction of the detail of the action, will require intensive study involving a range of techniques from pollen and soils analysis through to open field mapping, using a combination of both archaeological evidence and documentary sources.

For later battlefields the combination of documentary and archaeological evidence will be far more extensive, yet even in the central province as at Bosworth, the challenge is still a major one, to recover the fine detail necessary to understand the impact of terrain on military action.[23] It must also be recognized that the archaeological evidence for these open field landscapes is under severe threat, being rapidly eroded by intensive arable agriculture. If the necessary recording is not done in the near future, then the potential for terrain reconstruction on many of our battlefields may be severely reduced.

The complexity of the task will vary. Because of the high stability of the open field systems, where a battlefield remained open until the eighteenth or nineteenth century, then the recovery of the broad character of the historic terrain may be relatively simple using later sources. At Naseby, for example, the Ordnance Surveyors' Drawings of circa 1815 show the extent of open field and the pattern of the roads of the southern half of the battlefield, in Naseby township, prior to enclosure.[24] But the northern part of the battlefield, in Sibbertoft township, was enclosed in 1650, just five years after the battle. Though the documentary sources for the latter enclosure are exceptional for the date, it still represents a significant challenge to establish the exact extent of anciently enclosed fields that already existed by 1645. Indeed in our reconstruction of the battlefield the exact position and extent of one small hedged field called Archwrong Close remains a problem, yet it lies in a critical location within the battlefield and probably had great tactical significance in the action.[25] It is this great difference in the chronology of the evolution of the landscape between one township and another, and indeed the vagaries of documentary creation and survival between townships, which makes the study of historic terrain so difficult. In the case of Edgehill for example, Radway has a draft enclosure map of the mid-eighteenth century which shows each furlong and every hedge, whether part of ancient enclosures or not. In contrast Kineton has no enclosure or pre-enclosure map at all and so here we must depend on a written parliamentary enclosure award, yet these never record field closes, only the extent of ancient enclosure.[26] But then in both cases we must, if possible, employ pre-battle documents to confirm that any such enclosures and hedges were not created in the intervening period between the battle and parliamentary enclosure. Thus our knowledge of one part of a battlefield may be exceptionally good while that of another part may always remain far less complete.

Placing the Deployments and the Action within the Historic Terrain

The next step is to characterize the armies involved in the action. For the student of the seventeenth-century Civil Wars there are a wide range of sources. In the case of Naseby for example we have detailed contemporary plans of the deployments, each regiment in the Royalist army being named and its troop numbers specified. There are also many thousands of documents that tell us of the composition and equipping of the New Model Army. In contrast, the earlier in time one goes and the more obscure the battle then the poorer the evidence becomes. Even for the Wars of the Roses of the second half of the fifteenth century there are many uncertainties, while for earlier medieval battles the evidence becomes almost nonexistent in many cases, with the very notable exception of Hastings (Sussex, 1066). But for these earlier battles one can still draw upon more general principles of military practice to guide the interpretation.[27] With such information, however limited, we can begin to consider the problem of placing the troops in the field.

It is now that some of the major limitations of most previous interpretations of our battlefields become apparent. Once one has recovered with reasonable accuracy the historic terrain of the battlefield at the time of the action, it can immediately reveal problems with previous depictions of deployments, which have usually been reconstructed in relation to the modern landscape. This is clearly seen in relation to the various studies over the last 40 years of the initial deployments at Edgehill.[28] Such suggested deployments were viewed in the 1970s by Pannett against the extent of open field and hedged enclosures that he had reconstructed on a small scale in his mapping of the historic landscapes of Warwickshire. He realized immediately that, viewed in this seventeenth-century context, the published deployments by Burne, Young, and others are difficult to accept. On the basis of his limited reconstruction of the historic terrain he suggested a somewhat different alignment for the two opposing armies.[29] Ongoing research on the battlefield tends to support Pannett's conclusions. A more complex pattern of hedgerows has been revealed than that depicted by Pannett and these, together with the broader pattern of ancient enclosures, seem to reveal an even closer correlation between the reconstructed terrain and the topographical clues provided in the accounts of the military events.[30]

It is also necessary to have a detailed knowledge of the military practice of the period. First it enables one to build upon Burne's principle of Inherent Military Probability, in which one explores a problem on an historic battlefield by considering what a modern soldier might do in the same context.[31] A detailed understanding of the relevant historic military practice enables one to better consider what a soldier contemporary with the actual battle would have done, to assess the Inherent *Historic* Military Probability. Second, the evidence contained in the manuals often allows one to calculate the deployment of the armies on the field with a remarkable degree of accuracy, within the limitations of the evidence of troop numbers provided by the historic documents for the battle or for the armies themselves. When dealing with post-medieval battles the manuals specify exactly what space a particular number of infantry or cavalry will take up in both frontage and in depth, depending on whether the commander was using Dutch, Swedish, or German tactics,[32] and the documentary sources often provide clues if not detailed information on the exact formations, while one may also draw conclusions from the military experience of the commanders. Using such evidence, a detailed reconstruction of the initial deployments was prepared for Naseby.[33]

It seems likely that similar principles can be applied, with various important caveats, to the deployment of medieval and earlier armies. This is because there are certain fundamental principles in the deployment of men on a battlefield in pre-industrial warfare that almost inevitably recur for clear practical reasons from century to century. Moreover there are military manuals of the period,[34] mostly drawing heavily upon the manual by Vegetius written around AD 400, which provide the basic rules of deployment. For example Vegetius wrote: "We said that 6 ft. ought to lie between each line in depth from the rear, and in fact each warrior occupies 1 ft. standing still. Therefore, if you draw up six lines, an army of 10,000 men will take up 42 ft. in depth and a mile in breadth."[35] Even for the study of battles as early as the eleventh century we may be able to apply some of these principles and calculations, for the description of a shield wall formation by Vegetius seems, at least at first sight, to bear a striking resemblance to the nature of the shield wall deployments used in Anglo-Saxon and Viking battles. This should not perhaps be considered surprising, for it is known that Vegetius's manual was read by English commanders from at least the time of Alfred up to the late fifteenth century and beyond. Moreover the housecarls of the eleventh century were the highly professional and disciplined core of the English army whose soldiers, in exile after the fall of Anglo-Saxon England, earned a reputation as excellent troops in the service of the Byzantine emperor.[36] But above all where we lack vital evidence for these early periods is in the numbers of troops available on the field in the battles of the period, though many estimates or guesstimates have been made. It is quite clear using such calculations that the troop numbers sometimes suggested for the battle of Towton, on the basis of the evidence in the chronicles, could simply never have been deployed on the field. Only when one reduces the numbers to a figure similar to that of other contemporary battles of the period does deployment become viable in the restricted terrain at Towton, with impassable scarps on one side and lowland marsh on the other.[37] The available frontage is not enough to enable more than perhaps 15,000 men to be deployed 10 deep, the maximum depth recommended by Vegetius, and 6 deep is the more normal depth of deployment he quotes. Moreover this assumes that all the troops are deployed on foot. The more cavalry that actually fought on horseback the more rapidly the numbers possible within a given frontage fall.[38]

Battle Archaeology

While it is true that the analysis described above can enable many impossible and improbable interpretations to be dismissed, up to this point, almost without exception, all that such analysis can produce is a hypothesis or a number of alternative hypotheses. It is with the battle archaeology that the potential exists to apply wholly independent evidence to test these hypotheses.

On only a very few battlefields were defenses constructed or existing structures employed in some way in the action. On a battlefield such as Northampton (Northamptonshire, 1460), where the action took the form of an assault on an embanked and ditched camp, archaeological investigation to identify the ditch may well enable the exact location where the two armies clashed to be pinpointed with high accuracy.[39] Where defenses took the form of upstanding and surviving walls, there may be shot impact scars to indicate the direction and intensity of the firefight, though on battlefields such evidence is exceptionally rare whereas it is more common on siege sites.[40]

On most battlefields there will be mass graves at various locations, the main concentration of burial probably in most cases being, as Burne remarked, at the point where the main engagement began.[41] Other graves may well be scattered far more widely across the landscape, as in the case of Towton where the mass grave excavated in 1996 lay more than a mile from the core of the action.[42] However, such graves are notoriously difficult to locate and, although they can provide dramatic evidence of the nature of the action, may be relatively limited in what they can tell about the distribution of the action.

As has been demonstrated on several seventeenth-century battlefields in the UK and many more eighteenth- and nineteenth-century battlefields in the USA,[43] it is the distribution of projectiles which provides the most valuable evidence as to the extent, intensity, and character of the fighting. The other military equipment and the nonmilitary artifacts lost during the action by the troops can also be of great value in the interpretation. However, there are fundamental problems with the nature of the evidence the earlier one goes. It is particularly at the point of change from lead to iron projectiles in the late fifteenth and earlier sixteenth centuries that the problems really begin. Whereas lead is relatively inert, iron is highly unstable. The work at Towton shows that iron arrowheads exist in the topsoil of at least some battlefields, but it is as yet uncertain if they remain across most of the area in which they were originally deposited on the battlefield. They may only survive where exceptional conditions of preservation occurred.[44] This is why a high proportion of the evidence recovered from the action at Towton has been in the form of artifacts other than projectiles. While Towton, Bosworth, and the other battles of the Wars of the Roses took place just over 500 years ago, Hastings was fought more than 900 and Maldon over 1,000 years ago. The problems of survival on these earlier battlefields may therefore be further compounded by the enormous length of time that the artifacts have lain in the ground.

As with the archaeology of terrain, so with the archaeology of battle there is likely to be great variation both between battlefields and across an individual battlefield, in terms not only of deposition of artifacts during the action but also their survival to the present. In order to establish the nature of the original unstratified deposits before they were depleted through the effects of later agriculture, particularly for the battlefields from before the sixteenth century, it will be essential to identify areas of exceptional preservation, for example beneath alluvial deposits or where waterlogging has occurred. Preservation, particularly of ferrous artifacts, will also vary greatly according to soil pH and the current and past land use, with the mechanical damage occurring during arable cultivation being particularly influential. Hence, for example, where a battlefield has areas of surviving ridge and furrow, as at Bosworth, which have not been cultivated since at least the early seventeenth century, then the preservation of unstratified artifacts may be far better than in surrounding arable land. Burial beneath alluvium or colluvium may even preserve a largely undisturbed area of battlefield surface. Identifying such special conditions will be a key task in assessing the potential of early battlefields. It may provide a crucial guide as to what may once have existed more generally across the battlefield but now no longer survives. A good example of such preservation may exist at Battle, the site of the battle of Hastings, where an abbey was built soon after 1066, in commemoration of the dead, supposedly on the site where the English king fell. It is possible that the terracing for construction of the abbey may have preserved limited areas of battlefield surface from the impact of later activity. In contrast, on battlefields where intensive arable cultivation has continued for long periods, the preservation may be very poor and the continuing rates of destruction of artifacts, through influences such as modern chemical application and mechanical damage, may be exceptionally high. It is therefore particularly urgent that we establish what may survive on battlefields of different dates, types, and locations and how rapidly that battle archaeology is being destroyed by modern agriculture.

Even where the evidence is in the form of highly stable projectiles, particularly the lead shot of seventeenth-century battlefields, major problems still need to be addressed. Our primary objective is to use the projectile distributions to test and refine our hypotheses about the location and nature of the maneuvers, initial deployments, and action that have been based on the evidence of the military history set within the historic terrain. The artifact patterning that exists in the ground relates largely to specific elements of the action and to the effects of battlefield clearance in the hours and days following the battle. The interpretation of the relationship between the events of the battle and the artifact distribution that it left is a complex problem. In order to begin to make effective use of the evidence, the distribution that we recover needs to be as representative a sample as possible of that which actually exists in the ground. Despite having seen, in the 1970s, what were probably the first intensive modern battlefield surveys, England never fully developed the systematic survey and recording techniques for battlefield study that have been applied since the early 1980s in the USA. Almost without exception the work conducted in England has been neither sufficiently systematic nor well recorded to enable the level of analysis that is needed. Neither has most of the work been published. There has thus not been a developing body of work available that could be reviewed, nor has there been until very recently sufficient pooling of expertise to encourage the production of an effective methodology.

This is most clearly seen with the previously unpublished fieldwalking survey of Marston Moor battlefield conducted in the 1970s by Newman and Cammidge, to complement Newman's work on the documentary sources for the battle and the historic terrain.[45] The plan of the distribution of finds from this survey, published here for the first time, has been digitized from an annotated plan and other information provided several years ago to the author for this purpose by the late Peter Newman (see figure). However, we still lack sufficient information to be able to fully understand the methodology and thus the limitations of his pioneering survey of the battle archaeology.

The problems with the 1970s survey become strikingly apparent if one compares the Newman and Cammidge data with that recently published from

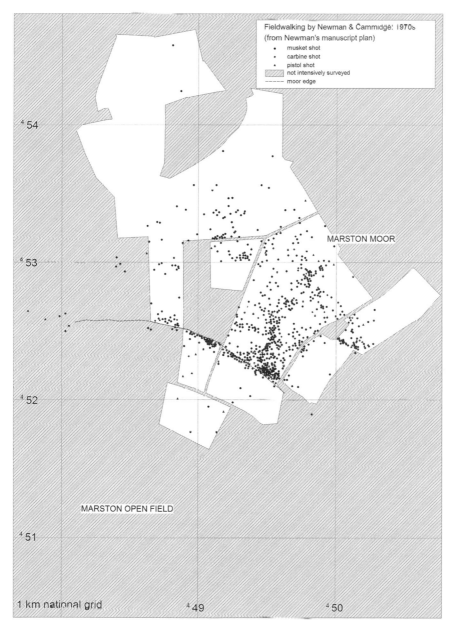

Newman and Cammidge's fieldwalking survey of Marston Moor battlefield in the 1970s.

Roberts's metal detecting survey of the battlefield in the 1980s and 1990s (see figure).[46] The latter produced a far wider distribution of bullets on the moor itself, while most striking is the extension of the distribution to the south of the moor. A major phase of the battle had been missed by the 1970s survey. To a large degree

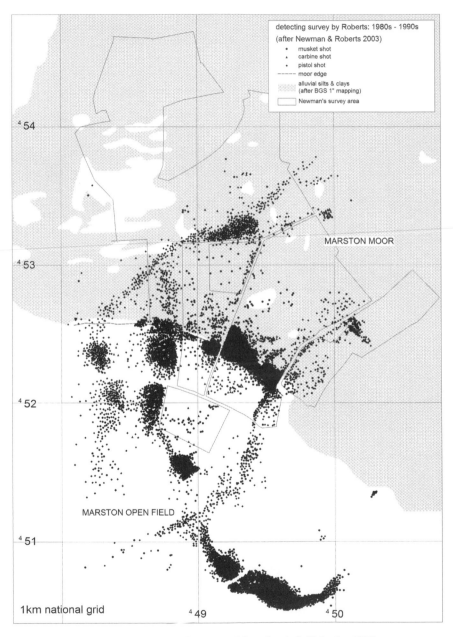

Roberts's metal detecting survey of Marston Moor battlefield in the 1980s.

this difference reflects the limited spatial extent of the Newman and Cammidge survey, while the gross differences on the moor were due to both land use (the pasture being inaccessible to the fieldwalking survey) and land ownership (because Newman was unable to gain access to the western part of the battlefield). However, the pattern to the south of the moor is far more problematic. It is true that Newman and Cammidge carried out very little survey work in this area, but this seems to have been because very little was being recovered as they moved south from the moor. It is possible this was because the dark soils of the moor itself provided an exceptional potential to recover shot from fieldwalking (visual inspection of the field surface, rather than by metal detecting), whereas the higher, sandy ground was far less conducive to the recovery of shot in this way (see figure for the boundary between the major soil types). For the metal detector user such specific biases of land use and soil type were not apparently a significant factor. Yet if one compares the area where both surveys overlap to the south of the moor boundary Newman and Cammidge seem to have sampled an area of relatively light shot distribution and may simply have stopped surveying too soon on the south side, believing they had reached the limit of the scatter.

But other equally important questions must be asked about the patterning right across the battlefield, for in the areas where both surveys were conducted intensively, both on and off the moor, one sees that the two maps often do not coincide in the finer detail of distribution. Yet it is on the analysis of such finer detail that much of the interpretation is likely to rest when analyzing the battle archaeology on this and other battlefields. Marston Moor would appear to be the only battlefield in England where there is extensive comparative data from two completely independent surveys conducted on the same area. The differences revealed in the distribution patterns provide great cause for concern. For example, in the area 4495/4525 Newman's plan shows a broad scatter across the moor, with lesser concentrations within it. In contrast Roberts shows relatively little across the moor but a dramatic density from the moor edge. Similar contradictions between the two datasets are seen elsewhere across the battlefield, as for example at 4492/4532 where the dense concentration on the north side of the track in the Roberts survey is not repeated by Newman. If both plans represent an accurate record of the actual number of bullets recovered, then one can only conclude that there has been dramatic variation in the intensity of surveying or in the effectiveness of recovery. The focusing of survey activity on areas producing the greater number of artifacts is a typical problem with an unsystematic survey. This certainly does appear, from limited personal observation and discussion about it, to be a partial explanation of the variations in the Roberts survey. It is unclear whether similar focusing of attention was a factor in the Newman survey, something that only Cammidge could now answer, for there is no data from either survey indicating the intensity of survey, though unlike Roberts, Newman did, on request, define the extent of intensive survey. The implications of this for the representativeness of the Marston data are substantial and highlight the difficulties of working with unsystematic or poorly recorded surveys from any battlefield.

Despite such limitations of such work it is still essential that we encourage and assist fieldworkers who have done such battlefield surveys in the past to bring the data to publication at as great a level of detail as is possible, as has been done with such good effect in Bonsall's analysis of McGovern's survey of Cheriton.[47] This is not only because such publication provides valuable insights into the nature of the battle archaeology on each site. It also provides key information as to the quantity and distribution of at least some of the material that has been removed from the battlefields. The removal, according to Roberts's published plan, of more than 10,000 bullets from Marston during his survey must have had a significant impact on the in situ pattern of distribution on that battlefield. Knowing approximately from where the bullets have been removed and in what numbers will at least enable the impact of that recovery to be taken into account in analyzing the results of any future systematic survey of that battlefield. With the exception of treasure hunting rallies, of which there was one in 2004 in the general area 4500/4510 at Marston, it is probably intensive but unsystematic and poorly recorded metal detecting surveys of our battlefields that are one of the greatest threats, simply because they remove so many artifacts.

So, while unsystematic surveys have provided a valuable body of evidence for some of our battlefields, one must conclude that such work, as well as simple treasure hunting, should no longer be allowed to continue on nationally important sites. In future only systematic surveys and recording to current standards of best practice ought to be accepted, at least on our Registered battlefields.

The problem can be further considered using the small-scale metal detecting survey conducted on Edgehill battlefield in the late 1970s by Captain Grant, which is analyzed and published here for the first time from data in the Warwickshire Sites and Monuments Record (See Figure). Up to April 1979 Grant recovered 52 musket balls from the battlefield. Given the concerns over the biases in the Marston Moor data the validity of interpretations based on a simple distribution map such as this have to be taken into account. Grant's survey is however exceptional for its time because it includes not only apparently highly accurate mapping of finds at 1:10560 and 1:2500 scale, but also records the amount of survey time spent in each area or on each transect. This enables consideration as to the degree to which absence of evidence may genuinely represent evidence of absence. If the data is processed to indicate the approximate amount of time spent in each hectare of the National Grid across the battlefield, one can begin to draw more secure and detailed interpretations based on the survey (see figure). This method of analysis should enable direct comparison between Grant's dataset and future survey data from the site. However, what has not yet been taken into account are the variable effects of land use on the recovery rates, because unfortunately Grant did not record the land use at the time of his survey. This is important because it would appear, from work undertaken by Kings on one

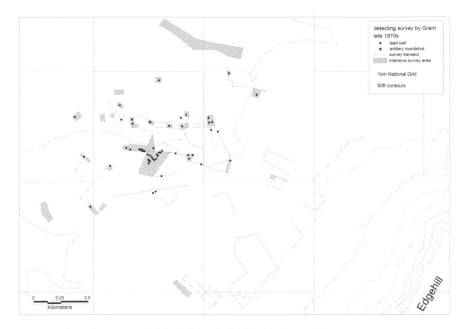

Captain Grant's survey of Edgehill battlefield in the late 1970s.

small area at Naseby, that on land which has remained under pasture for several hundred years, lead bullets collect at the base of the topsoil and are thus far more difficult to recover than on land which is or has recently been under arable cultivation, where the shot is more broadly distributed through the full depth of the topsoil.[48]

The processed data from Grant's survey seems to support a first stage of re-interpretation of the initial deployments and distribution of the action at Edgehill, based on a re-examination of the primary accounts of the battle in the light of the reconstruction of the historic terrain (see figure above).[49] The major shot concentration probably reflects the Royalist initial advance and the infantry engagement in the center. In contrast the cavalry action on the parliamentarian left wing seems to have produced almost no evidence, as one might expect, because Rupert's Royalist cavalry were instructed to not stand to fire their pistols but to charge home immediately. However, the absence of any evidence of the documented firing by parliamentarian musketeers standing behind the hedgerows on this wing might be considered surprising. But the intensity of survey on this wing can be seen to be considerably lower than in the center of the battlefield, where the main concentrations have been recovered, while the northernmost survey area remains wholly under ridge and furrow and hence has not been plowed since 1757 or 1792. Further analysis is required to reveal the full potential in Grant's dataset, but what has been done so far demonstrates very clearly how essential it is to have a well-recorded

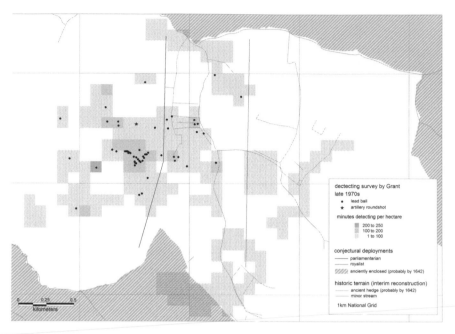

Captain Grant's data integrated with historic terrain evidence.

survey while the limitations it has revealed emphasize the need for comprehensive survey and a systematic survey methodology. In response to these conclusions a new two-year investigation was begun at Edgehill in August 2004, in which a systematic approach is being applied, initially using 10-m spaced transects across the whole of the accessible area in an attempt to recover a consistent dataset across the whole battlefield. Handheld GPS units, fixed to each metal detector, are being used to record individual find locations, to an accuracy of better than 10 m, and to collect track information every 15 seconds to record the exact location and intensity of survey by each detectorist.[50]

There is also the need for comparative study between battlefields, as can be seen from the crude graph comparing the balance of musket versus carbine/pistol bullets from a range of seventeenth-century battlefields and one siege site (see figure on page 151). The Grafton siege assemblage stands out as having a remarkably high percentage of carbine/pistol as opposed to musket (in fact the vast majority appears to be carbine rather than pistol). This graph also reinforces the questions about the nature of the biases in the evidence from Roberts's survey of Marston Moor, for the balance of caliber is quite different in his survey to that from any other battlefield, including the other survey of Marston Moor by Newman and Cammidge. However, it is interesting to note how much closer the interim Edgehill assemblage is to that from Marston than any other assemblage. The Edgehill sample comes from 1.2 sq km

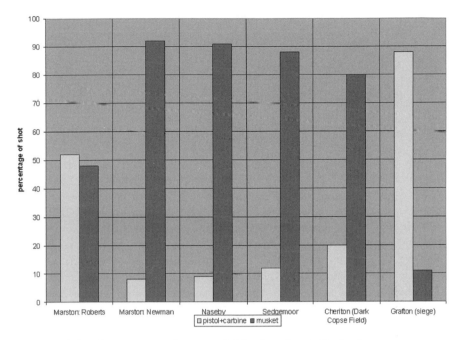

Caliber of shot from seventeenth-century fields of conflict in England.

covering much of the periphery as well as the core to battlefield, though the sample is as yet less than 200 bullets. The reasons for the variations seen in the graph are far from clear and are subject to ongoing research. Among other things this ultimately requires limited systematic sampling to a repeatable standard on each battlefield to attempt some form of calibration. It is possible that in part the differences may reflect sampling biases, with a focusing of attention to particular areas of a battlefield. It could in some cases also reflect a failure to recover the smaller bullets in some surveys, though this seems not to be a significant factor in the variation between Naseby and Edgehill because Burton has made a major contribution to both surveys, providing a degree of comparability between those two.

Such analysis raises many questions that can only begin to be answered by systematic survey on a range of seventeenth-century battlefields and points to the need for accurate recording of the caliber of shot. On most sites the best that has been done is a subjective assessment of caliber (musket, pistol, and sometimes of carbine) being made in the field. As work at Edgehill and Grafton Regis (Northamptonshire, 1643) in England and various battlefields in the USA have shown and are showing,[51] each bullet contains considerable information. The weight and size (caliber) can indicate in many cases the type of weapon it was meant for and thus to some degree the type of troops that probably used it. In the data from Edgehill not only can three very distinct calibers be recognized, there are hints at several possibly lesser subgroupings.[52] But the bullets also have surface evidence for manufacture and use, which shows whether it was dropped or fired and, if the latter, whether it was fired from an artillery piece as case shot rather than from a musket. Thus each bullet recovered from the battlefield needs to be individually bagged, numbered, and accurately located.

When one moves to battlefields of the medieval period, prior to or in the case of the Wars of the Roses at the very first stages of the introduction of firearms on the battlefield, the problems are compounded. As we have seen from the work at Towton, the projectiles in the form of iron arrowheads survive in relatively small numbers and in very restricted areas of the battlefield. Therefore far greater dependence has to be placed on the distribution of non-projectile military artifacts and especially on nonmilitary artifacts lost in the action. The implications that flow from this are drawn starkly into focus if we take the evidence of a Civil War battlefield, where shot distributions clearly reflect the distribution of key elements of the action. Here one finds that the number of non-shot artifacts that are of military character, and thus almost certainly relate to the battle, represent a tiny percentage of the finds compared with the shot.[53] If one was dependent upon these artifacts alone to determine the distribution of the action, then the investigation would need to be extremely intensive and the potential for interpretation might be very limited. Moreover, the majority of the finds would probably prove, as at Cheriton (Hampshire, 1644), to be of iron and thus very vulnerable to destruction, just as with the iron projectiles. The copper alloy and bronze artifacts are an even smaller percentage of the finds. To further complicate the situation, when one is dealing with artifacts that are not specifically military in character there is the added problem that an unknown percentage of them may have been deposited by agricultural and other activities over a period as long as a century or more. This is likely to be a major problem across large parts of England where intensive manuring has taken place for centuries and is known to have deposited large quantities of artifacts in the plough soil.[54]

So the study of a fifteenth-century battlefield such as Bosworth, where there has been some unsystematic survey across the wider landscape over the last decade, poses major difficulties. There may have been a very few lead shot deposited on the field from hand cannon, but the exact nature and likely quantity remains unknown and none has yet been recovered there. We are therefore dependent, as at Towton, on the other military and especially the nonmilitary artifacts. But finds like horse pendants may or may not actually relate to the battle. In order to address these problems what is needed is systematic survey which includes control samples from areas of nearby landscape that were certainly not affected by the action.[55] Only in this way may we be able to determine the level of "background noise," artifacts probably mainly deposited during manuring carried from village middens contaminated by domestic rubbish, which may be confusing the battle archaeology. These control samples will need to be representative of the different characteristics of the various areas of the battlefield. In the case of Bosworth this means areas historically under marsh and alluvium as well as open field, and areas close to villages as well as distant from them, for manuring patterns are known to have varied dramatically across the landscape.

If one adds to the current lack of such "control" the further confusion provided by surveying without accurate recording of the intensity of survey, as discussed for Civil War battlefields, then some apparent battle-related concentrations may prove to be largely an artifact of the survey method. In reality they might represent objects largely if not wholly deposited by agricultural activities, yet made to appear battle-related because of the concentration of detecting activity. This seems to be fairly clearly exhibited by the Bosworth survey. Where the artifacts are of exclusively military character, as with fragments of armor, or weaponry, then association with the battle may be a reasonable conclusion. However, the vast majority of artifacts recovered at Bosworth were in domestic usage as well as being used by soldiers present on the battlefield. Thus the concentration of finds to the southeast of Sutton Cheney village, which had been interpreted as perhaps representing Richard III's plundered camp, may prove to be largely or wholly the result of intensive survey where there had been intensive manuring in the fifteenth century.[56] After all, we do not yet know whether over a 100-year period the 200 or 300 people in a village might deposit many more nonmilitary artifacts across the landscape than 10,000 troops fighting for a few hours on one day. When systematic work is undertaken, as part of the planned investigation in 2005–2008, the other concentrations already seen at Bosworth, in the area between Shenton and Sutton Cheney, may be shown to reflect the intensity of metal detecting survey rather than concentration of military action.

CONCLUSIONS

To date almost all investigation and conservation of battlefields in England has been restricted to Registered sites. These certainly are the most important and best preserved examples, but there are also many more unregistered sites. Like one or two of the Registered battlefields, such as Newburn (Durham, 1640) or Neville's Cross (Durham, 1346), these unregistered sites often have extremely fragmentary survival of their historic environment and hence of the physical evidence of both battle and terrain. Yet this should not lead us to write them off. Even if there is no extensive, continuous distribution of unstratified projectiles surviving with which to study the course of the action, there is still likely to be limited battle archaeology. On badly preserved battlefields, for example where there has been extensive mineral extraction or urban development, limited areas of artifact scatters could still survive in the undisturbed areas. On other battlefields where the battle artifacts were mostly ferrous but the soil conditions and length of time since the action mean that no substantial unstratified scatters survive, there may still be some projectile preservation in features such as ditches that were open at the time of the battle, or where colluvium and alluvium have protected a battlefield surface, and where waterlogging or other special conditions prevail.

Such limited survival may not, in isolation, warrant a site being considered of national importance for its battle archaeology. However, the battle itself may well be of national importance in historical terms and so it may be particularly important that any surviving battle archaeology is assessed, because it may provide critical validation of hypotheses on the location and nature of initial deployments and action which have been developed from the documentary sources for the battle and the battlefield. Without such testing those interpretations would, almost without exception, remain purely hypothesis. Such potential will be the greater when we have a more detailed understanding of the character, distribution, and meaning of battle archaeology as a result of intensive studies on a few well-preserved "type sites." We may then be far better able to understand how to distinguish and interpret the finer detail of the archaeological signature of different types of action. Neither should it be forgotten that even where the battle archaeology is not well preserved it is still possible for good physical evidence for the earlier landscape to survive, sufficient to enable partial reconstruction of the historic terrain of the battlefield.

So not only must we strengthen the conservation of Registered battlefields and improve the methodology of battlefield study to exploit that resource; but even the poorly preserved battlefields, especially those which do not warrant Registration and have until now been largely ignored, must be considered for they too may prove to have a significant research potential.

NOTES

1. Sutherland and Richardson, in this volume.

2. Glenn Foard, "Bosworth Battlefield: A Reassessment," (Shocklatch: Chris Burnett Associates for Leicestershire County Council, 2004).

3. Michael K. Jones, *Bosworth 1485: Psychology of a Battle* (2002).

4. English Heritage, "Register of Historic Battlefields" (London: English Heritage, 1995).

5. The difficulty of assessment at a lesser scale is revealed in the inadequacy of their treatment in the Research Frameworks process promoted by English Heritage over the last few years. For example, Glenn Foard, "Medieval Northamptonshire" (paper presented at the East Midlands Archaeological Research Framework Seminar Series, 2001). http://www.le.ac.uk/archaeology/east_midlands_research_framework. htm.

6. http://www.battlefieldstrust.com/resource-centre/battlefieldsuk/.

7. For example, Robert Ward, *Animadversions of Warre* (1639). Roman Dyboski and Z. M. Arend, *Knyghthode and Bataile: A Fifteenth Century Verse Paraphrase of Flavius Vegetius Renatus' Treatise 'De re militari', Early English Text Society. Original series; no. 201* (London: Published for the Early English Text Society by H Milford Oxford University Press, 1935).

8. William Hutton and J. Nichols, *The Battle of Bosworth Field*, 1999. Alan Sutton, repaginated ed. (London: Nichols, 1813).

9. Richard Brooke, *Visits to Fields of Battle in England of the Fifteenth Century* (London: John Russell Smith, 1857).

10. Dave Johnson, *Adwalton Moor 1643: The Battle that Changed a War* (Pickering: Blackthorn Press, 2003). Glenn Foard, *Naseby: The Decisive Campaign* (Whitsable: Pryor Publications, 1995).

11. Francis Randle Twemlowe, *The Battle of Blore Heath* (Wolverhampton: Whitehead Bros. Printers, 1912).

12. Alfred Higgins Burne, *The Battlefields of England* (London: Methuen & Co., 1950).

13. W. G. Hoskins, *The Making of the English Landscape* (1955). Glenn Foard, "Sedgemoor 1685: Historic Terrain, the 'Archaeology of Battles' and the Revision of Military History," Landscapes 4, no. 2 (2003): 5–15.

14. Unpublished manuscript plan by David Pannett in English Heritage Battlefields Register file for Edgehill battlefield.

15. P. R. Newman, *Marston Moor, 2 July 1644: The Sources and the Site, Borthwick Papers; no. 53* (York: University of York Borthwick Institute of Historical Research, 1978), P. R. Newman and P. R. Roberts, *Marston Moor 1644: The Battle of the Five Armies* (Pickering: Blackthorn Press, 2003).

16. Daniel Williams, *The Battle of Bosworth, 22 August 1485* (Leicester: Leicester University Press, 1973). D. T. Williams, *The Battle of Bosworth Field* (Leicester: Leicestershire County Council, 2001).

17. Peter Foss, *The Field of Redemore: The Battle of Bosworth, 1485*, first edition. (Headingley: Rosalba Press, 1990), Peter Foss, *The Field of Redmore: The Battle of Bosworth, 1485* (1998).

18. English Heritage, "Battlefield Report: Maldon 991" (London: English Heritage, 1995).

19. G. R. Petty and S. Petty, "Geology and The Battle of Maldon," *Speculum*, 51 (1976): 435–446, George Petty and Susan Petty, "A Geological Reconstruction of the Site of the Battle of Maldon," (1993): 159–169.

20. Brian K. Roberts and Stuart Wrathmell, *An Atlas of Rural Settlement in England* (London: English Heritage, 2000).

21. For example, Foard, *Naseby: The Decisive Campaign*.

22. http://www.battlefieldstrust.com/resource-centre/medieval/battleview.asp?BattleFieldId=32.

23. Foard, "Bosworth Battlefield: A Reassessment." Glenn Foard, "Bosworth Battlefield Investigation: Project Design" (unpublished report for Leicestershire County Council, 2004).

24. Ordnance Surveyors' Drawings, British Library.

25. Foard, *Naseby: The Decisive Campaign*.

26. Glenn Foard, *The Battle of Edgehill Reinterpreted* (in preparation).

27. Flavius Vegetius Renatus, "Vegetius: Epitome of Military Science," ed. N. P. Milner (Liverpool: Liverpool University Press, 1996).

28. Peter Young, *Edgehill 1642: The Campaign and the Battle* (Kineton: Roundwood Press, 1967). Burne, *The Battlefields of England.*

29. Op. cit. in note 13.

30. Individual hedges and field closes were recorded on the draft enclosure map of Radway. Such features were normally omitted by enclosure records because they remained commonable with the rest of the open field, yet such hedges, as much as the ancient enclosures which were held in severalty and thus normally recorded in parliamentary enclosure documentation, seem to be key topographical features which influenced the action on both sides at Edgehill. Without the draft enclosure map their existence may have remained unrecognized.

31. Burne, *The Battlefields of England.*

32. A brief summary is given in Keith Roberts and John Tincey, *Edgehill 1642*, ed. David Chandler, vol. 82, *Campaign Series* (Oxford: Osprey, 2001).

33. Foard, *Naseby: The Decisive Campaign.*

34. Dyboski and Arend, *Knyghthode and Bataile: A Fifteenth Century Verse Paraphrase of Flavius Vegetius Renatus' Treatise 'De re militari.'*

35. Vegetius Renatus, "Vegetius: Epitome of Military Science."

36. Helen Nicholson, *Medieval Warfare* (London: Palgrave Macmillan, 2004).

37. For the terrain see Veronica Fiorato, Anthea Boylston, and Christopher Kunsel, *Blood Red Roses: The Archaeology of a Mass Grave from the Battle of Towton AD 1461* (Oxford: Oxbow, 2000).

38. For general specific information on the Towton battlefield see Sutherland and Richardson in this volume and the works referenced there.

39. English Heritage, "Battlefield Report: Northampton 1460" (London: English Heritage, 1995).

40. Of 25 Civil War battlefields in England examined by the author between 1992–1995, only that at Nantwich (Cheshire, 1644) revealed any extensive evidence of shot impact scars, on Nantwich church which was the focus of action for the royalist baggage train.

41. Burne, *The Battlefields of England.*

42. Fiorato, Boylston, and Kunsel, *Blood Red Roses: The Archaeology of a Mass Grave from the Battle of Towton AD 1461.*

43. For example, various papers in Philip Freeman and Tony Pollard (eds.), *Fields of Conflict: Progress and Prospect in Battlefield Archaeology*, proceedings of a conference held in the Department of Archaeology, University of Glasgow, April 2000, BAR International Series 958 (Oxford, England: Archaeopress, 2001).

44. Most notable in this is the work at Towton. See Sutherland and Richardson in this volume.

45. Newman, op. cit in note 14.

46. Newman and Roberts, *Marston Moor 1644: The Battle of the Five Armies.*

47. James Bonsall, "Archaeological Applications to Dark Coppice Field: A Scene of Retreat from the 1644 Battle of Cheriton" (BA dissertation, King Alfred's College, 2000).

48. Foard, *Naseby: The Decisive Campaign.*

49. Glenn Foard, "Integrating the Physical and Documentary Evidence for Battles and Their Context: A Case Study from 17th Century England" (PhD dissertation, University of East Anglia, in preparation).

50. Ibid. Limited information on the survey is also available online at http://www.battlefieldstrust.com/resource-centre/civil-war/battlepageview.asp?pageid=500.

51. For example, Sivilich in this volume.

52. Foard, "Integrating the Physical and Documentary Evidence for Battles and Their Context: A Case Study from 17th Century England". The Grafton survey is still largely unpublished, but a distribution plan is presented in Glenn Foard, "The Archaeology of Attack: Battles and Sieges of the English Civil War," in *Fields of Conflict: Progress and Prospect in Battlefield Archaeology*, ed. Freeman and Pollard, BAR International Series (2001), 87–103.

53. The best analysis of a Civil War collection in this context is Bonsall, "Archaeological Applications to Dark Coppice Field: A Scene of Retreat from the 1644 Battle of Cheriton."

54. For detailed evidence on manuring patterns in an example landscape of Midland England as revealed by pottery evidence see Steve Parry, *The Raunds Survey* (London: English Heritage, forthcoming).

55. Foard, "Bosworth Battlefield Investigation: Project Design."

56. Foard, "Bosworth Battlefield: A Reassessment."

REFERENCES CITED

Bonsall, James. 2000. Archaeological Applications to Dark Coppice Field: A Scene of Retreat from the 1644 Battle of Cheriton. BA dissertation, King Alfred's College.

Brooke, Richard. 1857. *Visits to Fields of Battle in England of the Fifteenth Century.* John Russell Smith, London.

Burne, Alfred Higgins. 1950. *The Battlefields of England.* Methuen, London.

Dyboski, Roman, and Z. M. Arend. 1935. *Knyghthode and Bataile: A 15th Century Verse Paraphrase of Flavius Vegetius Renatus' Treatise 'De re militari',* Early English Text Society. *Original series; no. 201.* Published for the Early English Text Society by II Milford Oxford University Press, London.

English Heritage. 1995a. Battlefield Report: Maldon 991. English Heritage, London.

English Heritage. 1995b. Battlefield Report: Northampton 1460. English Heritage, London.

English Heritage. 1995c. Register of Historic Battlefields. English Heritage, London.

Fiorato, Veronica, Anthea Boylston, and Christopher Kunsel. 2000. *Blood Red Roses: The Archaeology of a Mass Grave from the Battle of Towton AD 1461.* Oxbow, Oxford.

Foard, Glenn. 2001. The Archaeology of Attack: Battles and Sieges of the English Civil War. In Phillip Freeman and Tony Pollard (eds.), *Fields of Conflict: Progress and Prospect in Battlefield Archaeology*, 87–103. BAR International Series 958, Oxford.

Foard, Glenn. In preparation. *The Battle of Edgehill Reinterpreted.*

Foard, Glenn. 2004a. Bosworth Battlefield Investigation: Project Design. Unpublished report for Leicestershire County Council, Leicester.

Foard, Glenn. 2004b. Bosworth Battlefield: A Reassessment. Chris Burnett Associates for Leicestershire County Council, Shocklatch.

Foard, Glenn. In preparation. Integrating the Physical and Documentary Evidence for Battles and Their Context: A Case Study from 17th Century England. PhD dissertation, University of East Anglia.

Foard, Glenn. 2001. Medieval Northamptonshire. Paper presented at the East Midlands Archaeological Research Framework Seminar Series.

Foard, Glenn. 1995. *Naseby: The Decisive Campaign.* Pryor Publications, Whitstable.

Foard, Glenn. 2003. Sedgemoor 1685: Historic Terrain, the 'Archaeology of Battles' and the Revision of Military History. *Landscapes* 4(2):5–15.

Foss, Peter. 1990. *The Field of Redemore: The Battle of Bosworth, 1485.* First edition, Rosalba Press, Headingley.

Foss, Peter. 1998. *The Field of Redmore: The Battle of Bosworth, 1485.* Rosalba Press, Headingley.

Freeman, Philip, and Tony Pollard (eds.). 2001. *Fields of Conflict: Progress and Prospect in Battlefield Archaeology.* Proceedings of a conference held in the Department of Archaeology, University of Glasgow, April 2000, BAR International Series 958. Oxford.

Hoskins, W. G. 1955. *The Making of the English Landscape.* Penguin History, London.

Hutton, William, and J. Nichols. 1999. *The Battle of Bosworth Field.* Alan Sutton, London. Reprint of Nichols 1813 edition.

Johnson, Dave. 2003. *Adwalton Moor 1643: The Battle that Changed a War.* Blackthorn Press, Pickering.

Jones, Michael K. 2002. *Bosworth 1485: Psychology of a Battle.* Tempus, Shroud Gloucestershire, UK.

Newman, P. R. 1978. *Marston Moor, 2 July 1644: The Sources and the Site, Borthwick papers; no. 53.* University of York Borthwick Institute of Historical Research.

Newman, P. R., and P. R. Roberts. 2003. *Marston Moor 1644: The Battle of the Five Armies.* Blackthorn Press, Pickering.

Nicholson, Helen. 2004. *Medieval Warfare.* Palgrave Macmillan, London.

Parry, Steve. In press. *The Raunds Survey:* English Heritage, London.

Petty, G. R., and Petty, S. 1976. Geology and The Battle of Maldon. *Speculum* 51:435–446.

Petty, George, and Susan Petty. 1993. A Geological Reconstruction of the Site of the Battle of Maldon. In *The Battle of Maldon: Fiction and Fact,* edited by Janet Cooper, pp. 159–169. Hambledon Press, London.

Roberts, Brian K, and Stuart Wrathmell. 2000. *An Atlas of Rural Settlement in England.* English Heritage, London.

Roberts, Keith, and John Tincey. 2001. *Edgehill 1642,* edited by David Chandler. Vol. 82, *Campaign Series.* Osprey, Oxford.

Twemlowe, Francis Randle. 1912. *The Battle of Blore Heath.* Whitehead Bros., Wolverhampton.

Vegetius Renatus, Flavius. 1996. Vegetius: Epitome of Military Science, edited by N. P., Liverpool Milner. Liverpool University Press.

Ward, Robert. 1639. *Animadversions of Warre.* John Dawson, London.

Williams, D. T. 2001. *The Battle of Bosworth Field*. Leicestershire County Council, Leicester.

Williams, Daniel. 1973. *The Battle of Bosworth, 22 August 1485*. Leicester University Press, Leicester.

Young, Peter. 1967. *Edgehill 1642: The Campaign and the Battle*. Roundwood Press, Kineton.

Arrows Point to Mass Graves: Finding the Dead from the Battle of Towton, 1461 AD

Tim Sutherland & Simon Richardson

THE BATTLE OF Towton took place on Palm Sunday, March 29, 1461, between the armies of King Henry VI of the House of Lancaster and Edward Earl of March, later Duke of York, of the House of York. Preceding the conflict, Edward had been proclaimed the new king in London, which meant that at the time of the battle there were two kings fighting for the English throne. Shortly after his victory at Towton, Edward, Earl of March, was ceremonially crowned King Edward IV.[1]

The small village of Towton is situated four kilometers (two miles) to the south of the market town of Tadcaster and 18 kilometers (10 miles) southwest of the city of York, the medieval secular and ecclesiastical center of northern England. It is perhaps surprising that this tiny medieval hamlet gave its name to what is officially regarded as the largest battle ever fought on British soil,[2] with over 100,000 combatants allegedly taking part, and approximately 28,000 dead.[3]

Archaeological fieldwork on the battlefield at Towton developed as part of the Ph.D. research instigated by the author.[4] This followed the excavation and detailed recording of 37 skeletons from a mass grave, discovered at Towton Hall in 1996, which contained casualties from the battle.[5] The aim of the project was to record additional physical evidence of the conflict, including artifacts, possible earthworks, and the location of other mass graves on the main part of the battlefield, which lies one mile to the south of Towton.[6] This chapter describes the systematic way in which the battlefield was surveyed. This ultimately led to the discovery of a rare and important archaeological site: the mass graves of the combatants from the battle of Towton.

ARTIFACT DENSITY AND PATTERNING

An extensive survey of the Towton battlefield has been carried out using a multidisciplinary array of techniques including desk-based evaluation, geophysical survey, archaeological field walking, and excavation. The most successful survey technique used to identify the general area of the battlefield at Towton proved to be metal detector scanning of the whole battlefield landscape. Because of the considerable contamination of relatively modern ferrous objects, the metal detector search initially had to be limited to the recovery of non-ferrous artifacts. Artifacts that were probably lost during the conflict were generally found to be of a non-military nature, such as clothing fasteners, buttons, buckles, strap ends, and brooches.

Medieval arrowheads recovered as part of the Towton Battlefield Archaeological Survey Project. (The Trustees of the Royal Armouries)

Using a model based upon the location of over 1,300 of these fifteenth-century artifacts, it has been possible to identify the center of the conflict. This area has now been surveyed using more intensive and detailed survey techniques, targeting both ferrous and non-ferrous artifacts, which has led to the recovery of a substantial quantity of additional artifacts.

Although the ratio of the battle-related artifacts compared to that of the contamination is higher in the non-ferrous category, it has now been possible to locate and recover definite battle-related ferrous artifacts in the center of the battlefield. The proportion of ferrous artifacts identified as "background contamination" compared to that of fifteenth-century military artifacts is still approximately 50:1 within the target area, though the ratio is far greater in other parts of the battlefield, presumably because the fighting there was less intense. Due to logistical constraints, details of ferrous fragments from the background contamination are not usually recorded. The lower proportion of ferrous items from the target areas, however, means that it is now feasible to search for and record ferrous artifacts within intensively studied locations.

During a routine search of one of the target areas, a metal detector was being retuned and accidentally identified the presence of a ferrous artifact, which was identified as a medieval arrowhead. This meant that the signature of medieval arrowheads, which are often barely recognizable as such when

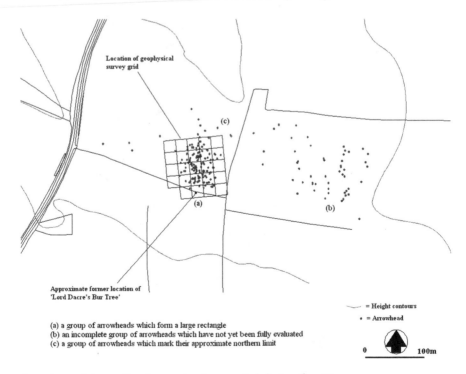

Location of geophysical survey grid

(c)

(a)

(b)

Approximate former location of 'Lord Dacre's Bur Tree'

(a) a group of arrowheads which form a large rectangle
(b) an incomplete group of arrowheads which have not yet been fully evaluated
(c) a group of arrowheads which mark their approximate northern limit

—— = Height contours
• = Arrowhead

0   100m

Locations of the medieval arrowheads recorded during the survey.

found, could now be positively identified despite their severely corroded nature. This discovery has led to the recording of over 200 arrowheads in areas that have previously been thoroughly searched using both metal detector and magnetometer geophysical survey (see figure).

When plotted, the locations of these arrowheads form three separate anomalies. One concentration forms a large rectangle located in one corner of a field. The second group of arrowheads is situated in the middle of another field, and has not yet been fully evaluated. The third group, which runs in an east-west direction across the center of the battlefield, appears to form an approximate northern limit of the arrowheads.

During metal detecting scanning, the remains of a human distal ulna (lower arm bone) were discovered on the surface of the plough soil. The location of the bone was recorded using a small handheld satellite navigation instrument (GPS).

GEOPHYSICAL SURVEY

Following the identification of the arrowhead concentrations, these areas were more closely investigated using a series of earth resistance and magnetic geo-physical surveys. Several distinctive anomalies were identified, the majority of which did not initially appear to be battle-related.

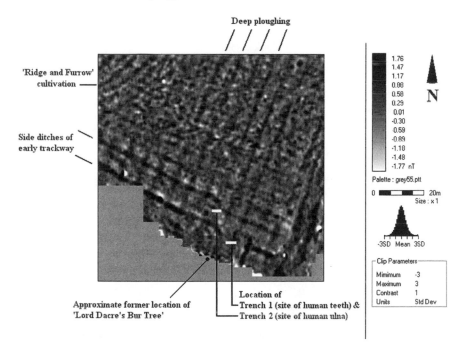

Fluxgate gradiometer (magnetic) survey of part of the Towton battlefield.

During the earth resistance survey, two human teeth were discovered on the surface of the plough soil within the survey grid and were precisely recorded. When the location of the teeth was superimposed over the magnetic geophysical survey results (see figure), they were found to lie directly over one of two short parallel anomalies which were located in the southeast corner of the survey area. These ran in an almost north-south direction, and consisted of some of the strongest readings recorded from the geophysical surveys. Additionally, when the location of the ulna—found during metal detector scanning—was superimposed over the geophysical survey results, it was observed to be closely associated with another linear anomaly.

EXCAVATION

Following the discovery of the human remains and the corresponding geophysical survey anomalies, it was decided to test their origin using archaeological evaluation. A test trench (Trench 2) was excavated at the location given by the GPS for the ulna, but no associated feature or other distinctive archaeological information could be identified.

Another test trench (Trench 1) was excavated at the location recorded for the teeth, revealing the fragmented remains of an arrowhead and several small

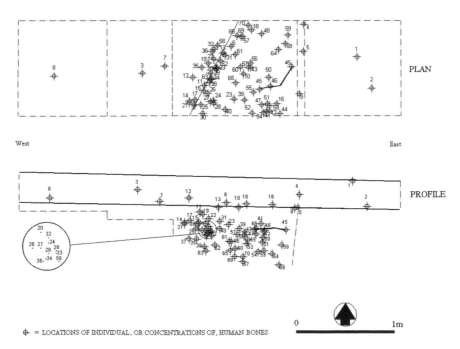

⊕ = LOCATIONS OF INDIVIDUAL, OR CONCENTRATIONS OF, HUMAN BONES

Plan and profile of Trench 1 showing locations of human bones.

human bones and teeth within the topsoil. As the trench was extended further, more human remains were uncovered, including fragments of skull, vertebra, patella, fingers, toes, and additional teeth. The precise location of each find was three-dimensionally recorded and the bones and artifacts removed (see figure). The test pit was excavated until a different soil matrix was encountered, not the expected solid limestone, but gray clay. This material was similar to clay, recorded during another local excavation, which was found to have derived from the silting up of a very large prehistoric ditch.[7] However, the clay in Trench 1 displayed a steeply sloping profile, suggesting that it must have been re-cut. It could also be observed that the feature in Trench 1 continued downward and sideways beyond the limits of the trench, and it was therefore decided not to excavate it further at the time, as the initial purpose of evaluating the feature had been fulfilled. The excavation was then fully recorded and backfilled. The evaluation suggested that the feature might originally have been an earlier ditch that had later been re-cut and re-used for later burial.

INTERPRETATION

The location of the ulna, found prior to the excavation of Trench 2, was not found near any archaeological feature. It might therefore have derived from the feature located in Trench 1 and have been moved, either in antiquity or by recent plowing. Alternatively it could have derived from a separate pit containing additional human remains. Its distance from Trench 1 suggested the latter hypothesis.

The location of the teeth found prior to the excavation of Trench 1 corresponded with an archaeological feature, which appeared to be part of a ditch or pit. The human remains recovered from this feature in Trench 1 were largely disarticulated, although the anatomical position of some bones suggested that the skeletal elements had been partially articulated when they were interred (see figure). It could not be determined, however, whether complete individuals had been interred and subsequently disturbed or whether fragmented parts had been buried in this feature. The distribution of the bones within the pit suggested that the bones had been interred as part of the fill matrix, pointing to the latter hypothesis. It was also observed that all bones and bone fragments recovered were small, and generally no larger than 10 cm in size.

The discovery of human remains in an area where a substantial number of arrowheads has been found suggests that there might be a link between the two. It is therefore possible that the arrowheads might originally have derived from the dead, the remains of which have subsequently been disturbed.

Importantly, it is evident that these arrowheads have deteriorated to such a degree that their ferrous content has largely been depleted and are therefore not immediately visible as "ferrous spikes," the term usually given to fragments of ferrous metal recorded by magnetic geophysical survey.[8] This

Semi-articulated human radius and ulna, recorded in Trench 1.

is important, as a magnetic geophysical survey carried out in 1997 on ''The Gastons,'' a part of the medieval battlefield at Tewkesbury, England (1471), failed to identify evidence from the medieval battle.[9] If it can be shown that the medieval arrowheads, which are known to exist, at Towton cannot be identified on the geophysical survey results of the same area, then it is doubtful whether similar evidence of battle will be identified, using the same methods, on other medieval battlefields. Similar forms of evaluation using fluxgate gradiometer should therefore not solely be used to locate such artifacts.

At Towton, a series of curvilinear anomalies had been identified in the north-western part of the magnetic geophysical survey, which is indicative of a medieval ridge and furrow field system (see figure). Notably, the lack of these features in the rest of the survey grid suggests that only part of the area had been cultivated during the medieval period. The clear lack of medieval cultivation in the corner of this field must have been due to obstructions, such as earlier earthworks, which prevented the plowing of this area. This, together with the discovery of the medieval arrowheads and human remains in concentrated areas, suggests one of the following scenarios: it is possible that burial pits or trenches were excavated coincidentally on the sites of earlier features. The lack of medieval cultivation in this area, however, suggests that these features may still have been recognizable during the medieval period and were therefore re-used following the battle by re-cutting them and using them as burial pits. These burial features might have been filled with the smaller human bones which remained on the battlefield following the clearance of larger skeletal elements. Alternatively, the features might have been used to inter the bodies of casualties following the battle, only to be removed at a later date. The spoil, together with any smaller bones that were overlooked, were then replaced in the burial pits.

Generally speaking, no patterning within the human remains could be observed. However, a linear alignment of several bones within one area of the pit, which ran in an approximate north-south direction across the trench, suggested that some bones had either been arranged in this manner, or that something had disturbed part of the pit fill and aligned some of its contents. The sides of the pit at this point also exhibited traces of a vertical disturbance which ran from the top of the pit fill downward. An on site visit from the local farmer clarified the reason for this disturbance. Some years prior to the excavation, an external contractor had been employed to plow the field in question. He had come from an area of Britain that required the subsoil to be deep-plowed in order to "break up the iron-pan and release nutrients." The subsoil beneath the field at Towton, however, is Magnesian Limestone rock and should not be deep-plowed—otherwise blocks of limestone are brought to the surface, resulting in the topsoil washing into the newly created ruts and becoming much thinner.[10] This is an important observation as it is therefore apparent that the deep-plowing of the site on a single occasion had caused the arrangement of bones within the feature as well as the linear anomaly in the sides of the test pit. The effects of the same deep-plowing had also caused a number of parallel linear anomalies that had previously been observed running north-south on the magnetic geophysical survey result displays (see figure).

The archaeological evaluation demonstrated that medieval arrowheads and human remains had been brought to the surface by a single episode of deep plowing, causing their identification but also deterioration and degradation through the effects of weather and additional annual plowing.

DISCUSSION

The results of the archaeological excavation of the burial feature are of major importance, as they represent an assemblage of human remains archaeologically recorded in the center of a medieval battlefield.

The current evidence suggests that long before the battle took place, a pre-existing feature, such as a pit or ditch, had been excavated and allowed to silt up. The feature was presumably still evident in the landscape during the medieval period to such an extent that this area was avoided by medieval cultivation. The feature was re-cut and filled with human remains following the Battle of Towton. It could not be determined whether or not the incomplete skeletons represent a primary burial of disarticulated human remains, or the secondary reburial of the human bones which remained after most of the larger bones had been removed.

A historical document dating to February 19, 1484, describes events 23 years after the battle of Towton and appears to confirm this latter hypothesis. It notes that in 1484 King Richard III gave a Royal Grant of Annuity[11] to

Saxton parish church (which lies to the south of the battlefield) so that the human remains from the Battle of Towton could be removed from the battle-field and placed in consecrated ground:

> and the people of this kingdom in a plentiful multitude were taken away from human affairs; and their bodies were notoriously left on the field, aforesaid, and in other places nearby, thoroughly outside the ecclesiastical burial-place, in three hol-lows. Where upon we, on account of affection, contriving the burial of the deceased men of this sort, caused the bones of these same men to be exhumed and left for an ecclesiastical burial in these coming months, partly in the parish church of Saxton in our said county of York and in the cemetery of the said place, and partly in the chapel of Towton, aforesaid, and the surroundings of this very place.

This grant provides primary documentary evidence for the removal of cas-ualties from the battlefield and may therefore refer to the pit identified in the geophysical survey and excavation.

Areas of graves have been highlighted on most post mid-eighteenth-century maps of the battlefield (e.g., Jeffries's map of Yorkshire)[12] but often in different locations. However, as previous archaeological excavations on such sites have proven,[13] these map locations are generally erroneous, and so it has not been possible to locate the graves using such evidence. However, there is a historical feature that is marked on the early ordnance survey maps, the meaning of which has since been lost or misinterpreted, that might originally have pointed to the location of the graves. As the location of the graves has now been determined by the discovery of the arrowheads and human remains within the pit, it can be shown to lie in close proximity to a position on the 1849 ordnance survey map that is annotated with the words

North Acres: Stump of the Bur Tree from which Lord Dacre was shot.[14]

Although it initially appears that there is little to connect the text and the graves, an understanding of the background relating to this piece of text is enlightening. It refers to Lord Dacre, a leading Lancastrian noble who was killed at the Battle of Towton and whose death is commemorated by a medie-val tomb in the nearby graveyard of Saxton church. Large quantities of bones, which were removed from the battlefield, were also allegedly reburied close to his tomb in a large ossuary outside the northern wall of the church.[15] In 1585, Glover recounted the tale of Lord Dacre and the tree thus.

> This Lord Dacres, as the report goeth, was slayne by a boy, at Towton Field, which boy shot him [with an arrow] out of a burtree, when he had unclasped his helmet to drink a cup of wyne, in revenge of his father, whom the said lord had slayne before, which tree hath beene remarkable ever since by the inhabitants, and decayed within this few yeares. The place where he was slayne is called the North Acres, whereupon they have this ryme, "The Lord Dacres, Was slayne in the North Acres."[16]

The tree allegedly marked the site of the death of Lord Dacre. There are therefore several historical and archaeological connections between the area highlighted by the human remains and arrowheads, and this story. Both relate to people killed in the Battle of Towton, both relate to arrows or arrowheads, both potentially have close connections to the dead from the battle that have been reburied in Saxton churchyard, and both relate to exactly the same location (see figure).

It is therefore feasible that the reference to Lord Dacre's tree also refers to the former site of a memorial or marker that might once have been situated near the mass graves of victims of the battle, but which has not been evident since before Glover's visit in 1585. It is also possible that Lord Dacre's remains were removed from the battlefield together with his comrades in 1484, after which a previous marker on the battlefield was allowed to deteriorate. The question must therefore be raised: were Lord Dacre's remains identifiable 23 years after the battle and if so, was this only possible because his grave had been marked? Alternatively, was Lord Dacre really buried inside his tomb in Saxton graveyard or was he interred together with the other bones from the mass grave, in the large ossuary on the northern side of the church?

The hypothesis of a grave marker on the battlefield is important, as it is possible that other sites of former markers on medieval battlefields, or the markers themselves, such as Lord Audley's Cross at Blore Heath, England (1459), might relate to the proximity of graves. A good example of this is the battlefield at Wisby (1361), Sweden, where a large stone cross still dominates the site of the graves of those who died in the battle.[17] It is also possible that other unmarked grave sites might be archaeologically evident by artifact scatters, such as arrowheads, reflecting the disturbed remains of battlefield casualties.

Importantly, it is also evident that deep plowing, even on the one occasion when it was accidentally carried out, has seriously disturbed previously secure archaeological deposits. This action has brought to the surface human remains and large quantities of archaeological artifacts, thereby enabling their discovery. However, unless recorded *in-situ* and collected, they will soon disintegrate due to their current fragile state.

A plan of the arrowhead distribution suggests that they were brought to the surface across a wide area in the approximate shape of a rectangle. It is probable that this concentration of arrowheads represents an area where bodies from the battle were dumped and left exposed, or were partly interred by being placed in shallow graves or pre-existing features. Alternatively, the arrowhead concentrations may reflect areas of an additional mass grave.

The magnetic geophysical survey highlights linear disturbances where the plow has brought deeply buried magnetic material to the surface. The location of arrowheads and human remains within this area of disturbance suggests that other mass graves similar to the two already highlighted might lie deeply buried below the ground. It is therefore possible that other graves, which might not have been emptied of their human remains in 1484, still exist in parts of the field. This hypothesis is strengthened by a reference in Drake[18] who wrote about a visit to the battlefield in the early eighteenth century. He states that

> about a year or two ago, two gentlemen and myself had the curiosity to go and see a fresh grave opened in these fields. Where amongst vast quantities of bones, we found some arrow piles, pieces of broken swords, and five very fresh groat pieces of Henry the fourth, fifth, and sixth's coin. These laid; near all together, close to a thigh bone, which made us conjecture that they had not time to strip the dead before they tossed them into the pit.

This description contains several similarities with the evidence from the test trench—human bones and arrowheads—and is almost certainly describing the same area, although Drake infers that the grave he observed was potentially intact, suggesting that not all of the graves were emptied in 1484.

CONCLUSIONS

The Towton battlefield research has clearly shown that a medieval battlefield can be analyzed and recorded using a multidisciplinary array of archaeological techniques. One such technique is the use of a good quality metal detector by a competent practitioner, with the aim of identifying non-ferrous and non-military artifacts. Once concentrations of these objects have been mapped, they can be specifically targeted using more intensive methods of analysis, including geophysical survey and archaeological excavation. The current investigation has shown that artifacts, which have previously been almost unrecognizable to most forms of prospection, can be located once their archaeological signature has been recognized.

The archaeological investigation at Towton has shown that concentrations of medieval arrowheads can point to areas of body deposition or burial. This suggests that it might not always have been possible to remove every arrowhead from the bodies prior to burial.

Using documentary evidence, as well as archaeological prospection, it has been possible to identify battle-related mass graves in the center of the Towton battlefield. These graves had apparently been inserted into earlier archaeological features, probably to reduce the size and number of new graves required. In 1484, however, only 23 years after the battle, according to Richard III's instructions, at least some of the graves were excavated and the dead reburied in Saxton churchyard and around a chapel in Towton. The recent archaeological excavation demonstrated, however, that not all of the smaller bones were removed from the pits, but that some were backfilled together with the excavated spoil. Partial articulation of some of these bones suggests that the dead were still partially fleshed when the mass graves were re-excavated in 1484.

Research of the battlefield, with the aim of identifying mass graves has also highlighted that archaeological features recorded using geophysical survey should be investigated through archaeological excavation if vital evidence is not to be overlooked.

This research has subsequently led to the first scientific analysis of medieval arrowheads, by the Royal Armouries, from a known conflict. Preliminary results suggest that these weapons were manufactured using previously undocumented technological procedures.[19] The Towton arrowhead collection is therefore, in itself, of great archaeological and scientific importance.

A disturbing outcome of the research is that now, despite the fact that archaeological evidence of a medieval battle has been identified and its location recorded, none of this unique evidence is legally protected. Every day artifacts are being removed from the topsoil by metal detectorists who are not recording where they find them. Such detectorists are destroying the very essence of what they have come to look for—tangible evidence of the Battle of Towton.

Other battlefields, such as at Shrewsbury, England, have suffered far worse and have almost been picked clean before their locations have been archaeologically proven.[20] If these nationally important sites cannot be legally protected, it is the duty of the archaeological profession to record them before it is too late. It is therefore necessary for sufficient grant aid and resources for funded projects to be made available to allow those already carrying out this important research, and others who will follow them, to be able to continue at a more efficient and productive rate before this finite resource disappears, unrecorded, forever.

NOTES

1. Myers 1969.
2. English Heritage 1995.
3. Hinds 1912.
4. Sutherland (forthcoming a).
5. Sutherland 2000a.
6. Sutherland 2000b.
7. Sutherland 2002.
8. Clark 1990.
9. Barker 1997.
10. Personal communication between T. L. Sutherland and the farm manager, Paul Saxon of the Hartley Estate, on whose land the excavation in Towton Dale took place, September 25, 2003.
11. Richard III 1484. *Royal Grant of Annuity to Saxton Parish Church, 19 February 1483/84.* From a document of unknown origin handed to the author by Dr. Donald Verity (formerly of Towton Hall; for which the author is duly grateful) from his private collection of works relating to Towton. The document was translated from a facsimile of a later copy written in Latin.

12. Margary 1973.
13. Sutherland (forthcoming b).
14. Ordnance Survey 1849. *The 6 Inch to 1 Mile Map of Towton and Saxton.* Sheet 205 (North Yorkshire County Council Record Office, Ref. MIC3357/191).
15. Brooke 1857.
16. Whitaker 1816.
17. Thordeman 1940.
18. Drake 1978.
19. Starley 2002.
20. Personal communication between T. L. Sutherland and Dr. T. Pollard at the Shrewsbury Museum on July 12, 2003, at a day meeting held by the Finds Research Group.

REFERENCES CITED

Barker, P. P. 1997. *A Report for Cotswold Archaeological Trust on a Geophysical Survey Carried out at The Gastons, Tewkesbury.* Stratascan, Geophysical & Specialist Survey Services Report.

Brooke, R 1857. *Visits to the Fields of Battle in England of the Fifteenth Century.* Russel Smith, London.

Clark, A. 1990. *Seeing Beneath the Soil: Prospecting Methods in Archaeology.* Batsford, London.

Drake, F. 1978. *Eboracum or the History and Antiquities of the City of York from its Original to its Present Time, 1736.* E.P. Publishing, London.

English Heritage. 1995. *The Register of Historic Battlefields.* English Heritage, London.

Hinds, A. B. (ed.). 1912. *Calendar of State Papers and Manuscripts in the Archives and Collections of Milan Vol.1. 1385–1618.* His Majesty's Stationary Office, London.

Margary, H. 1973. *A Survey of the County of York by Thomas Jefferys 1775.* Lymphe Castle, Kent.

Myers, A. R. (ed.). 1969. *English Historical Documents 1327–1485.* Eyre & Spottiswoode, London.

Starley, D. 2002. Unpublished report by Dr. D. Starley of the Royal Armouries, Leeds, for Mr. T. L. Sutherland, on the analysis of arrowheads from the battlefield at Towton.

Sutherland, T. L. (forthcominga). *The Application of an Integrated Prospection Methodology to the Understanding of the Archaeological Landscape of the Towton Battlefield.* PhD Thesis, University of Bradford, Bradford, England.

Sutherland, T. L. (forthcomingb). *Locating and Quantifying the Dead from the Battle of Towton: Analysing the Available Data.* A paper given at the "Fields of Conflict" Conference in Åland, Finland, September 2002.

Sutherland, T. L. 2000a. Recording the Grave. In V. Fiorato, A. Boylston, and C. Knüsel (eds.), *Blood Red Roses: The Archaeology of a Mass Grave from the Battle of Towton AD1461,* 36–44. Oxbow, Oxford.

Sutherland, T. L. 2000b. The Archaeological Investigation of the Towton Battlefield. In V. Fiorato, A. Boylston, and C. Knüsel (eds.), *Blood Red Roses: The Archaeology of a Mass Grave from the Battle of Towton AD1461,* 155–168. Oxbow, Oxford.

Sutherland, T. L. 2002. *An Archaeological Evaluation of an Enclosure Indicated by Crop Marks near Towton, North Yorkshire*. Unpublished report, carried out as part of the Towton Battlefield Archaeological Survey.

Thordeman, B. (ed.). 1940. *Armour from the Battle of Wisby 1361*. Vitterhets Historie Och Antikvitets Akademien, Stockholm.

Whitaker, T. D. 1816. *Loidis and Elmete*. Privately published, Leeds.

Indian Resistance in New Spain: The 1541 AD Battlefield of Peñol de Nochistlán, an Exemplar of Indigenous Resistance

Charles Haecker, Elizabeth A. Oster,
Angélica Medrano Enríquez, & Michael L. Elliott

THE MIXTÓN WAR of 1541–1542 AD is a virtually forgotten conflict of early Spanish Colonial Mexico, yet its consequences were far-reaching for both the Spanish victors and the vanquished native peoples of central Mexico. This war of rebellion derived from Spanish policies of forcibly replacing native cultural life ways with an alien European economy, social structure, and religion. Following their conquest of the Caxcan[1] homeland in 1530, the Spanish replaced uncooperative native leaders with those who were willing to accept Spanish rule and culture. At the same time, thousands of Caxcan people were rounded up to work on the newly created agricultural and ranching estates.

Growing resentment found a voice in one charismatic Caxcan leader, Tenamaxtle (var. Tenamaxtli), who planted the seeds of revolt. The opportunity for open rebellion came in the spring of 1541, after hundreds of Spanish had departed from Nueva Galicia with the Coronado and Alarcón expeditions. In the spring of 1541 Tenamaxtle's rebel armies, in a series of coordinated attacks, destroyed Spanish settlements of the province of Nueva Galicia with the goal of driving out the hated enemy from their land.[2] The Spanish viceroy in Mexico City, Antonio de Mendoza, realized that the rebellion had to be quashed as quickly as possible to prevent it from spreading to other regions of Mexico.

Accordingly, the lieutenant governor of Nueva Galicia, Cristóbal de Oñate, requested military assistance from Pedro de Alvarado—an experienced, ambitious, and especially brutal *conquistador*—to destroy the Caxcan centers of resistance within Nueva Galicia. Alvarado scraped together approximately 100 Spanish foot soldiers and cavalry, supported by one artillery piece. The small Spanish force also included a larger body of allied Tlaxcaltecan[3] warriors[4], who were armed with various types of native weaponry. From

Zapotlán Alvarado advanced first northward to the newly established city of Guadalajara to obtain supplies and reinforcements, and then headed north towards Peñol de Nochistlán, a Caxcan urban center situated on a high, rocky hill, or *peñol*. To prepare for the impending Spanish attack thousands of Caxcan warriors at Peñol de Nochistlán manned concentric rings of dry-laid rock walls that encircled the base, slopes, and escarpment of the hill city. Behind these defensive positions the warriors stockpiled an ample supply of sling stones, arrows, and javelins.

Accounts of the battle are sketchy and one-sided. One account states that Alvarado first invested the base of the peñol with a combined force of harquebusiers, crossbowmen, pikemen, and Tlaxcaltecans, "... and stationed squads of horsemen where it seemed fit ...".[5] The one artillery piece, firing solid shot, was intended to breach the concentric rings of rock walls. The Spanish had some initial success, having driven the Caxcan defenders away from two rock wall defensive positions. The cavalry, followed by foot soldiers and Tlaxcaltecan warriors, then chased the retreating Caxcan warriors up slope and toward the heavily defended escarpment. But fierce Caxcan counterattacks pushed the Spaniards and their native allies down slope and onto the rolling plain that surrounded the peñol. Caxcan warriors, now sensing victory, pressed their attacks. Alvarado, "with some recklessness," was in the forefront of a cavalry counterattack when a horse up slope slipped and tumbled on top of him. Unconscious and mortally injured, Alvarado was dragged away from the thick of battle.[6] The demoralized Spanish force, now under constant attack, made its way back to Guadalajara, which the Caxcan army immediately placed under siege. Other tribes, seeing an opportunity to annihilate the hated Spaniards, joined the Caxcan cause. Even Mexico City was in danger of falling.

The Caxcan victory, however, was short-lived. The Spaniards assembled another, even larger army that included over 800 horsemen and foot soldiers along with tens of thousands of allied warriors. They first lifted the siege of Guadalajara, and then methodically destroyed the centers of Caxcan resistance. The Spanish once again arrived at Peñol de Nochistlán. After two days of fierce fighting the overwhelming Spanish force finally reached the top of the peñol and breached its last defensive wall, but "... [the warriors] defended it with many stone weapons and arrows ...".[7] Thousands of Caxcan warriors fought to the death; many others committed mass suicide by jumping off a precipice of the peñol. It was reported that "... of the [Caxcan defenders] on the peñol, not even 20 escaped because those who were fleeing encountered the horsemen ...".[8]

By 1542 the Caxcan revolt was stamped out and Spanish authority re-established in Nueva Galicia, although conflicts would continue to the west in the lands of the Nayarita for decades longer. In the process all of the Caxcan urban centers were laid waste, the defenseless Caxcan people either slaughtered or forced to work for the Europeans as virtual slaves (Tenamaztle

1959).[9] Over the following decades, the region was wracked by Spanish-introduced diseases, which ultimately resulted in the obliteration of the remaining Caxcan peoples and their allies. The region was eventually re-populated by various other indigenous groups as well as Spanish settlers. Although Tenamaxtle's revolt ultimately failed, his memory became immortalized by the native peoples of central and western Mexico. In some of the Indian villages of this region, the Mixtón War is celebrated to this day as a symbol of indigenous resistance.[10]

The identification and recordation of Peñol de Nochistlán, the site of one of the greatest battles of the Mixtón War, would present an opportunity to define a rare event in human history. This is a place wherein soldiers of the Old World, utilizing the technology and tactics reflective of the early modern era, met in pitched battle warriors of the New World who employed a radically different technology with its corresponding appropriate tactics.

There is a respectable body of literature regarding early sixteenth-century Spanish battle tactics as they were applied in the New World. Especially useful are published eyewitness accounts of those who actively participated in the conquest of Mesoamerican peoples, or who fought against the Chichimec tribes of northern Mexico during the latter half of the sixteenth century.[11] Spanish methods of warfare underwent a revolution during the first decades of the sixteenth century, a revolution that aided the transformation of Spain from a regional to a global power. Cohesion, the social force that holds units together in combat and that makes the difference between a unit and a mob of individuals, was a Spanish strong point. The Spaniards fought as integrated units: sword, pike, and shot acted in seemingly automatic concert with horse. John Elliott[12] makes the cogent point that a balanced force of as few as 50 Spaniards, horse and foot, could hold their own against a numerically superior force of Mesoamerican warriors on open and level terrain, unless overcome by exhaustion.

The Spaniards' superior weapons are one of the favorite explanations as to why their soldiers usually could defeat their Mesoamerican counterparts. However, Spanish artillery, harquebus, and crossbows often broke down during battles, while their warrior opponents were known to charge through the hail of harquebus and crossbow bolt fire, and run past the cavalry. Thus, most of the fighting was hand-to-hand. The conquistadors, with their slender blades of steel, had an immense advantage over Mesoamerican warriors since they could strike much more quickly and with far more deadly force, advantages magnified by the warriors' lack of effective armor.

The Spanish invariably fought as a cohesive unit, both fighting well and keeping their ranks. When outnumbered, as they usually were, the Spanish typically formed a box formation that was seldom broken. Crossbowmen and harquebusiers worked as a team, with one set loading weapons while the other set fired, and so on. Swordsmen slashed at the enemy's guts, while the cavalry and pikemen aimed at their faces. Before the enemy warriors could use their slings and bows, Spanish cavalry would charge the group and force them to fight hand-to-hand, and hold them at bay long enough for infantry to come into the fray and effectively end the fight. Pikemen would also form up in lines and present an impenetrable wall of pikes. Cannon and harquebusiers presented firepower sufficient to break up a massed charge of warriors, whereupon swordsmen and cavalry would move in and finish the slaughter. Horses gave the Spaniards crucial advantages in striking power, shock effect, and speed. The well-mounted Spaniard could strike harder and more swiftly and reach farther with his sword than could his companion on foot. He could use the speed and mobility of his mount to drive home the point of his lance, and could do so without coming within reach of his enemy's handheld weapon. Yet even with their unquestioned superiority in weaponry and tactics, conquistador companies owed their amazing victories largely to the support of thousands of native warriors that fought with them.[13]

There are extant codices of the period that suggest the tactics and orders of battle as practiced by the various native military powers encountered by the Spanish.[14] Mesoamerican combat involved an orderly sequence of weapons use and tactics, usually beginning with projectile fire. Although there were specialist archers and slingers, the opening salvo of projectiles was cast by all the combatants, employing whichever projectiles they possessed, and causing considerable harm. Battle descriptions indicate that the initial engagement took place at approximately 150 feet (50 meters) and continued until the projectiles were almost depleted. The armies then closed during the waning moments of the mass barrage to take advantage of the covering fire. Once the armies closed the slingers and archers lost their massed targets and could strike only at individuals. They were also used to counter enemy archers and slingers and to harass reinforcements and prevent encirclement. Sling stones were said to be capable of shattering a horse's thigh, fracturing a skull, or snapping a sword blade in two with a square hit at short range, and the Spanish feared these missiles as they feared no other indigenous weapon. On the whole, however, sling stones usually could only wound whereas crossbow bolts and harquebus balls killed, so the overriding advantage went to the conquistadores.[15]

Codices depicting pre- and post-Hispanic battle scenes indicate that opposing Mesoamerican battle formations favored relatively open ranks in which the combatants were widely dispersed. This spacing was necessary to allow *macuahuitl* or sword-wielding warriors at least a six-foot (two-meter) radius—the length of the extended arm and weapon—to swing these weapons. Thrusting spears were used for jabbing and some restricted lateral movement. Codices frequently depict placement of spearmen between the macuahuitl warriors, with the length of the spear shafts allowing the spearmen to thrust at the enemy without getting in harm's way of a nearby comrade's swinging macuahuitl. The dislodging and breaking of obsidian and chert blades on these and other lithic blade-edged weapons such as spears typically occurred but did not seem to seriously affect the fighting abilities of the warriors who used them.[16] Mesoamerican warfare was highly ritualized in concept, with man-to-man heroic combat between peers of rank considered the ideal match. In contrast, their European enemies were intent on killing and maiming indiscriminately and, whenever possible, at safe distances using long-reaching projectiles. In the eyes of Mesoamerican warriors such fighting behavior was barbaric and cowardly. Unfortunately for them, however, it was also quite effective in getting the job done.

Documents of the period are silent as to how, or even if, Spanish military companies integrated with comparable units of their native allies. Phrased another way, would a Spanish commander mix a company of pikemen with allied warriors armed with javelins and atlatls? Would warriors armed with obsidian-edged hand weapons be supported by crossbowmen? Were companies of Spanish soldiers used as frontline shock troops, with their native allies used solely in a secondary, auxiliary role? Neither do we have a clear idea as to the typical order of battle employed by the various Mexican tribes during the early Colonial periods. As in any other battlefield study, we depend on identifying and interpreting the patterned detritus of battle toward answering these, and other, questions regarding applied tactics.

The findings from Spanish conquistador sites of comparable age suggest the detritus of this battle would include iron and/or copper bolt heads and lead balls, the projectiles fired from crossbow and harquebus, respectively. Other metal objects reflecting a Spanish presence would be fasteners such as buckles, hooks and eyes, buttons, pins, and copper-alloy lace tags, termed "aglets." Aglets, used to prevent fraying of the ends of cords that tied together the doublet and hose, are commonly found on Spanish military sites of this period. These objects would be intermixed with chert and obsidian projectile points, and sling stones of riverine pebbles that were pecked into a more spherical shape. The indigenous counterpoint to fragments of steel-edged swords, daggers, and lance heads would be, for example, obsidian bifaces and blades that once fitted into that classic Mesoamerican hand weapon, the macuahuitl. A nineteenth-century redrawing of the *Lienzo de Tlaxcala* clearly illustrates the wood and metal elements of the macuahuitl carried by native warriors.[17] Metal fittings from crossbows, harquebuses, swords, lances, and pikes might also be present, as well as copper rings used to hold fabric hair braids, and copper bells. We know very little, however, as to what other typical metal objects of indigenous origin might also be present. Contemporary native and Spanish illustrations suggest that non-noble Caxcan warriors wore little more than a breech clout (if even that) and a grim visage.[18] It is possible that badges of rank, and jewelry made of precious metals and semi-precious stones, such as ear spools and lip plugs typically worn by the nobility, will be present on the battlefield.[19]

We have noted that, during both battles at Peñol de Nochistlán, the Spaniards utilized cavalry squads in their attempts to break through the Caxcan defenses, and to chase down any enemies that tried to escape the ensuing slaughter. The recovery of wrought iron horseshoe nails of a type typically used by Europeans during the mid-sixteenth century would be a major component in the determination of battle tactics. Associated artifacts would be horseshoes and horse equipage of the period, such as harness bells. We hypothesize that this location is where one might best attempt an ascent on horseback. Accordingly, we believe Caxcan warriors would have massed behind that segment of breastworks where the Spaniards directed their main attack.

We expect to find an intermixing of European and native-related artifacts along the slopes and base of the peñol. Specific battle locations may be identified by discrete concentrations of lithic projectile points, sling stones, and obsidian blades derived from native hand weapons, intermixed with metallic artifacts that reflect European missile and hand weapons, armor, and apparel. The primary lithic material used by native allies of the Spaniards may well have been obsidian obtained from various sources near Mexico City, located some 240 miles (400 km) to the southeast of Nochistlán. In contrast, the Caxcan had access to West Mexican obsidians[20] and local cherts for making their stone-edged weapons, as well as riverine pebbles as the source material for their sling stones.

Of course, the first issue that must be addressed is simply identifying Peñol de Nochistlán. One might assume that primary documents, complemented by oral tradition and collectors' finds, would make this task simple. However, as is often the case in archaeological investigations of battlefields, this is not so. Decades of historical research conducted prior to this present study has determined only that Peñol de Nochistlán is a steep-sloped hill of respectable height, and located somewhere north of the City of Guadalajara. The hilltop in question should hold archaeological evidence of a Caxcan urban center dating no later than the mid-sixteenth century, and there likely exist remnants of concentric rings of dry-laid rock walls. Recent archaeological reconnaissance suggests that, in fact, there are many hills within the estimated 140 mi^2 (360 km^2) study area that meet these basic qualifications. One must consider that the bellicose Caxcan typically occupied and fortified many habitable peñols within their domain; therefore, it follows that a considerable number of these peñols were battlefields during the 1541–1542 war. An archaeological survey that included all of these sites is ideal but hardly practical given the constraints of this present investigation. Instead, we have applied a more thorough research of primary documents that pertain to this specific battle, followed by archaeological reconnaissance of a few of the more promising sites. This approach considerably narrowed the count of hilly contenders for the honor of being identified as Peñol de Nochistlán, the first and arguably the greatest battle of the Mixtón War.

Nochistlán de Mejía is a town founded by the Spanish prior to the Mixtón War. The name of the town is an obvious clue that Peñol de Nochistlán is likely in its vicinity. According to a document dated 1584, Peñol de Nochistlán was "situated 16 leagues [on average, approximately 50 miles/ 80 km] from the Episcopal cathedral, which is in the city of Guadalajara."[21] Nochistlán de Mejía, in fact, is located approximately 55 miles (90 km) northeast of Guadalajara, and there exist several likely elevations within a 12-mile (20 km) radius of Nochistlán de Mejía.

Documents research includes analyses of three period pictorial representations of the battle of Penol de Nochistlán. One of the representations (see figure) is by the famous copper plate engraver, Theodor de Bry (1528–1598); the other two were created by anonymous Native Americans (see figures).[22] De Bry did not actually witness the battle; rather, he completed his circa 1596 engraving based on an illustration that was produced prior to 1565 by Giralomo Benzoni (1520–?), an Italian who journeyed to the New World in 1541 and toured the Spanish possessions for some 14 years before returning to Italy.

Woodcut by Theodor de Bry, showing the European version of the 1541 battle of Peñol de Nochistlán. (Courtesy of the Seaver Center for Western History Research, Los Angeles County Museum of Natural History)

Benzoni's *Novae Novi Orbis Historiae* (1857 [1578]:22) consisted of adaptations of a variety of previously written accounts, which, in turn, described Spanish actions directed against the native inhabitants of the New World. Benzoni included the first battle of Peñol de Nochistlán as an example of such actions. Benzoni never visited Nueva Galicia so his illustration was based on obtaining first- or second-hand accounts from Spanish soldiers who fought at this battle. Thus, one cannot accept at face value this or other scenes that are depicted by De Bry's inflammatory engravings. Nonetheless, it is possible the image depicting the battle of Peñol de Nochistlán presents certain battle events and topographic features that hold a kernel of fact; therefore, these illustrated features should be considered when searching for the battle site.

If taken at face value, the De Bry engraving indicates the battle took place at the base, slopes, and crest of a conically shaped hill. It also places trees on the hilltop, with Caxcan warriors defending a breastwork of felled trees and stacked rocks along the escarpment. There is also a flowing stream at the base of the hill. We see a body of steel-armored horsemen in the foreground and in the process of fording the stream; harquebusiers likewise are advancing up slope, while dead and wounded horsemen and infantry litter the slope of the peñol. Caxcan warriors positioned behind the breastwork appear to be successfully defending their position by rolling logs and boulders down upon their attackers; many of the Caxcan are armed with clubs. Pedro de Alvarado appears as a fallen horseman in the middle of the scene, a contradiction of written documents that indicate Alvarado was mortally injured some distance away from the peñol. There are no indications on the engraving of a troop of native allies that reportedly fought with the Spanish.

Interestingly, De Bry's copper engraving receives some limited corroboration by the Codex Telleriano-Remensis (see figure on page 182). This codex, which describes the major events for the year 1541, supports two features of the De Bry engraving. Besides indicating the importance of Alvarado's death during the battle of Peñol de Nochistlán, it shows a Caxcan warrior shooting an arrow behind defensive rings of rock walls, and a stylized representation of a flowing stream surrounding the defensive position.

Additional detail is provided by the Compostela Map (see figure), thought to have been created in approximately 1550 by a native scribe who had been taught Spanish mapping conventions and orthography. Via text and simple schematic drawings, the map illustrates the various locations of native uprisings during the Mixtón War. One of these drawings depicts a pinnacle ringed by four rock walls, with two warriors firing arrows from the crest (see figure). Adjacent to the pinnacle is a peaked roof structure that symbolizes a pueblo. This drawing is labeled *"P. nochiztlan y pueblo"* ("Peñol Nochistlán and pueblo"). Apparently, at the initiation of the Mixtón War, there existed a close juxtaposition of this Caxcan-occupied peñol and the Spanish-occupied pueblo of Nochistlán.

Detail from the Codex Telleriano-Remensis (Folio 46r), depicting the death of Pedro de Alvarado at the first battle of the Peñol de Nochistlán. (Manuscrit Mexicain 385, Bibliothèque nationale de France)

Cerro San Miguel is a hill within the caldera of an extinct volcano, located approximately 12 miles (20 km) from the present-day town of Nochistlán de Mejía. Local legend holds that this hill is, in fact, Peñol de Nochistlán. In addition, the conical appearance of Cerro San Miguel is evocative of De Bry's engraving of Peñol de Nochistlán. For these two reasons Cerro San Miguel was assigned first priority for a reconnaissance-level survey. The survey crew walked a series of sample transects that traversed the base, slopes, and crest of Cerro San Miguel. The surveyors inspected the ground surface for battle-related lithic artifacts, as well as indicants of the defensive rock

Compostela Map: "Zonas limítrofes entre las Audiencias de Mexico y Guadalajara, ca. AD 1550" (Archivo General de Indias, Mapas y Planos México 560). Probably drawn by a native scribe, this map illustrates the various locations of Mixtón War battle sites, including the Peñol de Nochistlán.

walls reportedly constructed by the Caxcan. In addition, one of the surveyors employed a metal detector. Previous archaeological investigations of a Caxcan urban center[23] indicated that a variety of well-constructed architectural elements typified Caxcan settlements. Residential architecture was represented by structures built from perishable materials, on foundations of vertically laid rock slabs (termed *cimientos*), while elaborate civic-ceremonial precincts— usually built on the hilltops—were characterized by monumental stone masonry structures that were plastered, and probably painted with bright colors when in use. Archaeologists documented small terraces, larger masonry platforms, a variety of stone walls and revetments, and dry-laid masonry constructions that appeared to be more hastily created.

The reconnaissance of Cerro San Miguel yielded some interesting results. The surveyors discovered a segment of vertical slab wall foundation near the base of the hill, substantial remains of a ceremonial platform on its crest, and collapsed remains of two parallel, dry-laid stone walls spaced approximately six feet (two meters) apart. These rock walls were likely not intended as a formal ceremonial boundary since they were built by simply stacking tabular rocks directly on top of the ground. In fact, the stones used to construct the walls on the top of the Cerro apparently derived from the nearby ceremonial platform, which is partially stripped of its construction stones. These findings appeared to corroborate an account that Caxcan defenders hastily constructed rings of defensive walls around the peñol.

A battle of the magnitude of Peñol de Nochistlán would have resulted in thousands of bodies of the slain. Many bodies of Caxcan warriors may have been interred in nearby mass burials, as per the custom of the Caxcan peoples.[24] This assumes, of course, there were Caxcan survivors sufficient to exercise this custom. The Spaniards, as victors, would have had some opportunity to collect and bury all or at least some of their own dead, following the custom of their religious beliefs. In contrast, the bodies of those native warriors that were allied with the Spaniards—the Tlaxcaltecans, Mexica, and Otomís—may have remained largely where they fell, unclaimed and undoubtedly unmourned by both Spaniard and Caxcan. Regardless of the numbers of bodies that were removed, the battlefield still would have been a ghastly place of human decomposition for many years following this event. Thus, the chemical signature of bone—calcium phosphate—should be identifiable in elevated total phosphorus readings of battlefield soil.

Following Eidt (1973, 1977, 1985), the researchers applied the "spot test" technique of measuring the total phosphorus content of soil samples. This technique provides a quick means of determining gross measures of the total soil phosphorus, which typically bonds with aluminum, iron, and calcium. Regardless of the wholesale removal of skeletal remains from the battlefield, any dense concentrations of bone will produce elevated levels of calcium phosphate in the soil as the calcium leaching from the decomposing bones chemically bonded with the phosphorus naturally present in the soil. Once formed, soil phosphates are known to be extremely durable and relatively immobile.[25] The expected result of the soil testing was to document if elevated soil phosphorus levels are present within the soils found on the crest of Cerro San Miguel.

The survey team used a commercially available testing kit that provides an accurate, albeit qualitative, measurement of the total phosphorus in the soil samples. Since its relative density is higher than the surrounding background levels, the calcium phosphate comprises the major component of the total phosphorus, which is revealed by the relative degree of color change during soil testing. If present in significant amounts, phosphorus in solution turns "molybdenum blue." Color change was compared to colors in the charts supplied with the test kits, labeled "L," "M," and "H," which indicated low, medium, and high levels of soil phosphorus, respectively. Intensity of the resulting color change in each sample would be an indicator of relative quantity of phosphorus in the sample. For consistency, color changes noted in the soil samples were evaluated by consensus.

The survey team tested relative quantities of soil phosphorus at four locations on the crest of Cerro San Miguel. The team conducted two soil tests at each location: one test at the surface as a control, another at six inches (15 cm) below surface. One of these test locations contained high levels of soil phosphorus; two contained a medium level; and one location contained a low level. These findings give some support to the likelihood that a battle took place at Cerro San Miguel. We realize, however, that the Caxcan employed ceremonial centers as places to conduct human sacrifice, so the presence of significant quantities of soil phosphorus at this location may not be the direct result of a battle.

The reconnaissance survey of San Miguel produced one sling stone recovered near the base of the hill. A metal detection sweep of the crest of the hill yielded a bar of wrought iron having a chisel-shaped end, an object that possibly functioned as the business end of a club. As a whole, these features and artifacts, though scant, represented elements that one might expect from a hilltop defensive position during the Mixtón War. The crest and slopes of Cerro San Miguel were calculated, however, as covering an area of less than 4,000 m² (0.4 ha/1.0 acres), an area far too small to contain the reported thousands of Caxcan warriors who defended the urban center of Peñol de Nochistlán. Finally, Cerro San Miguel exhibits very little evidence of habitation architecture, which would be a key identifier for this battle site. The survey team concluded that Cerro San Miguel was a Caxcan ceremonial center worthy of defense during the Mixtón War, and it may even have been attacked by the Spanish army. Yet the fractional acreage of its crest and absence of habitation architecture indicated Cerro San Miguel and Peñol de Nochistlán were not the same hills.

Attention then shifted to the next likely location for the battle, that is, Cerro El Tuiche. This hill is located approximately six miles (10 km) northeast of Nochistlán de Mejía (see figure). Cerro El Tuiche is steep-sided, with a sheer precipice on its northeastern side (see figure). A permanent flowing stream demarcates its northern and eastern approaches. The top of Cerro El Tuiche is flat and encompasses about 7.4 acres (3 hectares), upon which lie the archaeological remains of a Caxcan urban center. Recall the Compostela Map detail (see figure), which implies a close juxtaposition existed between the Caxcan-defended peñol and the contemporaneous pueblo of Nochistlán: one might say the same of Cerro El Tuiche and present-day Nochistlán de Mejía. Finally, one side of Cerro El Tuiche is a sheer-sided precipice. As noted in the history of the battle the last of the Caxcan defenders, when faced with choosing either an ignominious submittal to the hated Spaniards or en masse suicide, chose the latter by jumping off Peñol de Nochistlán.

Utilizing a metal detector, the survey team investigated the base and slopes of Cerro El Tuiche. The surveyors soon discovered artifacts diagnostic of a mid-sixteenth-century battle: iron crossbow bolt heads (see figure on page 187); lead shot of a caliber range appropriate for harquebus; and two undated coins appropriate to the period of the Mixtón War. At Cerro El Tuiche project forensic anthropologist Angélica Medrano Enríquez employed the above-

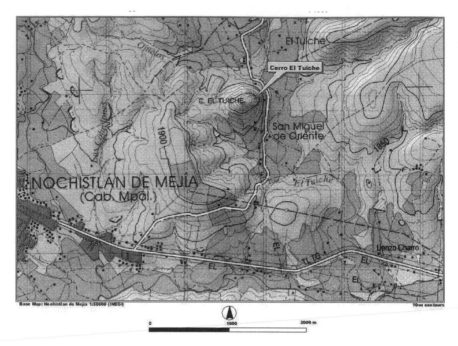

Topographic map showing the locations of Cerro El Tuiche and the present-day town of Nochistlán de Mejía. (from Carta Topográfica, F-13-D-37, INEGI, México)

Cerro El Tuiche, believed by researchers to be synonymous with Peñol de Nochistlán.

described "spot test" method for assessing relative amounts of calcium phosphate at this location. One tested location produced strong evidence that concentrations of subsurface calcium phosphate are present. Medrano Enríquez, who has excavated and analyzed Caxcan mass burials will eventually sample excavate this location.[26] Human skeletal remains, if encountered, will be monitored for battle-related trauma, pathological anomalies due to metabolic and infectious diseases, as well as indicants of the overall health status of the sample population.

These archaeological findings lend strong support to the researchers' present theory that Cerro El Tuiche and Peñol de Nochistlán are one and the same landforms. A comprehensive survey of this archaeological site is now being planned. We believe that, once the physical evidence of this battle is discovered and fully recorded, it will contribute a rarely viewed perspective of past actions and behavior in early Colonial Mexico. All too often, the victors of a war—or, even more frequently, their apologists—recount the events of their day, perhaps believing that they had silenced the vanquished forever. In this instance, we hope to once again give voice to those individuals who took part in a pivotal

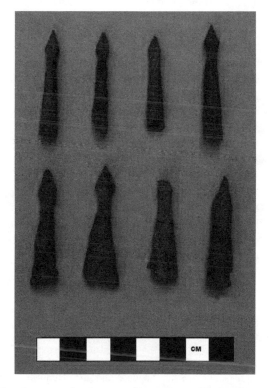

Crossbow bolt heads, recently discovered at Cerro El Tuiche as a result of an archaeological reconnaissance survey.

encounter in the New World, the result of social and political turmoil that marked the end of one era, and ushered in the next.

NOTES

Acknowledgments: The authors wish to acknowledge and thank the pueblo of Nochistlán de Mejía and its presidente for providing us with lodging, hospitality, and information during our stay there. We also are grateful to Richard and Shirley Flint for conducting documentary research related to this topic, and for reviewing and commenting on drafts of this article. *¡Gracias a todos!*

1. At the time of the Spanish Conquest, the Caxcan occupied a series of city-states or *cacicazgos independientes* in the region known today as "Los Altos" of Zacatecas and Jalisco. They enjoyed a sophisticated material culture that featured monumental architecture, utility and lapidary stoneworking, and complex ceramics. As was characteristic for their notorious Mexica cousins, Caxcan heads of state were referred to as *tlatoanis* (speakers). Their religious/ceremonial customs were focused on the interlocking intricacies of the *tonalamatl* or annual calendar round and the 52-year calendar cycle observed by most urban or semi-urban Mesoamerican peoples. Caxcan sites feature ballcourts, civic-ceremonial centers, and residential architecture apparently used by occupants belonging to a variety of social statuses, from *macehualtin* to privileged elites. As the Spanish Conquest moved north, the Caxcan settlements were the last outposts of "civilized" peoples participating in the life ways that have come to typify Mesoamerican culture as archaeologists define it. Due north, as depicted on the Compostela map, lay the *tierras de guerra* occupied by the Chichimeca.

2. Brother Juan Calero, a missionary, was killed near Tequila on June 10, 1541, when he attempted to pacify a group of Caxcan renegades holed up in the mountains. Calero thus attained the dubious honor of becoming the first European martyr in the New World (McCarty 1982:155).

3. Variants of the term "Tlaxcaltecan" that appear in professional and popular literature include "Tlascalan," "Tlaxcalan," "Tlazcalan," and even "Tezcalan." "Tlaxcaltecan" is the closest to the referent in Classical Nahuatl—the language spoken by the Caxcan, the Tlaxcaltecans, the Mexica or Aztec, and a number of other Central Mexican groups—and so is used here. With approximately one and a half million speakers, Nahuatl is spoken today by more people than any other indigenous language in Mexico.

4. Ibarra 1584.

5. Flint and Flint 2005.

6. Tello 1968.

7. Torres 1577.

8. Muñoz 1541.

9. Post-war relations between the Spanish and the vanquished Caxcan rebels are detailed in the *Relación de Agravios*, a petition made to the Royal Council of the Indies in Spain in the 1500s by Don Francisco Tenamaztle, a Caxcan nobleman (believed to be

the brother, and perhaps the betrayer, of the leader of the rebellion) who survived the Mixtón War. According to Reynoso (1959), the petition was written out and probably edited by Fray Bartolomé de las Casas, and incorporates many of las Casas's beliefs about appropriate treatment of indigenous peoples undergoing "Christianization." Don Francisco—or Petecatl, to use his Caxcan name—was believed to have succeeded the *cacique* who ruled at Nochistlán prior to the arrival of Nuño Beltran de Guzmán and his army of adventurers. Unlike his more famous brother who led the Caxcan during the Mixtón War, Don Francisco had behaved in a friendly and accommodating manner toward the Spanish and had even—by his own account—treatied with Don Antonio de Mendoza, leading his own people to suspect his motives (1959:7). At the time that he made his petition, however, he had been declared responsible for the uprisings, arrested, and transported to Spain by Mendoza's successor, Viceroy Don Luis de Velasco (1959:7).

10. The story of the war's end has become ritualized as an important ceremony still celebrated in the Mexican towns and villages located in what was once the Gran Caxcána. The rite celebrates the divine intervention of St. James, patron saint of the conquistadores, in convincing the natives to lay down their arms. The saint's appearance and the capitulation of the native leaders are re-enacted as part of a series of encounters that take place on St. James's feast day. The ritual, referred to as the dance of the "tlastoanis" [sic], features an individual dressed as the saint as well as numerous men garbed in motley costumes topped by elaborate masks, the "tlastoanis."

11. Diaz 1963 [1576], Powell 1975, Sahagún 1978.

12. Elliott 1984:174.

13. Diaz 1963 [1576]: 101–103, Towsend 1993:24, White 1971:171.

14. Davies 1972, Hassig 1995: 95–109.

15. Hassig 1995:98–99, Hemming 1970:192.

16. Diaz 1963 [1576]:103.

17. The *Lienzo de Tlaxcala* is a painted document, created by Tlaxcaltecan scribes around the middle of the sixteenth century. According to Gurría Lacroix (1988:210) two copies were originally painted. Of these, one remained in Tlaxcala while the other was sent to Spain. Both were subsequently lost, although a copy of the version which remained in Mexico had been made by the French Scientific Commission during the Second Empire. A copy was also made in 1773 by Manuel Illañes. This copy is stored today in the National Museum of Anthropology. Copies by Chavero (1892 and 1964) and Cahuantzi (1892) are available for consultation today. The *lienzo* recounts the participation of Tlaxcaltecans in the episodes of conquest directed by Cortés, Alvarado, and Guzmán. The portions of interest with respect to West Mexico are Láminas LVI through LXXI. These pages detail the participation of Tlaxcaltecan allies in the campaigns led by Guzmán and his captains. Lámina LVIII is denominated as "Xuchipila."

18. Note, for example, the contrast in complexity of dress and equipage between the Tlaxcaltecan allies, many of whom were noblemen, with the defenders of "Xochipillan" (Juchipila or Cerro de las Ventanas) illustrated in a fragment from the *Lienzo de Tlaxcala*.

19. Anawalt 1981, Arnold and Weddle 1978, Ewen and Hann 1998:80, Hosler 1988.

20. Darling (1998) reports on sourcing studies for samples of utilized obisidian from Caxcan sites, which point to the Tequila Source Area in Jalisco and the Huitzila-La Lobera Source Area in Durango as important procurement areas for the Caxcan.

21. Calderon 1584.
22. Oster 2006.
23. Oster 2006.
24. Medrano, Enríquez, 1995 a and b, Oster 2006.
25. Bethell and Máté 1989:9, Eidt 1977, Lillios 1992:500, Neff 2002:18–19; Proudfoot 1975:103–104; Sanchez et al. 1996.
26. Medrano Enríquez, 1995a and b.

REFERENCES CITED

Anawalt, Patricia Rieff. 1981. *Indian Clothing Before Cortés, Mesoamerican Costumes From the Codices*. University of Oklahoma Press, Norman.

Arnold, J. Barto III, and Robert Weddle. 1978. *The Nautical Archeology of Padre Island: The Spanish Shipwrecks of 1554*. Academic Press, New York.

Benzoni, Giralomo. 1857. *History of the New World*. Translated by W. H. Smith, originally published in 1578 by the author in Geneva. The Hakluyt Society, London.

Bethell, Philip, and Ian Máté. 1989. The Use of Soil Phosphate Analysis in Archaeology: A Critique. In *Scientific Advances in Archaeology*, edited by Julian Henderson, 1–29. Oxbow Books, Oxford.

Calderón, Juan Gutiérrez. 1584. *Relación geográfica*. Bancroft Library, University of California, Berkeley.

Chavero, Alfredo. 1892. *Antigüdades mexicanas publicadas por la Junta Colombina de Mexico en el cuarto centenario del descubrimiento de América*. México, Oficina Tipográfica de la Secretaria de Fomento.

Darling, J. Andrew. 1998. Obsidian Distribution and Exchange in the North-Central Frontier of Mesoamerica. Ph.D. dissertation, University of Michigan. University Microfilms, Ann Arbor.

Davies, Nigel. 1972. The Military Organization of the Aztec Empire. *Atti del XL Congresso Internazionale degli Americanisti* 4:213–221.

De Bry, Theodor. 1978. *Conquistadores, Azteken en Inca's/Conquistadores, Aztecs and Incas*. A Facsímile Edition of 16th Century Engravings by Theodor De Bry. Van Hoeve, Amsterdam.

de la Torre, Mario. 1983. *El Lienzo de Tlaxcala*. Mario de la Torre, editor. Cartón y Papel de México, México, D. F.

Diaz, Bernal. 1963. *The Conquest of New Spain*. Translated by J. M. Cohen. The Folio Society, London. Originally published in Spain in 1576.

Eidt, Robert C. 1973. A Rapid Chemical Test for Archaeological Site Surveying. *American Antiquity* 38:206–210.

Eidt, Robert C. 1977. Detection and Examination of Anthrosols by Phosphate Analysis. *Science* 197(4311):1327–1333.

Eidt, Robert C. 1985. Theoretical and Practical Considerations in the Analysis of Anthrosols. In *Archaeological Geology*, edited by George R. Rapp and John A. Gifford, 155–189. Yale University Press, New Haven.

Elliott, John H. 1984. The Spanish Conquest and Settlement of America. In *Colonial Latin America*, Vol. I of *Cambridge History of Latin America*. Cambridge University Press, Cambridge.

Ewen, Charles R., and John H. Hann. 1998. *Hernando de Soto Among the Apalachee, The Archaeology of the First Winter Encampment*. University Press of Florida, Gainesville.

Flint, Richard, and Shirley Cushing Flint. 2005. *Documents of the Coronado Expedition, 1539–1542, "They Were Not Familiar with His Majesty nor Did They Wish to Be His Subjects,"* Document 25, Letter to Fernández de Oviedo, October 6, 1541, *from* Segunda Parte, Libro XXXIII, Capitulo LII, *Historia general y natural de las Indias*, 1547, Academia Real de la Historia, Madrid Colección Salazar/Castro 9/555 (H-32), 309–316. Southern Methodist University, Dallas.

Gurría Lacroix, Jorge. 1988. Historigrafía de la conquista de Occidente. In *Conquista Hispánica de la Provincias de los Tebles Chichimecas de la America Septentrional*, by José Luis Razo Zaragoza, Apéndice IX, 210–234. Universidad de Guadalajara, Guadalajara, Mexico.

Hassig, Ross. 1995. *Aztec Warfare, Imperial Expansion and Political Control*. University of Oklahoma Press, Norman.

Hemming, J. 1970. *The Conquest of the Incas*. Harvest Books, San Diego, CA.

Hosler, Dorothy. 1988. Ancient West Mexican Metallurgy: South and Central American Origins and West Mexican Transformations. *American Anthropologist* 90:832–853.

Ibarra, Diego de. 1584. Testimony, *In* AGI Patronato 78, R1, N1: Informacion de parte en la audiencia de Mexico, año 1584. Ms. on file, Bancroft Library, University of Southern California, Berkeley.

Lillios, Katina T. 1992. Phosphate Fractionation of Soils at Agroal, Portugal. *American Antiquity* 57:495–506.

Lopez Portillo y Weber, José. 1935. *La Conquista de la Nueva Galicia*. Secretaria de Educación Pública, Departamento de Monumentos, Talleres de la Nación.

McCarty, Kieran R. 1982. Los franciscanos en la frontera chichimeca. *Lecturas Históricas de Jalisco antes de la Independencia* Vol. 1, 143–181. Unidad Editorial Guadalajara, Jalisco.

Medrano Enríquez, Angélica. 1995a. *Informe: Rescate Arqueológico: Entierro Múltiple, El Mirador*. Consejo de Arqueología, Instituto Nacional de Antropología e Historia, México, D.F. Unpublished ms.

Medrano Enríquez, Angelica. 1995b. *Restos Oseos y Malacológicos, Sitio Arqueológico Las Ventanas, Juchipila, Zacatecas*. Tésis profesional de licenciatura, Universidad Autónoma de Guadalajara.

Muñoz, Col. 1541. Document XI, Carta de don Antonio de Mendoza al Obispo de Mexico. De junto al Coyna, October, 1541. Academia de la Historia, t. LXXXII, fol. 223, p. 171. Manuscript on file, Bancroft Library, UCLA, Berkeley.

Neff, Loy C. 2002. Archeological Survey and Soil Testing at Washita Battlefield National Historic Site, Roger Mills County, Oklahoma. National Park Service-Intermountain Region. Western Archeological and Conservation Center, *Publications in Anthropology* 82, Tucson.

Oster, Elizabeth A. 2006. Cerro de las Ventanas: A Northern Mesoamerican Frontier Site in Zacatecas, Mexico. Unpublished Ph.D. dissertation in Anthropology, Tulane University, New Orleans.

Powell, Philip Wayne. 1975. *Soldiers, Indians and Silver*. Center for Latin American Studies, Arizona State University, Tempe.

Proudfoot, B. 1975. The Analysis and Interpretation of Soil Phosphorus in Archaeological Contexts. In *Geoarchaeology: Earth Science and the Past*, edited by D.A. Davidson and M. L. Shackley, 93–113. Yale University Press, New Haven.

Quiñones Keber, Eloise. 1995. *Codex Telleriano-Remensis; Ritual, Divination, and History in a Pictorial Aztec Manuscript*. University of Texas Press, Austin.

Reynoso, Salavador. 1959. Introduccion. In *Colección Siglo XVI*, Ernesto Ramos, ed., 7–9. México, D.F.

Sahagún, Fray Bernardino de. 1978. *The War of Conquest: How It Was Waged in Mexico*. Translated by Arthur J. O. Anderson and Charles E. Dibble. The University of Utah Press, Salt Lake City.

Sanchez, A., M. L. Cañabate, and R. Lizcano. 1996. Phosphorus Analysis at Archaeological Sites: An Optimization of the Method and Interpretation of the Results. *Archaeometry* 38(1):151–164.

Tello, F. Antonio Fray. 1968. *Crónica Miscelania de la Sancta Provincia de Jalisco*. Book Two, Volume One. Universidad de Guadalajara, México. Originally published in 1650.

Tenamaztle, Don Francisco. 1959. [1584]. Relación de Agravios. In *Colección Siglo XVI*, Ernesto Ramos, ed., 11–20. México, D.F.

Torres, Francisco de. 1577. Testimony of Francisco Torres, *In* AGI, Patronato, 75, R3, N1, Servicios de Cristóbal de Oñate en las conquista del nuevo reyno de Galicia. October 31, 1577. Ms. on file, Bancroft Library, University of Southern California, Berkeley.

Townsend, Richard F. 1993. *The Aztecs*. Thames and Hudson, Inc., New York.

White, Jon Manchip. 1971. *Cortes and the Downfall of the Aztec Empire: A Study in a Conflict of Cultures*. St. Martin's Press, New York.

Tatars, Cossacks, and the Polish Army: The Battle of Zboriv

Adrian Mandzy

IN EVERY NATION's history certain events take on mythological significance. Names like Queenston Heights and Dieppe, Rorke's Drift and Agincourt, Verdun and Dien Bien Phu, Gettysburg and San Juan Hill have taken on almost mythological status. Perception, more than fact, create national myths. Victories and defeats were massaged to serve current political considerations and the identities of the combatants shift in accordance to a regime's ideologies.

Ukrainian history has not been immune to such manipulations. Situated on the crossroads between Berlin, Moscow, Vienna, Istanbul, Stockholm, Warsaw, and Bucharest, each foreign "liberator" rewrote Ukraine's history for its own purpose. Conversely, Ukrainians used their past as a source of identity and modified it to fit their needs. Perhaps no myth is as enduring in Ukraine as that of the events of the late 1640s.

In 1646, a Ukrainian (or, to use the seventeenth-century term, Rutherian) land-owning Cossack[1] by the name of Bohdan Khmelnytsky had his property raided and his youngest son killed by a Polish nobleman. He tried to find redress to his claims in the courts of the Polish-Lithuanian Commonwealth,[2] which then ruled Ukraine. In January 1648 Khmelnytsky fled to the Zaporozhian Sich[3] and persuaded the local Cossacks to seek out justice through the use of force. Unlike other previous Cossack rebellions, which failed due to the lack of cavalry,[4] Khmelnytsky created an alliance with the Muslim Crimean Tatars. Together, these two traditional enemies faced the largest and one of the most powerful states in Europe—the Polish-Lithuanian Commonwealth.

In April 1648, Hetman[5] Khmelnytsky defeated the Polish-Lithuanian army at Zhovti Vody and in May 1648, he was again victorious at Korsun. Ukrainian regiments, who served in the Polish-Lithuanian armies, defected to Khmelnytsky's banner. Invigorated by the success of the Cossacks, serfs, peasants, and urban dwellers also rebelled. In this "Great Revolt," Jews, Catholics, and Polish nobles were killed or driven out from what is today central Ukraine. Polish nobles responded to the massacres in kind and employed their own terror tactics. Following the destruction of a third Polish-Lithuanian army at Pyliavtsi, Khmelnytsky returned to Kiev where the Ukrainian Orthodox hierarchy treated him as a liberator.

Yet in spite of these dramatic victories, the relationship between the rebellious Ukrainians and the Commonwealth remained unclear. The Cossack elite and long-serving rank-and-file had fought to secure the rights and privileges of noblemen. Others within the Orthodox hierarchy fought for parity with Catholics. Serfs, peasants, and the lower urban classes struggled against economic exploitation. Since neither Khmelnytsky nor the monarch could propose a peaceful solution to the ongoing conflict, the war continued into 1649.

Following the initial successes of the previous year's rebellion, Cossacks, Tatars, peasants, and nobles engaged the forces of the Polish-Lithuanian Commonwealth. A Polish-Lithuanian army attacked, but quickly became trapped in the city fortress of Zbarazh. The king personally led a second army to free this trapped army. Khmelnytsky's forces ambushed the monarch's army as it crossed the Strypa River outside the town of Zboriv, less than a day's ride from Zbarazh. Suffering heavy losses, the Polish-Lithuanian forces established a defensive perimeter and as evening fell, the king's army constructed earthworks in preparation for the coming battle. In the morning, Cossacks and Tatars breached the partially completed defensive works. German troops in the service of the crown successfully counterattacked and sealed the breaches in the line, but in doing so the king exhausted his only remaining military reserves. Surrounded, outnumbered, and with no hope for rescue, the crown opened negotiations with the rebels. The resulting Treaty of Zboriv created an autonomous Ukrainian Cossack state.[6]

Although this conflict did not end with the Treaty of Zboriv, the images of the Cossack Wars would be manipulated to further political agendas. With the dismemberment of the Polish-Lithuanian Commonwealth at the end of the eighteenth century, Poles looked to the past for inspiration to build a national Polish state. Despite the Commonwealth's inability to ever suppress the Cossack movement, particular military events, such as the 1649 siege of Zbarazh, were to become important elements in contemporary Polish national consciousness. Although Jan Casimir had made a strong effort to claim the Battle of Zboriv as a major victory for the Polish-Lithuanian Commonwealth, it was the nineteenth-century romantic writer Henryk Sienkiewicz who turned the seventeenth-century Siege of Zbarazh into a call for the restoration of the Polish state. In his work, Poles are noble, civilized, and honorable while the Cossacks are barbarous, petty, and cruel. On the cusp of the twenty-first century, Sienkiewicz's 1884 novel *With Fire and Sword* remained mandatory reading for Polish students. Jerzy Hoffman's recent adaptation of the novel to film strove to address some of the worst excesses of the novel and made the Great Revolt accessible to yet another generation.

Both the Tzarist and Soviet governments have used the Cossacks and Khmelnytsky for their own political purposes. In 1654, Khmelnytsky, unable to secure a lasting peace with the Commonwealth, signed a treaty with Moscow. Russians have traditionally interpreted this 1654 Treaty of Pereiaslav as the natural culmination of the events of 1648. Though early Soviet historians had no purpose for a land-owning "aristocrat," by the late 1930s Khmelnytsky was recast as a national military hero who led his peo-ple to unification with the Tsar of Moscow. In October 1943, the Soviets created the Order of Bohdan Khmelnytsky, the only Soviet military order to include a non-Russian hero in Stalin's hagiography of "our great ances-tors."[7] In 1954, the Soviet regime celebrated the 300-year anniversary of the Treaty of Pereiaslav to commemorate "the everlasting friendship between two people."[8] Works, such as Kozachenko's, made it clear that the purpose of the 1648 conflict was to bring about Ukrainian unification with Moscow and the liberation to the poor.[9] To this day, many scholars in Ukraine continue to look at Khmelnytsky's action in terms of a "War of National Liberation."

Part of Moscow's long-standing view of Ukrainians and Cossacks was that these people were backward provincials. As early as the eighteenth century, when during the reign of Catherine II the Imperial government sought to modernize by abolishing regionalism, the Cossack elite circulated copies of their own histories which strove to underline their ancient nobility. By the beginning of the nineteenth century, as the Ukrainian Cossack elite became assimilated into Russian society, a new romantic image of Cossack emerged— that of a frontiersman. As the century progressed, new tales of wild and exotic Cossacks riders were popular in the Russian Empire and the world. Although the line between Russian and Ukrainian Cossacks became blurred at the beginning of the twentieth century, Ukrainians during the Revolution of 1917 drew inspiration from the Cossack era. Many Ukrainian military units used the names of Cossack generals and at least one leader, Hetman Skoro-patski, based the legitimacy of his rule on the claim of being from the old Cossack elite.

Yet for most of the twentieth century, the terms "Ukrainian" and "Cossack" became synonymous with plebeian. For all the rhetoric of cultural equality, high culture in the Soviet state was Russian. Russian literature, music, ballet, art, and architecture were elevated to the equal of those in the West, while ethnic achievements were considered in the best of times as "rustic." Those who pushed the envelope too far in trying to gain recognition for non-Russian achievements were often branded as "nationalists," a crime which carried the penalty of losing one's job or one's life. Thus, the Soviet pantheon reduced the Cossacks to simple, primitive farmers.

Over the course of generations, the Cossacks, in popular imagery, are often portrayed as simpletons, but an examination of the Battle of Zboriv illustrates the sophistication of the Cossack forces. Although scholars have provided differing analyses of the events at Zboriv, little work has been pre-viously attempted to incorporate the local landscape, the documentary evidence, and the archaeological record into a holistic interpretation.[10] The first endeavor to link the historical accounts of the battle with the topography was undertaken by the Ukrainian historian Ivan Krypiakevych, who in July 1929 created a series of maps of the battle based on his two-day visit to Zboriv.[11] The Soviet regime made a concerted effort to downplay the significance of the events of 1649 and Krypiakevych's initial survey work did not continue. While new information related to the Treaty of Zboriv was published in the West, it was only in the early 1990s that Ukrainian and Polish scholars had the opportunity to focus on the 1649 campaign.[12] Perhaps the most important contribution of the last decade was the publication of two engineering field military maps created during the 1649 campaign (one from Zboriv and one from Zbarazh), which illustrate the disposition of forces and the extended fieldworks.[13]

In Ukraine, battlefield studies have a long tradition, but as elsewhere, it has focused almost exclusively on sites such as camps, castles, and fortresses. The best-known exception to this was Shveshnikov's excavations at the 1651 Battle of Berestechko, where, over the course of multiple field seasons, he excavated numerous graves from a swamp bog.[14] The waters of the swamp prevented the looting of the dead and preserved significant amounts of organic materials. These particular environmental conditions preserved significant quantities of military arms and accoutrements as well as many personal items. By focusing on the swamps to the rear of the actual battlefield, Shvechnikov recovered items such as stocked muskets, arrows with preserved shafts, belts, and leather cartridge boxes. Since he found these artifacts with individual combatants, it is possible to reconstruct how these forces were armed and equipped.[15]

While the Berestechko excavations provide an unparalleled look at the peasants and Cossacks who died while fleeing after their defeat, Shvechnikov's excavations follow the traditional archaeological field methods of digging in a very small area. Since battles occurred over a wide area, sometimes encompassing hundreds of square kilometers, an excavation method that relies on the analysis of a few square meters produces, in most instances, very few results. At Berestechko, researchers did not subject the rest of the battlefield to significant testing.[16] Even with the identification of individual artifacts, no research methodology existed at that time which could document the distribution of artifacts over many square kilometers. Not surprisingly, when in the mid-1990s, archaeologists employed traditional testing methods at Zboriv, they failed to find any material from the seventeenth-century battle.[17]

The study of open warfare, besides a few well-publicized successes such as Berestechko or Wisby,[18] began in earnest only after the work on the Little Bighorn battlefield was published.[19] The use of metal detectors at the Little Bighorn provided a way for archaeologists to deal with the limitations of identifying the distribution of battlefield artifacts over great distances. This data, coupled with extensive primary historical research and topographic information, allowed scholars to deal with the conditions specific to the study of battlefields.

Unlike the area around the Little Bighorn battlefield, where very little human activity had taken place before or after the battle, people farmed the territories around Zboriv and Zbarazh for centuries. Thus scholars recovered artifacts from many periods, including the seventeenth century, during the course of the survey. As on seventeenth-century English Civil War battle-fields, generations have used the same areas and many objects were lost or deposited during manuring.[20] On the European continent, military ordnance from later conflicts, especially from the two world wars, is likely to overlay earlier materials.[21]

In 2002, working with Bohdan Strotsen, the regional director in charge of preservation of historical and cultural monuments for the Ternopil Region in Ukraine, the author conducted a joint survey with the purpose of identifying any possible remaining cultural resources associated with the military events of 1649.[22] After integrating the primary accounts of the battle with the historical and geographic topography of the area, we conducted a visual inspection of the territory. Based on this preliminary analysis, we selected areas that appeared to have been least impacted by modern development.[23]

The methodology employed was a variation on the one initially used in the archaeological investigations at the Little Bighorn. After identifying a possible area, students swept the fields with metal detectors. Once a detector registered an object, the artifact was retrieved from the disturbed soil to identify its relevance to the battle. Since locals plowed the areas around Zboriv for generations, all the artifacts lacked stratigraphic provenience and essentially came from the surface. Using a handheld global positioning system (GPS) unit, we recorded the co-ordinates of each find and collected the artifacts from the field. Given the scale of the battlefield and number of square kilometers associated with it, an accuracy of ±5m provided by the GPS was considered to be acceptable. Following the cleaning of the finds, members of the project weighted, measured, drew, and photographed each artifact. At the end of the field season, Bohdan Strotsen presented all of the artifacts to the local regional museum in Zboriv.

Unlike medieval battlefields where very little datable material exists, seventeenth-century battlefields provide quantities of lead shot and iron shot. We recovered quantities of musket balls and iron shot during the survey, but the recovery of hundreds of WWI shrapnel balls, which are only slightly smaller and lighter than the majority of seventeenth-century musket balls, complicated our work. In spite of the contamination of the battlefield with modern lead shrapnel balls, when we plotted out the distribution of musket balls along an X and Y grid, we identified two distinct lines of seventeenth-century ordnance. Based on this preliminary information, we believed that we had discovered the eastern portion of a battle line in an area not yet subject to residential or industrial development (see figure).

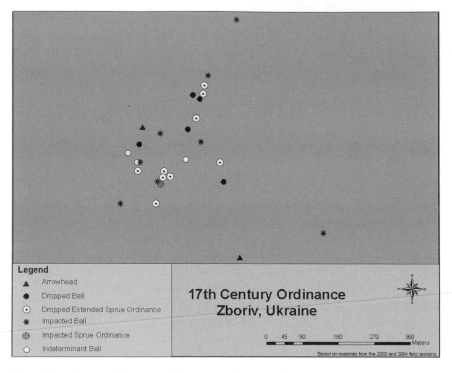

Spatial distribution of seventeenth-century military ordnance at Zboriv.

If we take this distribution of military artifacts and compare them with the local topography, we see that one line of ordnance is on top of a military crest of a small hill. Since the "choice of ground on which to fight and the exact deployment of troops in battalia were based on sound military principles," it is clear that the topographic environment predetermined the establishment of the firing line in this particular location.[24] The fragmentary primary sources provide the historical context in which to further interpret this battle. If we add to our dataset the existing contemporary map of the 1649 battle, which unfortunately is out of scale, we see that these artifacts are all found along what appears to be the eastern defensive line of the Polish camp. The map also shows the disposition of particular units, but it remains unclear to what degree units shifted during the course of the engagement.

To recognize the implications of the distribution patterns of the recovered ordnance, it is essential to understand the way firearms were used in the seventeenth century and how military units functioned. The reorganization of Polish infantry in the 1630s borrowed from both Swedish and Dutch models, which divided regiments into six companies.[25] In the 1640s, musketeers generally represented only two-thirds of a European infantry regiment, as the remaining one-third were pikemen. Within each army this arrangement may have been slightly different. The Swedish armies of King Gustavus Adolphus maintained a theoretical proportion of 216 pikes to 192 musketeers, while slightly larger Dutch battalions strove to maintain a ratio of 250 to 240.[26]

Scholars encounter additional difficulties when trying to link a particular military unit to the recovered ordnance distribution pattern. The general military practice of the period placed pike-armed troops in the center, with musketeers on each flank. Thus when we notice gaps between groups of lead balls it may indicate the space occupied by pikemen, rather than two separate units. Similarly, as throughout the century the number of ranks within particular types of units decreased, the frontage of the same type of unit occupied increased accordingly. Thus, an infantry battle line from the 1630s may have presented a completely different appearance from an infantry battle line of the 1660s. Finally, since most military units were rarely at full strength, the distribution of balls will not necessarily coincide with the theoretical dimensions of a combat unit.

According to a contemporary account of the battle, written shortly after the end of hostilities, the Crown forces built earthen fortifications to strengthen their battle lines.[27] Although the eastern line of these earthen fortifications witnessed no major military engagements, the fragmentary documentary record is quite clear that Tatar troops demonstrated in this area to draw attention of the enemy.[28] The recovery of buttons and metal buckles among dropped musket balls, which we believe troops dropped when they prepared for battle, confirms the location of the eastern section of the Polish defensive earthworks.

The construction of the earthen walls on the night between the first and second day of the battle, while undertaken primarily by attached servants, required the assistance of combat troops. The dire situation in which the Crown army found itself required haste and they would have used any item to build up a barricade. The Commonwealth commonly used heavy military wagons, similar to the fifteenth-century *wagenburg* initially developed by Jan Ziska, the commander of the Hussite Armies of Bohemia, as mobile field defenses. The recovery of so many metal hardware wagon parts found alongside seventeenth-century military ordnance suggests that the army added any broken or damaged wagons to the defensive barriers.

Contemporary descriptions of the Cossack regiments suggest that up to a third of the peasant troops lacked proper armaments during the 1649 campaign. The Cossack army fielded at Zboriv, however, consisted of Khmelnytsky's best troops. Since it was necessary to maintain an active siege of Zbarazh, only a fraction of the army made the march to Zboriv. The majority of these troops, we believe, carried projectile weapons. Cossacks often made use of Tatar-style bows which had a faster rate of fire than a seventeenth-century firearm, could fire in adverse weather, and did not give away the position of the bowman.[29] The recovery of seventeenth-century Tatar style arrowheads from both Zbarazh and Zboriv confirms the continued use of bows in warfare (see figure).

Seventeenth-century Tatar arrowhead recovered at Zboriv.

In the middle of the seventeenth century, there was a great variation in the types of infantry weapons in use. Along the northeastern frontier of the Commonwealth, flintlocks replaced hazardous matchlocks and expensive wheel locks. Excavations at the Berestechko battlefield indicated the overall dominance of flintlock weapons, while the recovery of large quantities of iron spanners suggests the use of wheel locks. The lack of matchlock weapons, however, is surprising. Cheap and somewhat reliable, matchlocks were the dominant firearm during the English Civil War (1642–1648)[30] and remained in use by Austrian military units at least until the 1683 Siege of Vienna.[31] French and English armies retained matchlocks until the turn of the century. Yet among the "poorly armed Cossacks," matchlocks were obsolete by the middle of the seventeenth century.

Another common assumption is the lack of firearm standardization. Rebel armies often have logistical nightmares and given the significant variations in the firearm calibers, one would expect to find a wide range of musket ball calibers. Since all seventeenth-century gunpowder left a residue of unburned soot after only a few shots, the barrel quickly became fouled and increasingly difficult to load. Conventional wisdom is that soldiers usually carried a variety of smaller balls to use as the battle progressed. Yet the recovery of complete bullet pouches and cartridge cases from Berestechko indicates no significant variations of ammunition calibers carried by each combatant. From this information we can make a much stronger argument that the caliber of ball corresponds closely to the weapons used.

A study of collections of seventeenth-century military arms in both the National Army Museum in Warsaw (Poland) and the Historical Arsenal Museum in L'viv (Ukraine) clearly illustrates that seventeenth-century armies standardized their weapon systems. Muskets, usually of Western European design, were predominantly large-caliber weapons with a bore diameter between 24 and 18 mm, with 20 mm being the most common. In 1649 and at the beginning of 1650 the arsenal in Warsaw acquired 1,300 muskets from Holland and 210 Dutch muskets.[32] Most Oriental "Turkish" weapons in the museums of Poland and Ukraine have a much smaller caliber bore, while mid-seventeenth-century Dutch muskets have a barrel bore that approaches 21 mm.[33] Given latitude for windage—that is, the difference between the actual barrel diameter and the size of the ball—the large-caliber musket balls recovered from Zboriv may have come from the Dutch guns imported by the Polish Crown. The battlefield museum at Berestechko identified similar large musket balls as "bullets that killed Cossacks."[34]

Most musket balls recovered from this area of the battlefield of Zboriv are between 11 and 16 mm. Given the close proximity of these finds along a line of battle, it is possible that these rounds all belonged to a particular military unit. In the seventeenth century, dragoons carried a specific type of firearm, called a *bandolet*. This weapon was of a smaller caliber and preserved examples in the museums of Poland and Ukraine have a bore diameter of between 11 and 18 mm, with diameters of 15 to 16 mm most common. At the same time, however, other cavalry units used smaller caliber weapons. In addition, Eastern firearms tended to be of a smaller caliber. While some have suggested that it may be possible in the future to identify certain types of units by the caliber of the shot, the use of small-caliber weapons on both sides of the conflict precludes such an analysis.

During our survey we discovered a great variation in the actual musket balls. Unlike most projectiles that are round or exhibit uncut sprue from their casting, many of those recovered at Zboriv had an added or modified tail along the sprue, which is far more elaborate than a simple by-product of the casting process (see figure). Such additions are unusual, and besides being recovered at Berestechko and Zbarazh, are rarely recognized as such in the archaeological record.[35] Saint Remy, an eighteenth-century French scholar, noted that these tails were previously used to facilitate the construction of paper cartridge.[36] Unlike eighteenth-century cartridges, however, where both the ball and powder were inside a paper tube, makers of these earlier cartridges attached the paper tube to the sprue (see figure on page 202). Sometimes they added a special flange to the ball to help tie the paper cartridge. It is more than likely that the musket balls recovered at Zboriv were modified in such a manner to allow for the production of semi-fixed ammunition. An examination of the Cossack bullet molds recovered at Berestechko indicates that at least some of the molds were specifically modified to create extended sprue musket balls (see lower figure on page 202).

Examples of seventeenth-century bullets recovered at Zboriv.

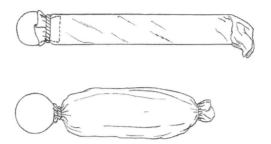

Early type of paper cartridge used with bullets with flanges (after Saint Remy). (Pierre Surirey de St Remy, Memoires d'Atillerir, Paris 1707)

Single cavity bullet mold for the creation of extended sprue ordnance. (Berestechko, Ukraine)

The production of cartridges simplified the loading process. Previously, musketeers relied upon bandoleers of pre-measured powder charges. Lord Orrery, a seventeenth-century military writer, noted that "bandeleers are often apt to take fire, especially if the matchlock musket be used."[37] The results of such accidents could be quite lethal. Although mounted units used small metal cartridge boxes as early as the second half of the sixteenth century,[38] the overwhelming majority of European infantry continued to rely on bandoleers. The numerous leather and wood cartridge boxes recovered at Berestechko are among the earliest known examples of infantry cartridge boxes used in Europe but it is more than likely that the Swedes first developed infantry cartridge boxes. Cartridge boxes quickly became popular and in 1656, 17 cartridge boxes were included in an inventory list of munitions sent to the South River of New Netherlands.[39] Nevertheless, the lack of the recovery of any traces of wooden or metal powder holders from Zboriv, Zbarazh, or Berestechko suggests that these types of containers were no longer used along Europe's eastern frontier. Conversely, the recovery of gunflints from Zbarazh and Berestechko is a good indication that the more modern ignition system, one based on a spark rather than a match, was common along the Pontic Steppe.

While some may argue that the reduced diameter of the barrel reduced the overall effectiveness of "Eastern" firearms (an inherent low muzzle velocity and an increased tendency for the fouling of the barrel), the addition of an extended sprue to the musket ball may have produced a weapon system as effective as Western models. The result of adding an extended sprue to a small-caliber bullet is that when it is fired at a low muzzle velocity, the bullet may not fly symmetrically but rather wobbles through the air. Upon striking its target, the tumbling round bounces through the soft tissue of the body, while large-caliber bullets simply tear through both flesh and bone and exit the body. While such a small-caliber tumbling weapon system does not have the range of a more powerful large-caliber firearm, the wounds inflicted in such a manner can be horrific. Provided that the barrel had not become fouled after repeated firing, such small-caliber weapons could have proved to be just as effective as their larger-caliber counterparts. At this time, ballistic testing of this hypothesis is needed to verify the effectiveness of the "sprue ordnance."

The recovered military ordnance challenges many of the commonly held assumptions of the Cossack armies of the mid-seventeenth century. Most scholars agree that the Cossack rebels wanted to create a new political system that replaced the religious, economic, and cultural elite in the southeastern territories of the Commonwealth, but few also note that the military innovations employed by Cossacks were just as revolutionary. Not only were the rebel armies under the direction of innovative leaders who had significant military talent and expertise in engineering, but the weapon systems used by the rebels were among the most modern and technically developed in both Europe and Asia. Clearly, these armies may have looked rather raggedy, especially when compared to the silver and gold encrusted troops of the Commonwealth, but the Cossack army was a professional force equal to any on two continents.

Without a doubt, the Cossack army was a professional fighting force. The image of a rag-tag mob, although burned in the collective memory, is a stereotype of questionable utility. Rather, while turned out in non-regulated clothing and perhaps intermittently fed, these rebel long-serving Cossacks, former serfs, nobles, and Orthodox clergy adapted new military tactics and weapon systems. This may not be all that unusual, since these same revolutionaries were by their very nature vying to bring about a new social reality. Although existing military establishments are often among the most conservative segments of society, the results of the research from this program suggest that this rebel army, much like earlier and later revolutionary armies, adapted and incorporated the most recent and successful of the new technologies.

The identified section of the Polish defensive earthworks serves as a point of reference for further research. By taking into consideration any minute topographic features in the terrain that contemporary military commanders would have exploited to their advantage, it is possible to correlate the terrain with the features noted on the preserved 1649 map. Using this information, it becomes much easier to see how the actual battle developed. Additional analysis will allow us to identify sections of the battlefield where cultural resources may be present and will let us extrapolate the locations of fieldworks even in areas significantly impacted by modern development.

When compared with other battlefield surveys, our results at Zboriv were not unusual. For 10 years Dan Sivilich and his group of excavators have been returning to the same areas of the American Revolutionary War battlefield of Monmouth (New Jersey) and continue to flesh out the original model. After a decade's worth of research, they are now able to show how and why the battle developed the way it did. Clearly, the results achieved at Zboriv reflect the possibilities offered in studying battlefields and need to be continued. By using new technologics, coupling them with local topography, and comparing this information with the available documentary evidence, it is possible to gain new insights into one of the most important events in the history of Ukraine and East Central Europe.

NOTES

1. The term Cossack has evolved over time. Initially the term was used as a verb to indicate a specific part-time activity that men undertook when in the wild lands of the steppe. Throughout the sixteenth century, as magnates began to place ever increasing restrictions on peasants and subjugate them to ever-increasing servitude, many villagers fled to the steppe frontier. Not all Cossacks, however, were previously farmers—nobles, burghers, and former priests could also be found among this social estate. Though the majority of the Cossacks were ethnic Ukrainians, not all were, as Poles, Germans, Tatars, Russians, and even a few West Europeans joined their number. Over time, as these social outcasts became ever more skilled in the military arts, Cossack year-round fortified camps developed. Royal officials of the Commonwealth, fearful of the growing number of armed Cossacks, began recruiting these freemen as border guards.

2. While the modern-day Polish state considers itself to be the direct successor of the Polish-Lithuanian Commonwealth, it was in fact a multi-ethnic and multi-religious state where class was more important than nationality or religion. During the mid-seventeenth century, many old established Ukrainian nobles held key offices within the Polish-Lithuanian Commonwealth.

3. The Zaporozhian Sich refers to the Cossack armed camp located south of the Dnipro River rapids. Cossacks who chose to live in the Sich did so in stern simplicity without wives or families. The men were organized into military units and worked together for a common good.

4. Although most people think of Cossacks as horse-mounted troops, their earliest renown was as sailors who raided the Ottoman settlements along the Black Sea coast. During the middle of the seventeenth century, most Cossacks fought on foot or served as artillerymen.

5. Originally from the German word *Hauptmann*. Among the Ukrainian Cossacks, the Hetman was the highest military, administrative, and judicial office. This is not to be confused with the use of the title in the Commonwealth, where the term of hetman simply meant commander-in-chief and the highest military authority in the realm.

6. Although the text of the Treaty of Zboriv has survived and the register of Cossacks has been previously published, Ukrainian scholars such as the eminent historian Mykhailo Hrushevsky has interpreted the Zboriv Agreement as "hopeless" (2002: 575–654) or "compromised" (Krypiakevych 1954:165–172). More recently, the Canadian Ukrainian historian Frank Sysyn has indicated that "the guarantee of a forty-thousand-man Cossack army ensured Hetman Khmel'nyts'kyj his place as an almost independent ruler of the Ukraine" (Sysyn 1985:173).

7. As illustrated in a letter from Khrushchev to Stalin, Khmelnytsky was chosen not because he fought for Ukraine's liberation, but because of the union of Ukrainian and Russian peoples (Yekelchyk 2002:69).

8. Basarab 1982.

9. Kozachenko 1954.

10. While many scholars have devoted their attention to the battle of Zboriv, among the earliest and most influential studies remain Kubala 1896 and Fras 1932.

11. I. Krypiakevych published five separate accounts of the battle of Zboriv, but the most detailed description appears in 1929. A later account published by the same author in 1931 includes two maps, one which showed the disposition of forces at the time of the initial ambush and the second map illustrates the attacks of the second day. These two maps were later reprinted by Tyktor (1953).

12. Matskiv 1985.

13. Alexandrowicz 1995:15–23.

14. Sveshinkov 1993.

15. Vasyl'ev and Dzys 1988:2 6.

16. Such a result is not unexpected, since archaeologists who have relied on traditional testing methods of digging in depth rarely have been successful in identifying resources related to military engagements. Using traditional archaeological field methods at the American Civil War First Manassas (Bull Run) battlefield, for example, "only one artifact was found by shovel testing, while several hundred were found using metal detectors" (see Babits 2001:118).

17. Artifacts from these excavations are on display at the local museum in Zboriv.

18. Excavations of a burial pit from the Battle of Wisby, for example, provided a good indication of medieval warfare (Thordeman et al. 1939).

19. Scott and Fox 1987; Scott et al. 1989.

20. Foard 2001:90.

21. The most common artifacts recovered from the 2002 and 2004 survey are from later battles fought at Zboriv. Shrapnel balls, rifle cartridges, bullets, and artillery shell fragments litter the area of the 1649 battlefield. While the majority of these finds are thought to relate to an engagement fought during WWI, the recovery of dated American-manufactured Mosin-Nagaunt rifle cartridges from 1918 indicates that at least some of this early twentieth-century military ordnance relates to an engagement fought during the Chortkivs'ka Offensive in the summer of 1919, almost exactly on the 270th anniversary of the 1649 Battle of Zboriv.

22. The battlefield research at Zboriv was undertaken as a component of Strotsen's 2002 survey of the Zboriv region and was sanctioned by the archaeological license (*vidkrytyj lyst*) No. 216 (Strotsen 2003).

23. As during Scott's (Scott et al. 1989) research at Little Bighorn, where both Native Americans and European Americans took part in uncovering their joint history, the research of the 1649 campaign included both Polish and Ukrainian team members. Since the initial funding for this research project came from a Fulbright-Hays Faculty Research Fellowship, peace building and preservation of historical memory was a critical component of the research and thus it was important that all sides be represented. The students from the departments of history and archaeology who took part in this research came from various institutions, including the University of Warsaw, L'viv Polytechnic University, and Drohobychskyj Pedagogic University.

24. Foard 2001:89.

25. Wimmer 1978:202.

26. Griess 1984:48.

27. Valerij Smolij and Valerij Stepankov, *Bohdan Khmel'nyts'kyj*, Kiev, 2003, 200.

28. Ivan Krypiakevych, "Z Istorii Zborova," 25.

29. Guillaume Le Vasseur, le Sieur de Beauplan, *Description D'Ukranie* [1660], L'viv, 1998.

30. Pollard and Oliver 2002:211.

31. Das Heeresgeschichtliche Museum (Museum of Military History), Vienna, Austria.

32. Górski 1902:121.

33. For a discussion of exported arms from Holland, see Puype 1985.

34. Museum of the "Cossack Mounds," National Historical Memorial Preserve "Field of the Berestechko Battle," Pliasheva Village, Radyvylivs'kyj Region, Rivnens'ka oblast, Ukraine.

35. A sprue is normally created as part of the casting process, but usually it is removed before the ball is fired. As such, unless a scholar is specifically looking for such sprues, they would most likely conclude that these were unfinished balls.

36. Saint Remy 1707.

37. Peterson 1956:63.

38. Krenn and Karcheski 1992:88.

39. O'Callaghan 1855:645.

REFERENCES CITED

Alexandrowicz, Stanislaw. 1995. Plany Obronnych Obozów wojsk Polskich pod Zbarażem i Zborowem z Roku 1649. *Fortyfikacja*, Vol. 1.

Babits, Lawrence E. 2001. Book Archaeology of the Cowpens Battlefield. In P. W. M. Freeman and A. Pollard (eds.), *Fields of Conflict: Progress and Prospect in Battlefield Archaeology*, 117–126. BAR International Series 958.

Basarab, John. 1982. *Pereiaslav 1654: A Historiographic Study*. Edmonton.

Foard, Glenn. 2001. The Archaeology of Attack: Battles and Sieges of the English Civil War. In P. W. M. Freeman and A. Pollard (eds.), *Fields of Conflict: Progress and Prospect in Battlefield Archaeology*, 97–104. BAR International Series 958.

Fras, Ludwick. 1932. Bitwa pod Zborowem w r. 1649. *Kwartalnik Historzcynz* 46.

Górski, Konstanty. 1902. *Historya Artyleryi Polskiej*. Warszawa.

Griess, Thomas E. (ed.). 1984. *The Dawn of Modern Warfare*. West Point Military History Series, Wayne.

Hrushevsky, Mykhailo. 2002. *History of Ukraine-Rus'*. Canadian Institute of Ukrainian Studies Press, Vol. 8. Toronto.

Kozachenko, A. I. 1929. *Zhyttia i Znannia*, No. 10–11, L'viv.

Kozachenko, A. I. 1931. *Litopys Chervonoi Kalyny*, No. 10, L'viv.

Kozachenko, A. I. 1954. *Bor'ba Ukrainskoho naroda za vossoedinenie s Rossiei*. Moscow.

Krenn, Peter, and Walter J. Karcheski Jr. 1992. *Imperial Austria: Treasures of Art, Arms and Armor from the State of Styria*. Munich.

Krypiakevych, I. 1954. *Bohdan Khmelnyts'kyj*. Kiev.

Krypiakevych, Ivan, 1942. Z Istorii Zborova, In Istoriia Ukrainy by Ivan Krypiakevych. Vernyhora, Vienna.

Kubala, L. 1896. *Oblężenie Zbaraża i pokój pod Zborowem, Szkice historyczne*. Krakow.

Le Vasseur, Guillaume le Sieur de Beauplan, 1998. *Description D'Ukranie* [1660], L'viv.

Matskiv, Teodir. 1985. Zborivs'kyj Dohovir u svitli nimets'koi j anhlijs'koi presy z 1649. *Zborivshchyna*, Naukove Tovarystvo im Shevchenka, Ukrains'kyj Arkhiv, Vol. 38. Toronto.

O'Callaghan, Edmund B. (ed.). 1855. *Documents Relative to the Colonial History of New York*, Vol. 1. Albany.

Peterson, Harold L. 1956. *Arms and Armor in Colonial America 1526–1783*. Stackpole, Harrisburg, PA.

Pollard, Tony, and Neil Oliver. 2002. *Two Men in a Trench: Battlefield Archaeology—The Key to Unlocking the Past*. London.

Puype, Jan Piet. 1985. Dutch and Other Flintlocks from Seventeenth century Iroquois Sites. Proceedings of the 1984 Trade Gun Conference, Research Records, No.18, Vol. 1. Rochester Museum and Science Center, Rochester, NY.

de Saint Remy, Pierre Surirey. 1707. *Memoires d'Artillerie*, second edition, 2 vols. Paris.

Scott, Douglas D., and Richard A. Fox Jr. 1987. *Archaeological Insights into the Custer Battle: An Assessment of the 1984 Field Season*. University of Oklahoma Press, Norman.

Scott, Douglas D., Richard. A. Fox Jr., Melissa A. Connor, and D. Harmon. 1989. *Archaeological Perspectives on the Battle of the Little Bighorn*. University of Oklahoma Press, Norman.

Smolij, Valerij and Valerij Stepankov, 2003. *Bohdan Khmel'nyts'kyj*, Kiev

Strotsen, B. S. 2003. *Zvit pro arkheolohichni rozvidky v okolytsiakh m. Zborova (Ternopil's'ka obl.) u 2002 r.* Ternopil's'ka oblasna komunal'na inspektsia okhorony pam'iatok istorii ta kul'tury, Ternopil.

Sveshnikov, I. K. 1993. *Bytva pid Berestechkom*. L'viv.

Sysyn, Frank. 1985. *Between Poland and Ukraine: The Dilemma of Adam Kysil 1600–1653*. Cambridge, MA.

Thordeman, Bengt, Poul Noörlund, and Bo E. Ingelmark. 1939. *Armour from the Battle of Wisby, 1361,* Vol. 1, Kungl. Vitterhets Historie OCH Antikvitets Akademien, Stockholm.

Tyktor, Ivan. 1953. *Istoriia Ukrains'koho Vijs'ka*. Winnipeg.

Vasyl'ev, Aleksej, and Igor Dzys. 1988. Bytva pod Berestechkom, *Zeughaus* 8(2)1988:2–6.

Bytva pod Berestechkom'', *Zeughaus* No 8. Moscow.

Wimmer, Jan. 1978. *Historia Piechoty Polskiej do 1864*. Warsaw.

Yekelchyk, Serhy. 2002. Stalinist Patriotism as Imperial Discourse: Reconciling the Ukrainian and Russian "Historic Pasts," 1939–45. *Kritika* 3(1):51–80.

Camden: Salvaging Data from a Heavily Collected Battlefield

James B. Legg & Steven D. Smith

THE REVOLUTIONARY WAR Battle of Camden, August 16, 1780, was a disaster for the American cause, destroying the second of three armies sent south to oppose the British occupation of the Carolinas and Georgia.[1] While the fighting spread over an area of some 600 acres, until recently commemoration was limited to a six-acre tract owned by the Daughters of the American Revolution, while the remainder of the battlefield was an expanse of pine plantation. In 2000, Katawba Valley Land Trust and the Palmetto Conservation Foundation (PCF) negotiated a conservation easement for the 310-acre core of the Camden Battlefield, and in 2003 PCF purchased the remaining property rights (see figure). Preservation and interpretation of the battlefield are now the focus of a well-organized consortium of preservationists and historians called the Battle of Camden Project, including archaeologists from the South Carolina Institute of Archaeology and Anthropology. A critical component of this effort is an attempt to define battlefield boundaries and to document battle events across the modern terrain. Controlled metal detector collection, now *de rigueur* in battlefield interpretation, would seem to be the obvious means of addressing these questions archaeologically.

Unfortunately, the battlefield has been very heavily collected by relic hunters for at least three decades. Some collectors consider the site virtually "hunted out," and report having spent entire days detecting there without recovering an artifact. Our approach to this problem has been two-fold. First, in 2001 we initiated the Camden Battlefield Collector Survey, a pragmatic effort to salvage as much information as possible from private collectors. This survey, while not providing the kind of well-controlled data we would prefer, has, at a minimum, assisted in defining battlefield boundaries, and provided new insights into battle events. Interestingly, the synthesis of collector and historical data suggests two very different battle scenarios, each with its camp of supporters. Second, we have defied the predictions of the collector community, and have begun a controlled metal detector sampling regime across the

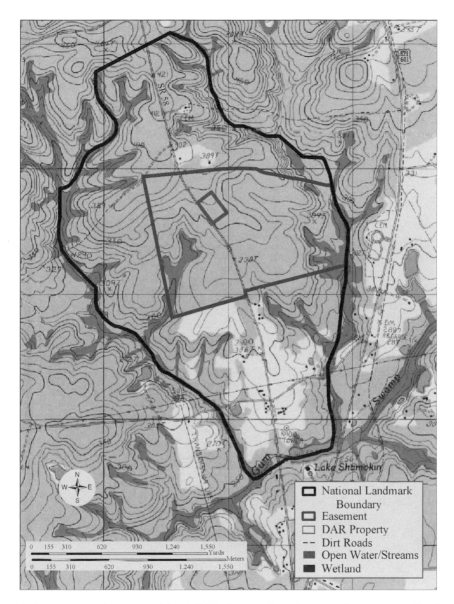

Modern topographic map of battlefield showing boundaries and easements. (South Carolina Institute of Archaeology and Anthropology)

battlefield in the hope of acquiring even a small sample of precise data that would enhance our collector survey data. The metal detecting project is in a preliminary stage, but has already shown surprisingly good results. This chapter describes the first of our two-fold approach, the Camden Battlefield

Collector's Survey, and our struggle to accurately interpret the combined historical and collector evidence.

THE BATTLE OF CAMDEN

The broad outlines of battle chronology are generally agreed upon, if the precise geographic placement of various units and timing are not.[2] When Horatio Gates led his Southern American army from North Carolina into South Carolina in early August of 1780, he was hoping to force the British from their fortified post at Camden, South Carolina. But Lord Cornwallis saw Gates's approach as an opportunity rather than a threat. At 10:00 in the evening of August 15, Cornwallis led his army out of Camden with the intention of attacking the superior force of Americans in their camp at Rugeley's Mill, 13 miles north of Camden. Gates, at that same hour, began a march south from Rugeley's Mill, intending to occupy favorable terrain about six miles north of Camden. At about 2:30 on the moonlit morning of August 16, the two columns collided on a sandy, forested plateau about seven miles north of Camden, and after a brief but fierce skirmish both sides drew off to wait the dawn only two hours away.

Battle participants agreed on certain battlefield terrain features that help in interpreting the battlefield today. Both sides were pleased that they could anchor their flanks on swamps at opposite ends of their lines. The battlefield was wooded, but very unlike the present pine plantation; it was an old-growth longleaf pine forest, the huge trees widely spaced, with their limbs starting 40 feet above the forest floor. No eyewitness indicated any problems maneuvering in the woods. The ground was clear of brush, but covered with pine straw and tall wiregrass. The sandy road from Rugeley's to Camden bisected the battlefield from north to south, perpendicular to the opposing lines, and it was used by both sides to guide the placement of their units. The relative positions of the two armies at the opening of the battle (see figure) are well documented, and while these unit dispositions are not controversial, the placement of the entire array on the present landscape *is*, as we shall see, in dispute.

Gates deployed four small regiments of the 2nd Maryland Brigade, including the Delaware Regiment, with their right flank anchored on a swampy draw. In the center was the North Carolina militia. On the left was Virginia militia, light infantry, and a few cavalry. Two hundred yards to the center rear of the front line, straddling the road, was the 1st Maryland Brigade, in reserve. American artillery included two guns with the 2nd Maryland Brigade, three straddling the road, and two in the reserve line with the 1st Maryland Brigade. Total American strength was about 3,500, but of this number only 900 were Continentals. While the Continentals and North Carolina militia had had a two-day rest before the march, the Virginia militia had arrived at

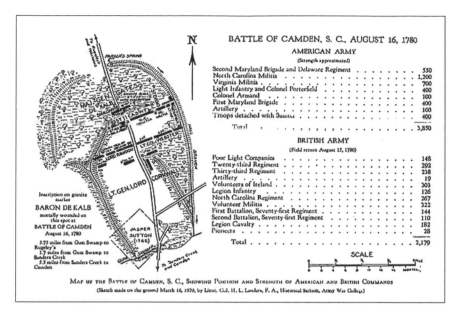

BATTLE OF CAMDEN, S. C., AUGUST 16, 1780	
AMERICAN ARMY	
(Strength approximated)	
Second Maryland Brigade and Delaware Regiment	550
North Carolina Militia	1,200
Virginia Militia	700
Light Infantry and Colonel Porterfield	400
Colonel Armand	100
First Maryland Brigade	400
Artillery	100
Troops detached with Sumter	400
Total	3,850
BRITISH ARMY	
(Field return August 15, 1780)	
Four Light Companies	148
Twenty-third Regiment	292
Thirty-third Regiment	238
Artillery	19
Volunteers of Ireland	303
Legion Infantry	126
North Carolina Regiment	267
Volunteer Militia	322
First Battalion, Seventy-first Regiment	144
Second Battalion, Seventy-first Regiment	110
Legion Cavalry	182
Pioneers	28
Total	2,179

MAP OF THE BATTLE OF CAMDEN, S. C., SHOWING POSITION AND STRENGTH OF AMERICAN AND BRITISH COMMANDS
(Sketch made on the ground March 16, 1929, by Lieut. Col. H. L. Landers, F. A., Historical Section, Army War College)

Colonel H. L. Landers map of the Battle of Camden showing combatants. ("The Battle of Camden, South Carolina, August 16, 1780" by Lieutenant Colonel H. L. Landers, F.A.U.S. House of Representatives House Document No. 12, 71st Congress, 1st Session, Washington, DC)

Rugeley's only the day before. They were exhausted. But none of the American soldiers were in much shape for the upcoming fight as they had been fed a full meal of bread, meat, and a gill of molasses that evening before the march, and it was having an obvious effect on their digestive systems.

Cornwallis did not fully deploy his troops until dawn, when they quickly and professionally deployed left and right of the road. East of the road to the British right, Cornwallis deployed a regular brigade including light infantry companies, the 23rd Regiment and the 33rd Regiment. Left of the road, he deployed his Loyalist brigade, under Francis Lord Rawdon, including the Volunteers of Ireland Regiment, the British Legion infantry, and Loyalist militia. Cornwallis's artillery, consisting of two 6-pounders and two 3-pounders, were placed near the center. The 71st Highland Regiment was in reserve, one battalion behind the British right and one behind the left, along with the British Legion dragoons under Banastre Tarleton along the road. Cornwallis's force consisted of 2,179 officers and men.

At dawn, an American artillery captain on the front line announced to Colonel Otho Williams that he could see the British right advancing some 200 yards in front of the American left. Williams ordered the officer to open fire and immediately rode to General Gates who had just placed himself behind the American second line. Williams reported to Gates that the British were displaying to their right and that an advance by the Americans might have a "fortunate effect."[3] With Gates's approval Williams quickly made his way to General Stevens, commander of the Virginia militia, and passed on the order to advance. Williams also saw that a few skirmishers in front of the Americans might blunt the British attack. But his effort was futile since, by that time, the British were closing. The sight of British fixed bayonets was more than the militia wanted and they immediately took flight, most without firing a shot. The effect along the line was devastating, and like dominos, the North Carolina militia followed the Virginians. Within mere seconds, the American left melted away. Only a small body of North Carolinians anchored on the artillery and Continental right held firm. After Williams rode off with orders for the militia to advance, Gates had ordered the 1st Maryland to advance to the left in support of the militia and also ordered the American right to advance. Gun smoke soon mixed with the moist morning air, obscuring the combatants.

The British right quickly moved through the position vacated by the American militia, but were met by the advancing 1st Maryland Brigade who had opened their ranks to let the militia through, reformed, and were attempting to form a new line with the 2nd Maryland. However, two Continental brigades were never able to connect and they remained widely separated throughout the battle—in effect, the American left and right fought different battles. Pressed on their front and left flank, the 1st Maryland Brigade had to refuse their exposed left and eventually their line ended up at a right angle with the 2nd Maryland Brigade. From there the 1st Maryland rallied and fell back as many as three times before eventually being overpowered. Meanwhile, the American right advanced and nearly broke the Loyalists on the British left. Unable to see what was happening to the 1st Maryland Brigade, the 2nd Maryland pushed forward, thinking they were winning the battle. With the two American forces fighting in isolation, Cornwallis ordered Banastre Tarleton's dragoons and the 71st Highlanders into the gap and against the 1st Maryland's left. The American Continentals were out-flanked and overrun. Totally disorganized, many Continentals died on the battlefield, while others fought their way off in small groups.

Gates and much of the senior command on the American left were not around to watch the destruction of the Continentals. They had attempted to rally the militia and been swept away in the panic. Gates had been pushed off the battlefield and on up the road past Rugeley's. He rode on to Charlotte, North Carolina, and eventually reached Hillsboro. American casualty figures for Camden are not exactly known. Cornwallis reported 800 to 900 Americans killed and about 1,000 prisoners taken, but this was certainly an inflated figure. A good number of Continentals dragged into Charlotte over the next few days. But not the General Johann Baron de Kalb, who led the American 2nd Maryland and Delaware Regiments on the American right, and was mortally wounded. As for the British, although it is clear that they won a resounding victory, it was costly. Cornwallis listed 68 killed, 245 wounded, and 11 missing, all veterans that would be difficult to replace.

POST-WAR BATTLEFIELD HISTORY

The land use history of the Camden battlefield since 1780 is essential to understanding the archaeological resource today.[4] In 1786, a visitor reported seeing shattered trees and unburied bones of soldiers and horses, but a visitor in 1830 reported that not a vestige of the battle remained.[5] Historian Benson Lossing examined the Camden battlefield in January 1849, and recorded the first substantial description of the site:

> The hottest of the engagement occurred upon the hill, just before descending to Sander's Creek [Gum Swamp Creek] from the north, now, as then, covered with an open forest of pine-trees. . . . Many of the old trees yet bear marks of the battle, the scars of the bullets being made very distinct by large protuberances.... Within half a mile[6] of Sanders Creek [Gum Swamp Creek], on the north side, are some old fields, dotted with shrub pines, where the hottest of the battle was fought. A large concavity near the road, filled with hawthorns, was pointed out to me as the spot where many of the dead were buried.[7]

The Camden battlefield was still wooded at the beginning of the twentieth century, but Camden County historians Thomas Kirkland and Robert Kennedy reported that the character of the forest had changed:

> At the date of the battle the ground was occupied by a close array of tall and stately pines, limbless to a height of forty or fifty feet. These, by the process of turpentining, have been reduced to a scanty few, so that not many of those remain that witnessed the battle. Their thinning has allowed to come up a growth of scrub oaks, which in summer obscure the view much more than did the pines.... Those living in that neighborhood have found amongst the leaves of the woods many an old buckle, button, bayonet, bullet, cannon ball, flintlock....[8]

Kirkland and Kennedy found "grape shot and bullets in half-burnt and decayed trees."[9] Their map of the Camden battlefield shows the location of the "Pine where De Kalb lay wounded," which was replaced by the monument to Baron de Kalb erected by the Hobkirk Hill Chapter of the Daughters of the American Revolution in 1909.[10] In March 1929, Lt. Col. H. L. Landers visited the battlefield while researching the battle. His map, prepared for the War Department (see figure), depicts the battlefield south of the present DAR property as fields.

In 1930, the Hobkirk Hill Chapter of the DAR secured an option to buy 425.5 acres of the battlefield for about $6,500, but the land was not purchased. In 1942, the chapter did acquire five additional acres around the de Kalb monument, adding to a single acre acquired there in 1912.[11] An aerial photograph taken in 1949 shows that nearly all of the battlefield south of the DAR property was under cultivation, while the areas to the north and west of the DAR property were in woods, or pine savannah. By 1964, the fields seen in 1949 and the farm site east of Route 58 are in pine plantation, while the formerly wooded areas to the north have been timbered, but are *not* in agricultural fields. The DAR property stands out as a small rectangle of original (if thinned) longleaf pine forest. A massive clear-cutting timber program completed in 1998 stripped any remaining semblance of the battlefield's 1780 appearance.

In summary, it is clear that the local vegetation has gone through several changes since the battle, but importantly the topography is intact and undeveloped. The southern portion of the battlefield was cultivated, while the northern portion was repeatedly timbered but not plowed for agriculture.

THE CAMDEN BATTLEFIELD COLLECTOR SURVEY

The impetus for the present study dates to December 2000, when the first author was asked by the Palmetto Conservation Foundation (PCF) to assess the battlefield's archaeological integrity and potential, and to suggest ways in which archaeology might assist in the battlefield interpretation. He noted that the battlefield was undeveloped and relatively well preserved as a landscape, but as an archaeological resource it had suffered serious damage through decades of relic collecting. He suggested that a concerted effort be made to identify and interview individuals who have collected from the site in an effort to salvage whatever information they could provide and would be helpful in interpretation. PCF contracted with the South Carolina Institute of Archaeology and Anthropology in 2001 to conduct the Camden Battlefield Collector Survey, with funding provided by a grant from the National Park Service's American Battlefield Protection Program (ABPP).[12] The survey is now an ongoing project assisted by a second grant from the ABPP in 2003.

The primary goal was the compilation of a mapped record of artifact distributions from private collector information that might help to tie the Battle of Camden, as understood from the historical record, to the present landscape. Secondary goals included the location of unmarked battlefield burials, and the detailed documentation of artifacts from the battlefield in private collections. While the Collector Survey is by no means complete, it has long since yielded far more information than originally envisioned. There are currently 12 collections fully documented and three partially documented, and at least three additional collectors have been identified. In addition, three important Camden collections have been donated to the project for public ownership, and two more are informally promised.

Data collection methods have been simple and informal, involving on-site visits, phone conversations, and e-mail. Seven collectors were already known to the authors, PCF, or the Camden Battlefield Project, and these collectors introduced others. Initially, not knowing how best to proceed with the collectors, or what level of data to expect, it was hoped at a minimum to accomplish the following tasks for each informant:

1. A meeting on the site, with a walking discussion/interview regarding the collector's finds and impressions, and the individual's collecting history.
2. Recording on a standard base map of the "find spots" of as many particular, described artifacts as possible, together with any general observations.
3. Examination of the collection, if available, and photographic documentation of selected artifacts.

In the end, there was considerable variation among the interviews and the results, largely dictated by the kinds of information offered by the informant. All of the collectors recorded to date have shown great enthusiasm for both the battlefield preservation project and the archaeological project, in spite of the fact that the public effort has put an end to artifact digging. Only two collectors who were contacted ultimately did not follow through with formal recording, and there is still hope for both of those individuals. Two collectors insisted on anonymity, but were otherwise very helpful, and both donated their entire, intact collections to the project. Other collectors expressed willingness to eventually donate their collections if the material goes to a local public facility that will properly curate and exhibit their materials. Once it was clear around the collector community that our goals were to preserve and understand the battlefield, as opposed to confiscating collections or prosecuting the removal of artifacts, more collectors were happy to cooperate with the project. Overall, our informants were pleased with the project, even if some differ with our interpretations.

As noted, the quality of the data recorded varies considerably. No collector provided specific proveniences for ammunition specimens (below), but other battle artifacts of any sort were relatively rare finds, and consequently, their provenience was memorable. In every case, the informants were able to map nearly all of their individual finds *other than lead shot*. The confidence with which artifacts were plotted varied. On the poor end of the scale, a collector might indicate an artifact's location with a wave of a hand in the direction of a clump of weeds – perhaps a 20-meter margin of error. Much of this uncertainty is the result of the unfortunate clear-cutting in 1998, which eliminated the collector's visual frame of reference. On the opposite end of the scale, two collectors used GPS instruments to record their finds, which they cataloged, photographed, and presented on CD-ROM. Still other collectors previously had mapped their finds on their own sketch maps, and their information was readily transferred to a standard base map. Even the most general "plots" of individual items were recorded as points, and all such proveniences were considered adequate for the overall, large-scale distributional information that was sought. While some may question the precision of the provenience data, it is argued that even if every plotted item were reassigned to a random location within 100 meters of its original plot, it would not change any conclusions inferred from the large-scale artifact distributions provided by the data.

All data, from generalized ammunition distribution maps to precise GPS locations, were transferred onto enlarged USGS Camden North quad maps, and each plotted artifact was described in an accompanying catalog. Each artifact was assigned a functional class code, including:

S: Lead shot—musket balls, buckshot, and intermediate shot for pistols, rifles, etc.

A: Arms and accoutrement parts—gun parts, gun tools, bayonets, scabbard and cartridge box hardware, etc.

C: Clothing objects—military and civilian buttons, knee buckles, shoe buckles, neck stock buckles.

G: Iron and lead canister balls.

M: Miscellaneous objects that may or may not be battle artifacts, but which plausibly date to the eighteenth century—eating utensils, wrought iron hardware, iron and brass frame buckles, etc.

N: Miscellaneous objects that are clearly not battle artifacts, but were nevertheless recorded in a private collection or collected during the metal detector survey (e.g., an 1829 dime).

By far the most common artifacts recovered by the collectors were lead shot, chiefly musket balls, and buckshot from musket buck and ball cartridges. These mundane projectiles were ubiquitous, and as a result none of the collectors we have interviewed maintained specific location information for particular ammunition specimens in their collections. More than 2,000 musket balls and buckshot were collected by the informants, but their provenience is remembered only in very general terms. Two collectors had bagged most of their lead shot by various described proveniences (e.g., "west of highway, head of ravine"). Three other collectors maintained sketch maps that indicated quantities of lead shot recovered from different parts of the battlefield, but these notations were not linked to particular specimens. The remaining collectors combined all of their shot into a single collection. The collector ammunition data is rough and incomplete. Nevertheless, the data from the five collections about which something is known, together with observations from several collectors concerning lead shot distribution, have been combined to prepare a generalized lead shot density map (see figure). This distribution necessarily combines fired and unfired shot of all calibers, but it includes no areas that were dominated by unfired ammunition, which would indicate a camp or other non-combat episode. In the private collections as well as in the metal detector survey, the ratio of fired to unfired balls is consistently about three or four to one.

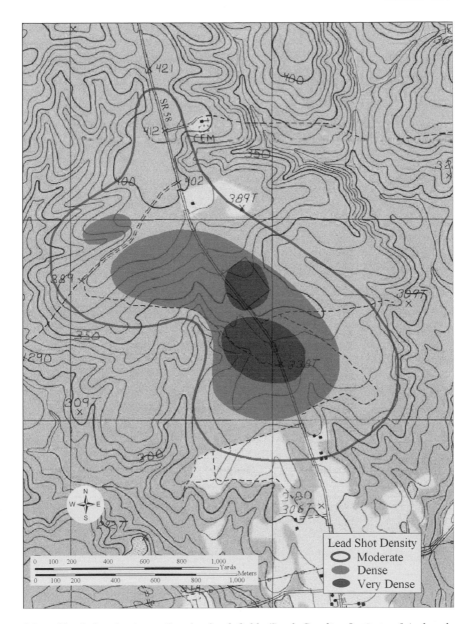

Map of lead shot density at Camden battlefield. (South Carolina Institute of Archaeology and Anthropology)

For artifacts other than lead shot, GIS map layers have been created that illustrate the plotted finds in each collection. The most useful product of the Collector Survey is the next step—maps showing finds, by functional class, of all collections combined. This has yielded distribution maps showing arms and accoutrement artifacts (see figure), clothing artifacts, and artillery canister balls (see figure) from all private collections. Combined with the admittedly less precise data on the ammunition density map (see figure), this information is proving very valuable in reconstructing the battle.

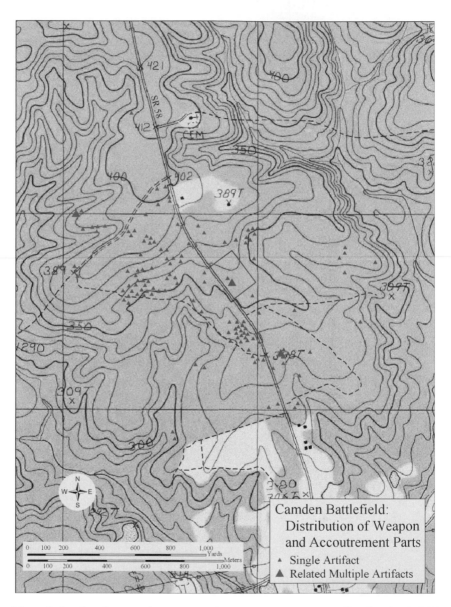

Map of the distribution of weapon and accoutrement parts at Camden battlefield. (South Carolina Institute of Archaeology and Anthropology)

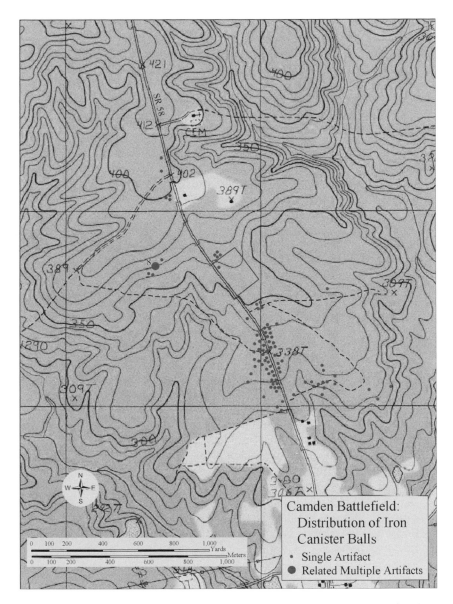

Map of the distribution of canister balls at Camden battlefield. (South Carolina Institute of Archaeology and Anthropology)

An important limitation in the Collector Survey results to date has been the failure to locate any informant who seriously collected from the site prior to 1979 or 1980, when "Anonymous Collector #1" first visited the battlefield. By that time metal detectors had been in use on Civil War battlefields for about 30 years, and indeed the most active and "productive" era of battlefield metal detecting was already over. This is unfortunate because an unprotected site as obvious as the Camden battlefield must have been heavily collected by many different individuals before 1979. Collector #1 reported that by then the entire battlefield as he understood it showed the tell-tale signs of heavy collecting in the past—small, eroded holes, discarded non-battle artifacts on the ground surface, and a scarcity of "easy" artifact readings. Thus, even the present collector data must be considered only a reasonably representative "shadow" of the material originally present, before the advent of metal detectors. The search for earlier informants continues.

One of the stated goals of the Collector Survey was to locate battlefield burials. Some or all of the men killed in action in the Battle of Camden were buried on the field in unmarked graves, and a number of these, confirmed or probable, have been reported by collectors. To date the Collector Survey has recorded the existence of eight burials, six of them certain and two more that are "probable." Of the six certain graves, only three can presently be plotted with any certainty—the others are now only generally located, due to the clear-cutting of 1998. Of the eight burials, one was British, four were Continentals, and three were indeterminate. There are probably between 200 and 300 burials on the field, but the only ones found happened to include metallic artifacts that were shallow enough to detect. Others may be too deep to detect, or the remains may have been stripped of clothing, shoes, and equipment—one of the "indeterminate" individuals bore no artifacts at all other than a musket ball embedded in his chest.

As discussed below, the Collector Survey and other information have indicated an interpretation of the battlefield that the authors believe is essentially correct. That interpretation is not free of controversy, but as the Collector Survey and other research efforts continue, it is hoped that a consensus can be arrived at that all interested parties (not merely the authors) can agree upon. The Camden Collector Survey has already resulted in three important conclusions that are not controversial:

1. Regardless of initial unit placements and subsequent movements, the outer-most density boundary encompasses the area of significant action during the Battle of Camden (see figure).
2. A minority, but substantial part of the battlefield is located outside of the present conservation easement, to the north and northwest, on property that is currently unprotected.
3. Unmarked battlefield graves exist both within the conservation easement and on unprotected private property.

CAMDEN BATTLEFIELD INTERPRETATION

The most important goal of both the Collector Survey and the metal detector sampling effort has been to better understand how the Battle of Camden unfolded across the present landscape. Where were the armies initially deployed, and where did they maneuver? In the interpretation below, we synthesize what has been learned into a battle scenario tied to the modern geography. As new data emerges, it is hoped that this scenario will be refined, improving our understanding of the historical events, illuminating factors such as visibility, timing, and duration of movements, and firepower effectiveness. Obviously, this is not the last word about the Battle of Camden, but this scenario is offered as a "line of departure" for future debate.

The significant action in the Battle of Camden can be confidently located within the outermost boundary (see figure on page 217). This area encompasses the traditional battlefield, and while there has been very little battle material found beyond the boundary, thousands of battle artifacts have been recovered from within it. Unfortunately this leaves more than enough terrain for a variety of possible interpretations, and the historical and material evidence is admittedly complex. Two possible interpretations have emerged, which for clarity, are called the Southern and Northern Solutions. The authors strongly favor the Southern Solution, while some other serious students of the battle champion the significantly different Northern Solution. Both interpretations are outlined below, followed by an analysis of why the authors favor the Southern Solution.

The Southern Solution

The initial positions of the opposing forces as championed in the Southern Solution are depicted in the figure on page 222. In this interpretation, the dense concentration of material in the south-central portion of the battlefield (see figures) marks the protracted fight between the American right wing under Baron de Kalb and the British left wing (and 33rd Regiment) under Lord Rawdon. The vicinity of the DAR property is the site of the isolated struggle by the American reserve, the 1st Maryland Brigade, against the British right wing. The heavy scatter of material stretching far to the west of the DAR property probably represents the envelopment and rout, and/or capture of the remnants of both American brigades. The small, isolated concentration in the extreme northwest appears to represent an undocumented "last stand" by some portion of the American army—on this last point both factions agree. This interpretation provides a plausible reading of the artifact densities in the three figures above—the southern artifact concentration represents the intense combat between the British left and the American right, while that in the area of the DAR property represents the struggle of the American left as they advance, fall back, rally and stand again, ultimately ending up entirely behind the American right, where they collapse and many surrender.

The Northern Solution

The alternate interpretation, the Northern Solution, begins the battle with the two armies positioned several hundred yards further north, with the British line crossing the road at about the middle of the DAR property, where the Southern Solution places the American reserve (see figure). In this scenario, the extensive concentration of artifacts running west from the vicinity of the DAR property (see figure) represents the entire day battle, with the artifact

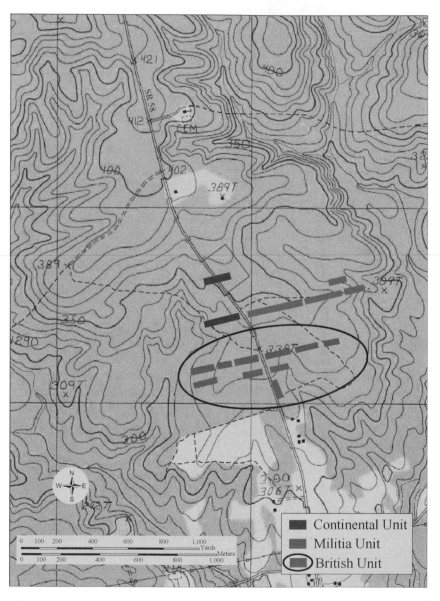

Initial deployment of combatants on modern topographic map at Camden battlefield. (South Carolina Institute of Archaeology and Anthropology)

concentration to the south interpreted as the site of the night meeting engagement only. The Northern Solution is favored by several collectors who found the bulk of their artifacts in the battlefield's northern section.[13]

Resolution

These "Southern" and "Northern" interpretations are so different that one or the other must ultimately be discounted as incorrect if the battle is to be tied to the present landscape. The strongest argument favoring the Northern Solution is the remarkable array of artifacts recovered by several collectors in an area running west from the DAR property for some 500 yards (see figure). This area yielded artifacts which were rare or absent on other portions of the field, including numerous complete shoe buckles (some in matching pairs), large gun parts, bayonets, and clusters of uniform buttons, as well as fired and unfired musket ammunition. In contrast, these same collectors found relatively little to the south, where the Southern Solution places the hardest fighting.[14] In spite of these intriguing findings, a careful study of all of the available evidence, including the artifact distributions, strongly favors the Southern Solution. Four important areas of evidence support the Southern Solution, including: (1) primary historical sources regarding the combatants' initial deployment; (2) artifact distributions in light of land use history; (3) artifact distributions in light of the chronology of relic collecting; and (4) projectile distributions.

There is no single, primary historical source that describes the battlefield in sufficient detail to place the action on the current terrain. Taken as a whole, however, the contemporary sources provide a location for the initial dispositions of the armies that can only match the Southern Solution (see figure). Of the six eighteenth-century maps of the battle known to the authors, one (Finnegan n.d.) is completely incoherent, and the other five all suffer from significant distortions of scale, among various other problems (these include Senf 1780, Barrette 1780, Barron n.d., Vallancy/DesBarres 1780, and Faden 1787).[15] Errors aside, the five usable maps share certain important consistencies, including reasonable agreement in the relative placement of units,[16] and the basic orientation of the two armies astride, and perpendicular to, a north-south road. All five maps show the right flank of the 2nd Maryland Brigade and the left flank (at least) of the British line resting on swamps. Eyewitnesses on both sides consistently state that their flanks were protected by swamps. Otho Williams reported, "It happened that each flank was covered by a marsh, so near as to admit the removing of the First Maryland Brigade to form a second line...."[17] Gates reported that Gist's 2nd Maryland Brigade took position "upon the Right – with His Right close to a Swamp," while Col. Senf recalled "an almost impassable swamp" on the American right.[18] Lord Cornwallis was "well apprized by several intelligent Inhabitants that the ground on which both armies stood, being narrowed by swamps on the right & left, was extremely favorable for my numbers...."[19] Stedman reiterated, "A swamp on each side secured [Cornwallis's] flanks, and narrowed the ground in front...."[20] A nineteenth-century British narrative based on now-unknown primary sources provides an additional, critical detail: "The ground... was a sandy plain with straggling trees, but a part of the ground on the British left was soft and boggy ... the Provincials were on the left, with the marshy ground in their front."[21] This same detail is depicted in the front of the Loyalists on the Faden Map of 1787. An examination of the figure readily reveals that the Southern Solution fits very well with the historical sources cited above, while the Northern Solution does not. The Northern Solution places the American army on a broad ridgeline with their right flank exposed and *not* anchored on any drainage, and places the British left with a swamp *behind* them. This swampy drainage is nearly impenetrable today, and it is unlikely that the British would have maneuvered into or around it during the early morning hours prior to the battle.

The second consideration concerns land use after 1780. The historic land uses detailed above have certainly impacted the available artifact evidence, and have affected the distributions recorded by the Collector Survey. Although more recently wooded, the southern portion of the battlefield is an expanse of old agricultural fields, with a plow zone as much as a foot in depth. A resident of one of the two farms on the site collected "buckets full of musket balls" in the fields, suggesting substantial surface collecting.[22] In contrast, the northern part of the battlefield apparently remained in old-growth turpentine trees through much of the twentieth century, and it generally does not exhibit an old, agricultural plow zone, as distinct from evidence of logging and pine-plowing. This would help to explain why artifacts like bayonets, musket locks, and pairs of shoe buckles survived undamaged as well as undiscovered by farmers and visitors in this northern area.

The history of relic collecting with metal detectors on the Camden battlefield is another important consideration, because the battlefield was not collected uniformly. A site as obvious as the Camden battlefield was almost certainly collected with metal detectors in the 1960s, if not in the 1950s. This is supported by the testimony of our earliest informant who began collecting from the battlefield in 1980. He reported that in 1980, the southern and northeastern parts of the battlefield already had been intensely collected by unknown parties. Although those areas were still quite productive in 1980, the artifacts removed before then are not reflected in the Collector Survey distribution data. Four of the earliest collections currently known, gathered mostly in the early- and mid-1980s, were derived substantially from the southern concentration. These four collectors combed the southern portion of the battlefield for several years, and found a seemingly endless supply of fired and unfired musket ammunition. Other artifacts were generally small objects, or fragments of larger items, contrasting with the larger, well-preserved objects and clusters of related objects later found to the northwest.

While they collected the evidence for the heavy fighting to the south, none of the four earlier collectors wandered far enough to the west and north to discover the artifact concentration that appears to support the Northern Solution. By the time the authors of the Northern Solution arrived on the scene in about 1986, the southern part of the battlefield presented only a weak ammunition scatter, while the as-yet-uncollected northwestern concentration (which they immediately discovered) was still an impressive trove of artifacts. Given their late arrival, their battle interpretation is not unreasonable, but it is not supported by a full understanding of land use and the history of collecting at the site.[23]

Finally, there is archaeological evidence in the form of lead shot and iron canister ball distributions. As discussed above, the musket ball provenience data from the Collector Survey is poor—only five collections include any plotting of musket balls, and no actual specimens are tied to particular locations. In spite of these limitations, an important observation can be made regarding the location of the heaviest small-arms fire during the battle. The concentration of arms artifacts (see figure) and clothing artifacts running west from the DAR property was accompanied by relatively few musket balls in comparison to the musket ball concentration to the south. The ratio of musket balls to other objects is dramatically higher in the southern concentration, where the Southern Solution places the Continentals' protracted struggle. This can be demonstrated in spite of the poor quality of the musket ball provenience data. For example, Collectors #5 and #7, who discovered the northern concentration, recorded finding a total of 212 musket balls in the area.[24] These were accompanied by 99 arms and clothing artifacts, including (for example) 13 shoe buckles and 46 buttons. In the southern concentration, Collectors #1, #2, and #3 together recovered at least 538 musket balls (actually many more), but only 29 arms and clothing artifacts, including no shoe buckles and only five buttons.[25] These are ratios of about 2.1 to 1 and 18.5 to 1, respectively. Furthermore, the ratio of fired to unfired balls appears to have been higher in the southern area, although we have no objective measure of this. The suggestion here is that there was comparatively less firing (suggesting less intense combat) in the northern concentration west of Highway 58. The concentration of arms and accoutrement material found in the northern concentration may be the archaeological expression of headlong flight, slaughter, and surrender, and the subsequent processing of prisoners and the wounded.

In contrast to the far more abundant musket balls, the locations of individual canister balls were more precisely remembered by Collector Survey informants, and their distribution is significant in our battlefield interpretation (see figure). There is a heavy concentration of canister along the road in the southern portion of the battlefield. In either interpretation, most of these balls would be behind the British lines; but in the Northern Solution, many would be 600 to 800 yards behind the British lines.[26] While it is physically possible to fire canister from an elevated six-pounder gun (the heaviest in use at Camden) to these ranges, the effective range of the load was only about 200 to 300 yards, with only a minority of the balls traveling further downrange—this assuming they did not encounter trees, personnel, or other obstacles. It is well documented that American guns were deployed along the road at dawn, and that they caused heavy British losses with their initial fire, apparently at a range of about 200 yards.[27] The southern concentration of canister in the figure fits much better with the Southern Solution, the guns being located in the road on the American front line (see figure).[28] The canister distribution on the battlefield also argues against the Northern Solution interpretation that the southern artifact concentration represents the night meeting engagement. We have found no source that indicates either side used artillery during that action.

CONCLUSIONS

The authors are convinced that the initial positions of the opposing forces in the Battle of Camden are those depicted in the figure on page 222. It is hoped that the arguments marshaled above will sway those individuals who have disagreed thus far, and that this interpretation can be refined in the future with additional historical and archaeological research.

A broader conclusion concerns the use of collector data from battlefields generally. We believe this study has clearly demonstrated the value and utility of collector data in reconstructing battle history on existing topography. Like metal detecting technology, however, the "collector informant" technique may be some time in gaining general acceptance. There was a time, perhaps 25 years ago, when most archaeologists objected to the use of metal detectors in any archaeological context, thanks to the association of the technology with private collectors and a general ignorance of its potential. With the exceptions of a few pioneers like Roy Dickens, and more recently Douglas D. Scott, the archaeological community was slow to recognize the great utility of metal detecting on non-architectural military sites, together with the futility of certain traditional methods such as shovel testing and block excavation. Metal detectors are finally in general use, however, and the literature of successful applications has grown dramatically over the last 20 years.[29]

While metal detectors now appear to be acceptable tools for many archaeological applications, most archaeologists still seem to have a poor understanding of the scope and time depth of nonprofessional metal detecting on military sites and its impact on battlefield interpretation. Questions such as, "Has this battlefield been metal detected?" or, "Will our work encourage pot hunters?" might have been pertinent 30 or 40 years ago, but they are merely naive today. With rare exceptions, all reasonably accessible battlefields, field fortifications, and campsites in North America have been collected for several decades by numerous individuals. Nearly all such sites have lost most of their easily detectable metallic artifacts.[30] This condition extends to even the most obscure skirmishes and bivouacs, thanks to the rigorous historical research conducted by thousands of collectors. The exceptions are those few sites or portions of sites that have both legal protection and 24-hour security, and sites where the use of metal detectors is not practical (e.g., developed areas or trash dumps). While the literature of archaeological metal detecting on military sites is growing, most reports fail to address how previous collecting might affect their interpretations or even mention that there are missing collections that were removed long before any archaeological effort was undertaken.

It is not surprising, then, that few archaeologists have recognized the collector community as a resource that can and should be carefully tapped for information. Certainly we would all prefer that metal detecting at military sites had not happened in the past, and that it was not so popular today. To ignore it, however, is to put one's head in the sand, and to settle for a less informed interpretation of previously detected sites. In many cases, collector data is now the best (or only) distributional evidence available. Thus we feel it is the obligation of archaeologists to salvage what information can be gained from relic collectors and integrate it into their work. While the quality of the provenience data is usually not as precise as we would like, it is unique and very usable information that is otherwise entirely lost. We encourage archaeologists to develop strong relationships with the collectors in their region. We also encourage relic collectors to allow professional archaeologists access to their material, and urge them to make arrangements for their collections to be protected in perpetuity.

NOTES

1. The authors thank the National Park Service, American Battlefield Protection Program, the South Carolina Palmetto Conservation Foundation, and the South Carolina Institute of Archaeology and Anthropology for their financial support of this research. Also supporting this project was the Katawba Valley Land Trust. Special individuals who we want to thank include foremost Brigadier General (Ret.) George D. Fields, Dr. Douglas D. Scott, and Dr. Lawrence E. Babits. We are also most grateful to the members of the Battle of Camden Project and the collectors who offered their knowledge and allowed us to inventory their collections. Ms. Tamara Wilson developed the maps for this project.

2. An essential component of Battle of Camden Project is an effort to compile a definitive archive of primary sources relating to the battle. This task has been undertaken by the project on a large website, *battleofcamden.org*. The website includes numerous participant accounts of the battle from both sides, as well as several eighteenth-century maps. The

following primary sources were used in the development of this battle narrative: Report of Earl Cornwallis to Lord George Germain, Camden, South Carolina, August 21, 1780 in, Walter Clark, editor, *The State Records of North Carolina*, Volume XV 1780–81 (Goldsboro: Nash Brothers, Book and Job Printers, 1898), 268–273; Guilford Dudley, "The Carolina's During the Revolution, A Sketch of the Military Services Performed by Guilford Dudley– Then of the town of Halifax, North Carolina, During the Revolutionary War," in *Southern Literary Messenger*, 1845, Volume XI, March 144–148, April 231–253, May 281–287, June 370–374; Report of General Gates to President of Congress, August 20, 1780, in John Austin Stevens, "The Southern Campaign, 1780, Gates at Camden," *Magazine of American History*, October 1880, V(4):241–301; General Thomas Pinckney, "General Gates's Southern Campaign, July 27th, 1822" in *Historical Magazine* (1866), Volume X (8):244–253; Thomas Pinckney, Letter to Judge James, dated July 31, 1822, Thomas Pinckney Papers, South Caroliniana, University of South Carolina, Columbia, SC; Lieutenant Colonel Banastre Tarleton, *A History of the Campaigns of 1780 and 1781 in the Southern Provinces of North America* (Reprint, North Stratford, NH: Ayer Company Publishers, 1999, original 1787), 103–116; Colonel Otho Williams, "A Narrative of the Campaign of 1780," Appendix A, in William Johnson, *Sketches of the Life and Correspondence of Nathanael Greene, Major General of the Armies of the United States in the War of the Revolution*, Volume 1 (Charleston: A.E. Miller, 1822), 485–503. A good secondary narrative is Lt. Col. H. L. Landers, *The Battle of Camden*, House Document No.12, 71st Congress, 1st Session (Washington, D.C.: U.S. Government Printing Office, 1929).

3. Williams, "Narrative," 495.

4. The most complete history of the battlefield thus far has been R. Bryan Whitfield's 1980 thesis, *The Preservation of the Camden Battlefield* (Department of History, Wake Forest University, Winston Salem, NC).

5. Whitfield, 56.

6. The southern end of the battlefield is actually nearly a mile north of Gum Swamp Creek.

7. Benson Lossing, *The Pictorial Field Book of the Revolution*. Volume II (New York: Harper and Brothers, 1855), 460.

8. Thomas J. Kirkland and Robert M. Kennedy, *Historic Camden, Part One: Colonial and Revolutionary* (Columbia, The State Company, 1905), 169.

9. Kirkland and Kennedy, 162n.

10. Whitfield, 58–61.

11. Whitfield, 64–65.

12. George Fields, Steven D. Smith, and James B. Legg, *Strategic Plan for the Battle of Camden National Historic Landmark* (Columbia: Palmetto Conservation Foundation, 2003).

13. Calvin Keys, "Map of Day Battle Lines," in Charles Baxley, *Camden. American Battlefield Protection Program, Battlefield Survey Form*, National Park Service.

14. The Northern Solution would also seem to be favored by the location of the de Kalb monument, which was erected at the location of a pine tree where tradition held that de Kalb "fell." There is other traditional evidence, however, that de Kalb fell on the west side of the road, "at the head of a little bay, in the deep shades of the forest"

(Kirkland and Kennedy, 188). This would fit de Kalb's position at the climax of the battle in the Southern Solution. A participant account of de Kalb's death is found in the same source indicating that de Kalb was riding away when shot. This might support the contention that the de Kalb monument is indeed the location of his fall.

15. Ed Barron, "Sketch of the disposition and commencement of the action near Camden," Duke of Cumberland Collection, Public Archives, Nova Scotia, Canada; William Faden, "Plan of the Battle fought near Camden, August 16th, 1780," 1787, British Museum, London, and Tarleton's *History*; Lieutenant Finnegan, "Plan of the Batel close Campton in South America between the British under Gen. Lord Cornwallis and the Americans under Command of Gen. Gates," North Carolina Collection, University of North Carolina, Chapel Hill, North Carolina; Lt. Colonel Johann Christian Senf, "Battle of Camden," in Senf, "Journal"; C. Vallancy, "Sketch of the Battle of Camden," Library of Congress, 71000873. These maps can be seen at www. battleofcamden.org.

16. The major exceptions are the Vallancy and DesBarre Maps, which are actually manuscript and engraved versions of the same map. These are the best of the lot cartographically, but the American unit dispositions and identifications are wildly incorrect. Among other problems, they depict half of the American militia west of the drainage on the American right.

17. Williams, 495.

18. Gates, 303; John Senf, "Extract of a Journal Concerning the Action of the 16th of August 1780 Between Major General Gates and General Lord Cornwallis." Ms, Library of Congress.

19. Cornwallis, 270.

20. Charles Stedman, *The History of the Origin, Progress, and Termination of the American War*. Volume II (London: J. Murray, 1794) 208.

21. Col. David Stewart, *Sketches of the Character, Manners, and Present State of the Highlanders of Scotland*. Volume II, 2nd cd., Reprint of 1877 ed. (Edinburgh: John Donald Publishers, 1977), 67.

22. Whitfield, 65n.

23. It has been the experience of the authors that when collectors locate an area abundant with artifacts they will stay in that area until the finds become rare. Only then do they radiate outward from the core area. In fact, we have observed that some military sites may exhibit a reversal of actual historic density. In this phenomenon the central historic location of a camp, battlefield, or skirmish has been collected to the extent that it is nearly devoid of archaeological evidence, while the site's peripheries still retain some artifacts. Archaeologists should be mindful of this manifestation when assessing sites that have been heavily collected.

24. For the purposes of this example the "northern concentration" is the area bounded by Highway 58 on the east, by the dirt roads on the north and west, and on the south by a line running west from the southwest corner of the DAR property; the "southern concentration" is the larger dense contour on figure, page 217.

25. These totals do not include burial artifacts—currently, two burials are recorded from the southern concentration, none from the northern sample discussed here.

26. In our own metal detector sampling survey, a canister ball was found even further south than any recorded on figure, page 219.

27. Pinckney, Letters, July 22 and 31, 1822, Williams, 1130.

28. The question of canister range is critical to the correct interpretation of the Camden Battlefield. According to Brent Nosworthy, "Canister was generally limited to targets within 350 yards, and the absolute range of the heaviest canister was less than 700 yards." Here Nosworthy is discussing Civil War field guns, which were generally heavier than Revolutionary War guns. See his *The Bloody Crucible of Courage: Fighting Methods and Combat Experience of the Civil War* (New York: Carroll and Graf, 2003), 64–65. Lawrence Babits suggests that individual canister balls from an elevated six-pounder gun might conceivably travel 800 yards (personal communication, February 2004), but certainly most would come to rest at much shorter ranges. Firing over nearly level ground at targets 200 yards away would have required little or no elevation of the gun, which would have brought most of the canister balls to ground at minimal ranges. See also Garry Wheeler Stone, Daniel M. Sivilich, and Mark E. Lender, "A Deadly Minuet: The Advance of the New England 'Picked Men' against the Royal Highlanders at the Battle of Monmouth, 28 June 1778," *Brigade Dispatch*, XXVI(2), Summer 1996. They found a few canister balls and "grape shot" more than 600 yards from presumed gun positions, but 500 yards was more typical, and the firing was over open terrain, and from higher to much lower topography.

29. For example, Melissa Connor and Douglas D. Scott, "Metal Detector Use in Archaeology: An Introduction," *Historical Archaeology*, 1998, 32(4):76–85; Christopher T. Espenshade, Robert L. Jolley, and James B. Legg, "The Value and Treatment of Civil War Military Sites," *North American Archaeologist*, 2002, 23(1):39–67; Charles M. Haecker and Jeffrey G. Mauck, *On the Prairie of Palo Alto* (College Station: Texas A&M University Press, 1997); James B. Legg and Steven D. Smith, *"The Best Ever occupied ...": Archaeological Investigations of a Civil War Encampment on Folly Island, South Carolina* (Columbia: South Carolina Institute of Archaeology and Anthropology, 1989); Richard A. Fox Jr., *Archaeology, History, and Custer's Last Battle* (Norman: University of Oklahoma Press, 1993); William B. Lees, "When the Shooting Stopped, the War Began," in Clarence R. Geier Jr., and Susan E. Winter, eds., *Look to the Earth: Historical Archaeology and the American Civil War* (Knoxville: University of Tennessee Press, 1994); Douglas D. Scott, "Oral Tradition and Archaeology: Conflict and Concordance from Two Indian War Sites," *Historical Archaeology*, 2003, 37(3):55–65; Douglas D. Scott, Richard A. Fox Jr., Melissa A. Connor, and Dick Harmon, *Archaeological Perspectives on the Battle of the Little Bighorn* (Norman: University of Oklahoma Press, 1989); Douglas D. Scott and William J. Hunt Jr., *The Civil War Battle at Monroe's Crossroads, Fort Bragg, North Carolina: A Historical Archaeological Perspective* (Tallahassee: Southeast Archaeological Center, National Park Service, 1998); Steven D. Smith, "Archaeological Perspectives on the Civil War: The Challenge to Achieve Relevance," in Geier and Winter 1994; Steven D. Smith and James B. Legg, "Archaeological and Historical Analysis of the Camden Battlefield, August 16th, 1780," Southeastern Archaeological Conference, Charlotte, NC, November 13, 2003; Bruce B. Sterling

and Bernard W. Slaughter, "Surveying the Civil War: Methodological Approaches at Antietam Battlefield," in Clarence R. Geier and Stephen R. Potter, eds., *Archaeological Perspectives on the American Civil War* (Gainesville: University of Florida Press, 2000).

30. Roy Dickens, "Archaeological Investigations at Horseshoe Bend National Military Park, Alabama," *Special Publications of the Alabama Archaeological Society*, No. 3, 1979. A remarkable overview of battlefield relic collecting as it was during its peak can be found in Stephen W. Sylvia and Michael J. O'Donnell, *The Illustrated History of American Civil War Relics* (Orange, Virginia: Moss Publications, 1978).

REFERENCES CITED

Barrette, Lt. Col. Thomas George Leonard. 1780. Map of the Battle of Gum Swamp Alias Sutton-Ford. Clements Library, University of Michigan, Ann Arbor. http://battleofcamden.org/barrette.gif.

Barron, Ed. n.d. Sketch of the Disposition and Commencement of the Action Near Camden, South Carolina, 16 August 1780. http://battleofcamden.org/ed_barron_map.jpg.

Baxley, Charles B. 2000. Camden. American Battlefield Protection Program, Battlefield Survey Form, National Park Service.

Connor, Melissa, and Douglas D. Scott. 1998. Metal Detector Use in Archaeology: An Introduction. *Historical Archaeology* 32(4):76–85.

Cornwallis, Lord Earl. 1780. Report of Earl Cornwallis to Lord George Germain, Camden, South Carolina, August 21, 1780. In Walter Clark (ed.), *The State Records of North Carolina*, Volume XV 1780–81, Nash Brothers, Book and Job Printers, Goldsboro, North Carolina, 1898, 268–273.

DesBarres, J. F. W. 1780. Sketch of the Battle of Camden. On file, Library of Congress. http://battleofcamden.org/desbarres.jpg.

Dickens, Roy. 1979. Archaeological Investigations at Horseshoe Bend National Military Park, Alabama. *Special Publications of the Alabama Archaeological Society*, No. 3.

Dudley, Guilford. 1845. The Carolina's During the Revolution, A Sketch of the Military Services Performed by Guilford Dudley–Then of the town of Halifax, North Carolina, During the Revolutionary War. *Southern Literary Messenger* XI(March):144–148, (April):231–253, (May):281–287, (June):370–374.

Espenshade, Christopher T., Robert L. Jolley, and James B. Legg. 2002. The Value and Treatment of Civil War Military Sites. *North American Archaeologist* 23(1):39–67.

Faden, William. 1787. Plan of the Battle fought near Camden, August 16th, 1780. British Museum, London.

Fields, George, Steven D. Smith, and James B. Legg. 2003. *Strategic Plan for the Battle of Camden Historic Landmark*. Palmetto Conservation Foundation, Columbia, South Carolina.

Finnegan, Lieutenant. n.d. Plan of the Batel close Campton in South America between the British under Gen. Lord Cornwallis and the Americans under Command of

Gen. Gates. North Carolina Collection, University of North Carolina, Chapel Hill, NC.

Fox, Richard A. Jr. 1993. *Archaeology, History, and Custer's Last Battle.* University of Oklahoma Press, Norman.

Geier, Clarence R., and Stephen R. Potter (eds.). 2000. *Archaeological Perspectives on the American Civil War.* University Press of Florida, Gainesville.

Geier, Clarence R. Jr., and Susan E. Winter (eds.). 1994. *Look to the Earth: Historical Archaeology and the American Civil War.* University of Tennessee Press, Nashville.

Haecker, Charles M., and Jeffrey G. Mauck. 1997. *On the Prairie of Palo Alto: Historical Archaeology of the U.S.–Mexican War Battlefield.* Texas A&M University Press, College Station.

Keys, Calvin. 2000. Map of Day Battle Lines, in Charles Baxley, *Camden. American Battlefield Protection Program, Battlefield Survey Form,* National Park Service.

Kirkland, Thomas J., and Robert M. Kennedy. 1905. *Historic Camden, Part One, Colonial and Revolutionary.* The State Company, Columbia, SC.

Landers, Lieutenant Colonel H. L. 1929. *The Battle of Camden, South Carolina, August 16, 1780.* House Document No. 12, 71st Congress, 1st Session, U. S. Government Printing Office, Washington, D.C.

Lees, William B. 1994. When the Shooting Stopped, the War Began. In Clarence R. Geier Jr. and Susan E. Winter (eds.), *Look to the Earth: Historical Archaeology and the American Civil War.* University of Tennessee Press, Knoxville.

Legg, James B., and Steven D. Smith. 1989. "The Best Ever Occupied…" Archaeological investigations of a Civil War Encampment on Folly Island, South Carolina. *Research Manuscript Series* #209, South Carolina Institute of Archaeology and Anthropology, Columbia.

Lossing, Benson. 1855. *The Pictorial Field-Book of the Revolution.* Harper and Brothers, New York.

Nosworthy, Brent. 2003. *The Bloody Crucible of Courage: Fighting Methods and Combat Experience of the Civil War.* Carroll and Graf, Inc., New York.

Pinckney, General Thomas. 1866. General Gates's Southern Campaign, July 31, 1822. *Historical Magazine* X(8):244–253.

Pinckney, General Thomas. 1822. Letter to Judge James, dated July 31, 1822. Thomas Pinckney Papers, South Caroliniana Library, University of South Carolina.

Scott, Douglas D. 2003. Oral Tradition and Archaeology: Conflict and Concordance from Two Indian War Sites. *Historical Archaeology* 37(3):55–65.

Scott, Douglas D., Richard A. Fox Jr., Melissa A. Connor, and Dick Harmon. 1989. *Archaeological Perspectives on the Battle of the Little Bighorn.* University of Oklahoma Press, Norman.

Scott, Douglas D., and William J. Hunt Jr. 1998. *The Civil War Battle at Monroe's Crossroads, Fort Bragg, North Carolina: A Historical Archaeological Perspective.* Southeast Archaeological Center, National Park Service, Tallahassee, FL.

Senf, Colonel John. 1780. "Extract of a Journal Concerning the Action of the 16th of August 1780 Between Major General Gates and General Lord Cornwallis," Library of Congress.

Smith, Steven D. 1994. Archaeological Perspectives on the Civil War: The Challenge to Achieve Relevance. In Clarence R. Geier Jr. and Susan E. Winter (eds.), *Look to the Earth: Historical Archaeology and the American Civil War*. University of Tennessee Press, Knoxville.

Smith, Steven D., and James B. Legg. 2003. Archaeological and Historical Analysis of the Camden Battlefield, August 16th, 1780. Southeastern Archaeological Conference, Charlotte, NC.

Stedman, C. 1794. *The History of the Origin, Progress, and Termination of the American War*. J. Murray et al., London.

Sterling, Bruce B., and Bernard W. Slaughter. 2000. Surveying the Civil War: Methodological Approaches at Antietam Battlefield. In Clarence R. Geier and Stephen R. Potter (eds.), *Archaeological Perspectives on the American Civil War*. University of Florida Press, Gainesville.

Stevens, John Austin. 1880. The Southern Campaign, 1780, Gates at Camden. *Magazine of American History* October V(4):241–301.

Stewart, Colonel David. 1977. *Sketches of the Character, Manners, and Present State of the Highlanders of Scotland*. Volume II, Second edition, John Donald Publishers, Ltd., Edinburgh, reprint, original 1877.

Stone, Garry Wheeler, Daniel M. Sivilich, and Mark E. Lender. 1996. A Deadly Minuet: The Advance of the New England "Picked Men" against the Royal Highlanders at the Battle of Monmouth, 28 June 1778. *Brigade Dispatch* XXVI(2), (Summer 1996):2–18.

Sylvia, Stephen W., and Michael J. O'Donnell. 1978. *The Illustrated History of American Civil War Relics*. Moss Publications, Orange, VA.

Tarleton, Lieutenant Colonel Banastre. 1787. *A History of the Campaigns of 1780 and 1781 in the Southern Provinces of North America*. Reprint, Ayer Company Publishers, North Stratford, NH, 1999.

Vallancy, Charles. 1780. Sketch of the Battle of Camden. On file, Library of Congress. http://battleofcamden.org/vallancy2.jpg.

Whitfield, R. Bryan. 1980. *The Preservation of Camden Battlefield*. MA Thesis, Department of History, Wake Forest University, Winston-Salem, NC.

Williams, Colonel Otho. 1822. Narrative of the Campaign of 1780, Appendix A. In William Johnson, *Sketches of the Life and Correspondence of Nathanael Greene, Major General of the Armies of the United States in the War of the Revolution*, Volume 1. A.E. Miller, Charleston, SC.